Intellectual Property Aspects of Ethnobiology

Australia
LBC Information Services
Sydney

Canada and USA
Carswell
Toronto

New Zealand
Brooker's
Auckland

Singapore and Malaysia
Sweet & Maxwell Asia
Singapore and Kuala Lumpur

Intellectual Property Aspects of Ethnobiology

Edited by Michael Blakeney

Perspectives on Intellectual Property Series
General Editor: Professor Michael Blakeney

In association with the Queen Mary Intellectual Property Research Institute, Queen Mary & Westfield College, University of London

LONDON • SWEET & MAXWELL • 1999

Published in 1999 by
Sweet & Maxwell Limited of
100 Avenue Road
Swiss Cottage
London NW3 3PF
http://www.smlawpub.co.uk
Typeset by Dataword Services Limited, Chilcompton
Printed and bound in Great Britain
by MPG Ltd, Bodmin, Cornwall

No natural forests were destroyed
to make this product, only farmed
timber was used and replanted.

A CIP catalogue record for this book
is available from the British Library

ISBN 0 421 684 305

Foreword

The field of intellectual property protection, traditionally somewhat obscure, has found that recent developments in science and technology have forced it firmly into the limelight. This is now an area of law in which some of the most profoundly important moral challenges of the twentieth century have arisen. Aside from the digital technology domain, with its massive impact on copyright issues and extraordinary consequences for the global economy and education, the ethnobiology and bioethnology fields, in particular with respect to the use of indigenous knowledge for commercial purposes and the patenting of "life" including the genes of indigenous persons themselves, represent two of the most important areas of debate. Indeed, they are both now front-page issues, with a potentially enormous impact on the economic, cultural, health and other aspects of the international order.

However, what is notable amidst the mass of opinion that presently fills the airwaves is the perhaps surprising lack of solid research and hans-on experience to provide the factual grounding in which considered and ultimately useful attitudes can be formed. *Intellectual Property Aspects of Ethnobiology* is therefore both timely and valuable, and I am delighted to support it on the simple grounds that all serious research at this stage is extremely welcome. I believe, however, that I may go further, and say that this work has the great advantages of not only providing helpful surveys of the prevailing legal framework in which what some have called a biological gold rush may be taking place, but also of containing overviews from opposite ends of the globe, from Brazil through India and Malaysia to New Zealand. By illustrating the similarities of experience in different regions, and also the specific differences, a comprehensive picture of the global situation emerges which will prove essential to all those working in, or simply interested by, the subject.

The importance of the interface between intellectual property rights and bioethics, particularly in the fields of ethnobiology, bioethnology, ethnoecology and conservation, and other related areas in anthropology and biology, is now firmly established. *Intellectual Property Aspects of Ethnobiology* is a pioneering work which extends out knowledge and contributes to the formulation of empirically-driven solutions critical to ensuring that humankind takes the correct steps forward in this remarkable, largely uncharted field at the frontier of our moral and ethical experience.

Dr Kamil Idris
Director General,
World Intellectual Property Organisation (WIPO)

Contents

Table of Cases

Table of National Legislation

Table of International Conventions, Treaties, Agreements and Declarations

1. The International Framework of Access to Plant Genetic Resources

Professor Michael Blakeney

Herchel Smith Professor of Intellectual Property Law, Queen Mary and Westfield College and Director of the Queen Mary Intellectual Property Research Institute. Formerly, Professor Blakeney worked with the Asia Pacific Bureau of the World Intellectual Property Organisation and has taught at Murdoch University and the University of New South Wales. His books include: *Legal Aspects of Technology Transfer to Developing Countries* (1989) and *Trade Related Aspects of Intellectual Property Law: A Concise Guide to the TRIPS Agreement* (1996)

The International Framework of Access to Plant Genetic Resources

1. Introduction

Access to the plant genetic resources of a country is governed by an evolving composite of national legislation pursuant to international legal conventions and agreements concerning biodiversity and intellectual property and voluntary codes of international practice developed within the context of the FAO Global System for the Conservation and Utilisation of Plant Genetic Resources for Food and Agriculture. Within this framework of legal as well as non-binding instruments attempts are on-going to harmonise the private proprietary intellectual property system with principles of unrestricted access to genetic resources.

2. The United Nations Convention on Biological Diversity

2.1 General Principles

The Rio Earth Summit which was convened in June 1992, promulgated the Convention on Biological Diversity (CBD), The Rio Declaration on Environment and Development and Agenda 21. Agenda 21 was the strategic plan of the Rio participants for achieving sustainable environmental and developmental goals into the next century.[1] The CBD represented an attempt to establish an international programme for the conservation and utilisation of the world's biological resources[2] and for the "fair and equitable sharing" of the benefits arising from the utilisation of genetic resources.[3] An obvious tension exists between the dual objectives of conservation and utilisation. This tension is further exacerbated by the acknowledgement in Article 3 of the sovereign right of nations to exploit their own genetic resources pursuant to their own environmental policies and a number of provisions of the CBD which require contracting parties to create conditions to facilitate access to genetic resources. An additional complication is the repeated incantation that access should be on mutually agreed terms and conditions on the basis of "prior informed consent" and with the provision of equitable remuneration.

---

[1] See Meyers, "An EIA for Rio: Assessing the Environmental Impacts of the United Nations Conference on Environment and Development", (1994) 1(2) *The Australasian Journal of Natural Resources Law and Policy* 1 at 15.

[2] See F. McConnell, *The Biodiversity Convention. A Negotiating History*, (Kluwer, London, 1996).

[3] CBD, Art. 1.

The architects of the CBD saw some possibilities for the reconciliation of the objectives of conservation and utilisation in the environmental management practices which had been evolved and were practised by the indigenous peoples of the world. Acknowledgement of the significance of this traditional environmental wisdom is made in the Convention. The knowledge of indigenous peoples had also informed the commercial bioprospecting of plant genetic resources and the CBD enjoins the equitable remuneration of that contribution. Outlined below are the key access and benefit sharing provisions of the CBD.

2.2 Access Regime of the CBD

(a) Scope

Article 1 of the CBD envisages "appropriate access to genetic resources" and "the fair and equitable sharing of benefits arising out of the utilisation of genetic resources". "Genetic resources" are defined in Article 2 as meaning "genetic material of actual or potential value". The term "genetic material" is then defined in Article 2 to mean "any material of plant, animal, microbiological or other origin containing functional units of heredity". On a strict analysis of this definition, it is suggested that biochemical extracts which do not contain DNA or RNA would be outside the scope of the CBD.[4] Thus the Convention would apply to seeds and cuttings and DNA extracted from a plant, such as a chromosome, gene, plasmid or any part of these such as the promoter part of a gene.[5]

Article 9 deals with "the conservation of components of biological diversity outside their natural habitats", for example, in germplasm and seed banks, botanical gardens, museums, laboratories and agricultural research institutions. This article calls for national legislation to provide for the acquisition, conservation, storage and management of these *ex situ* collections. The access and benefit-sharing provisions of the CBD do not apply to the genetic resources of a country which were collected prior to the entry of the CBD into force in that country.[6] Thus a country with a pre-existing collection of genetic material has the sovereign right to control access to that collection, but has no legal right to insist upon a share of any benefits derived from the use of that collection. Also, the CBD applies to those genetic resources which originate in the country of a contracting party.[7] As will be explored

[4] See L. Glowka, F. Burhenne-Guilmin and H. Synge, *A Guide to the Convention on Biological Diversity* (Gland, IUCN, 1994), p. 3.
[5] See L. Glowka, *A Guide to Designing Legal Frameworks to Determine Access to Genetic Resources* (Gland, IUCN, 1998), p. 4.
[6] CBD, Art.15(3) and see Yusuf, "International Law and Sustainable Development: The Convention on Biological Diversity" in A.A. Yusuf, (ed.) *African Yearbook of International Law*, (vol. 2, (Kluwer, London, 1995), p. 109.
[7] *ibid.*

below, complications arise from questions of access to the gene banks established by the Consulting Group of International Agricultural Research Institutes (CGIAR), which is administered by the Food and Agricultural Organisation (FAO). The GGIAR, established in 1971, is an informal association of 57 public and private sector members that supports a network of 16 international agricultural research centres.[8] This collection currently comprises over 600,000 accessions of more than 3,000 crop, forage and pasture species[9] which are held at the Centro Internacional de Agricultura Tropical (CIAT), Center for International Forestry Research (CIFOR), Centro Internacional de Mejoramiento de Maiz y Trigo (CIMMYT), Centro Internacional de la Papa (CIP), International Center for Agricultural Research in the Dry Areas (ICARDA), International Center for Living Aquatic Resources Management (ICLARM), International Center for Research in Agroforestry (ICRAF), International Crop Research Institute for the Semi-Arid Tropics (ICRISAT), International Livestock Research Institute (ILRI), International Institute of Tropical Agriculture (IITA), International Plant Genetic Resources Institute (IPGRI), International Rice Research Institute (IRRI) and the West Africa Rice Development Association (WARDA).

(b) Sovereign Rights over Genetic Resources (Article 15(1))

Article 15(1) of the CBD affirms "the sovereign rights of states over their natural resources" and provides that "the authority to determine access to genetic resources rests with the national governments and is subject to national legislation". This provision, dealing as it does with access to genetic resources, does not refer to the question of the ownership of genetic resources. These resources may be of two types: *ex situ*, in that they are preserved outside their natural habitats, in for example gene banks; or *in situ*, where genetic resources exist within ecosystems and natural habitats or, where domesticated or cultivated, they exist in their agricultural surroundings. Different ownership regimes may apply to these two categories of genetic resources. In recent years difficult questions have been raised concerning the legal status of the germplasm collections of the agricultural research institutes which are members of the CGIAR. Some of the gene banks which make up the CGIAR were established in the 1960s and 70s as a means of fomenting what became known as the "Green Revolution". At that time the questions of ownership and intellectual property rights in the collections were very much subordinated to the mission to increase crop yields to feed a burgeoning world population. It has only been in recent years that ownership issues have become important,

---

[8] See "About the CGIAR", http://www.cgiar.org:80/whatis.htm.
[9] *ibid.*

either as a bargaining counter in North-South negotiations or as a source of revenue.[10]

The question of the ownership of the CGIAR collections issue arises in two principal contexts. First, the status of the collection upon the dissolution of the relevant gene bank and, secondly, the related question of the authority of the centres to permit third parties to exploit their genetic resources. The starting place for these inquiries commences with an analysis of the legal status of these institutes themselves. The legal status of these collections has always been problematic. In 1986 the FAO had conducted a review of the legal status of all national and international institutions operating genebanks.[11] In relation to the CGIAR centres, the FAO report concluded that as control over their operation was shared between national and international representatives, they were not international in the strict sense, as they were not created by any international instrument or organisation. On the other hand the report concluded that because they were not either in the private sector or under the control of any state or national authority, the CGIAR centres were *sui generis*. Consequently, the report reached no firm conclusion on the ownership of the genetic resources controlled by the Centres.

For example, ownership concerns were raised recently as a consequence of Plant Breeder's Rights applications made in Australia by agricultural research institutes in relation to a peavine and a lentil which had been bred from genetic stock obtained from the CGIAR gene bank: International Centre for Agricultural Research in the Dry Areas (ICARDA), located in Aleppo, Syria.[12] A charter for ICARDA had been established in November 1975 on the basis of an agreement between the World Bank, FAO and UNDP and the Canadian International Development Research Centre (IDRC), as the executing agency. Subsequently establishment agreements were negotiated by IDRC with Syria (June 28, 1976), Lebanon (July 6, 1977) and Iran (July 20, 1976). These parallel agreements provide for the establishment of ICARDA in "the region" defined as the "Near East, North Africa and the Mediterranean region". ICARDA's headquarters were established in Aleppo, Syria. The agreements also provided for the Chairman of CGIAR to declare that ICARDA has been established as a legal entity allowing IDRC's role to lapse. This formal step does not appear to have been taken. The question of ownership of the ICARDA collection was raised in the context of whether its Director-General acted in breach of trust obligations, which he owed in relation to ICARDA genetic

[10] See Blakeney, "Access to Genetic Resources: The View from the South" [1997] 3 *Bioscience Law Rev.* pp. 97–103.
[11] FAO Commission on Plant Genetic Resources, *Legal Status of Base and Active Collections of Plant Genetic Resources*, Doc. CPGR/87/5, Dec.1986.
[12] "Editorial. Lest We Starve", *New Scientist*, No. 2121, February 14, 1998, p. 3; Edwards and Anderson, "Seeds of Wrath", *ibid*, p. 14.

material, in permitting the Australian agricultural research institutes to seek intellectual property rights in applications of that material.[13]

(c) Facilitating Access to Genetic Resources between Parties (Article 15(2))

National sovereignty over genetic resources is qualified by Article 15(2) which requires parties to "endeavour to create conditions to facilitate access to genetic resources for environmentally sound uses by other contracting parties" and the provision prohibits the imposition of conditions that run counter to the objectives of the Convention. Like much of the CBD,[14] this provision has a breadth and vagueness which will require its meaning to be settled through usage. Alternatively, national obligations to facilitate access will be formulated within the context of the FAO International Undertaking on Plant Genetic Resources, which is discussed below.

(d) Access Subject to Mutually Agreed Terms and Prior Informed Consent (Article 15(4) and (5))

Article 15(4) envisages that where access is granted it will be subject to mutually agreed terms. Currently the conventional form of access agreement is the Material Transfer Agreement (MTA).[15] The International Service for National Agricultural Research is currently formulating a standard form of MTA for use by research institutes within the CGIAR system.

Article 15(5) requires access to genetic resources to be subject to the "prior informed consent" of the contracting party providing those resources, unless it waives that right. Glowka suggests that the mutual agreement on terms could be part of a larger access determination regime administered by a designated competent authority.[16] As is discussed in the chapters below, a number of states already require bioprospecting to be subject to the grant of a permit. In this administrative process, full disclosure by the bioprospector is usually required.[17]

---

[13] See Blakeney, "Intellectual Property Rights in the Genetic Resources of International Agricultural Research Institutes — Some Recent Problems" [1998] 1 *Bioscience Law Rev.* pp. 3–11.

[14] For a full range of difficult interpretative phrases in the CBD see W. Lesser, *Sustainable Use of Genetic Resources under the Convention on Biological Diversity*, (CAB International, Oxford, 1998), pp. 10–11.

[15] See J.I. Cohen, C. Falconi, J. Komen and M. Blakeney, *The Use of Proprietary Biotechnology Research Inputs at Selected CGIAR Centres* (International Service for National Agricultural Research (ISNAR), The Hague, 1998).

[16] See L. Glowka, "Legal and Institutional Considerations for States Providing Genetic Resources" in J. Mugabe, *et al.* (eds), *Access to Genetic Resources: Strategies for Sharing Benefits*, (ACTS Press, Nairobi, 1997).

[17] See Downes, Laird, Klein and Carney, "Biodiversity Prospecting Contract" in W.V. Reid *et al.* (eds), *Biodiversity Prospecting; Using Genetic resources for Sustainable Development,* (WRI, Washington DC, 1993), pp. 255–287.

(e) Benefit Sharing and Access to Technology

The countries of the South have been the principal source of the genetic material which forms the basis of many or all of the agri-industries of the industrialised North.[18] This fact coupled with celebrated allegations of "biopiracy" by Northern corporations,[19] has resulted in agitation for the equitable sharing of benefits and technology by the providers and exploiters of genetic resources. A number of the provisions of the CBD refer to the equitable sharing of benefits arising from the utilisation of the genetic resources of a signatory. Article 15(7) requires each contracting party to "take legislative, administrative or policy measures, as appropriate" and in accordance with a number of specified provisions of the Convention, "with the aim of sharing in a fair and equitable way, the results of research and development and the benefits arising from the commercial and other utilisation of genetic resources with the contracting party providing such resources". Article 8(j) envisages the "equitable sharing" of benefits with indigenous and local communities, arising out of the use of the traditional knowledge, innovations and practices of those communities. Article 21 provides for the establishment of a "mechanism" for the provision of financial resources to developing country parties to the CBD.

Complementary to the equitable sharing of benefits, the CBD provides for the access of developing country signatories to technologies which may result from the utilisation of the genetic resources which they may provide. Article 16(1) recites the importance of access to biotechnologies to attain the objectives of the CBD and Article 16(2) provides for the access to technologies by developing countries on "fair and equitable terms, including on concessional and preferential terms". Article 19(1) requires parties to take appropriate measures to "provide for the effective participation in biotechnological research activities by those contracting parties, especially developing countries, which provide the genetic resources for such research". Article 19(2) requires parties to "take all practicable measures to promote and advance priority access on a fair and equitable basis . . ., especially developing countries, to the results and benefits arising from biotechnologies based upon genetic resources provided by those Contacting Parties" on mutually agreed terms.

(f) Indigenous and Local Communities

The Rio Declaration in Principle 22 stated that "Indigenous peoples and their communities . . . have a vital role in environmental management and development because of their knowledge and traditional

[18] *e.g.* see charts depicting the regional sources and utilisation of major food and industrial crops in Kloppenburg and Kleinman, "The Plant Germplasm Controversy" (1987) 37 *BioScience* 190 cited in Lesser, n.14 *above*.

[19] *e.g.* see Kocken and van Roosendoal, "The Neem Tree Debate", (1997) 30 *Biotechnology and Development Monitor* 8.

practices". Chapter 26 of Agenda 21 detailed the relationship which conference participants recognised between indigenous peoples and their lands. The Agenda, at paragraph 26.3(a), required governments:

> to establish a process to empower indigenous peoples and their communities' through measures that include:
>
> - recognition of their values, traditional knowledge and resource management practices with a view to promoting environmentally sound and sustainable development;
> - enhancement of capacity-building for indigenous communities based on the adaptation and exchange of traditional experience, knowledge and resource-management practices, to ensure their sustainable development;
> - establishment, where appropriate, of arrangements to strengthen the active participation of indigenous peoples and their communities in the national formulation of policies, laws and programs relating to resource management and other development processes that may affect them.

The Preamble to the CBD recognised the

> . . . close and traditional dependence of many Indigenous and local communities embodying traditional lifestyles on biological resources, and the desirability of sharing equitably arising from the use of traditional knowledge, innovations and practices relevant to the conservation of biological diversity and sustainable use of its components.

Article 8(j) of the Convention required each signatory

> . . . subject to its national legislation, respect, preserve and maintain knowledge, innovations and practices of indigenous and local communities embodying traditional lifestyles relevant for the conservation and sustainable use of biological diversity and promote their wider application with the approval and involvement of the holders of such knowledge, innovations and practices and encourage the equitable sharing of the benefits arising from the utilisation of such knowledge, innovations and practices.

The provisions of Article 8(j) require implementation through national legislation. It is expressed to be subject to national legislation, in order to preserve legislation on this subject which predates the CBD.[20]

---

[20] See Chandler, "The Biodiversity Convention: Selected Issues of Interest to the International Lawyer" (1993) 4 *Colorado Jnl of Int'l Law and Policy* 141.

3. International Intellectual Property Instruments Relating to Access to Plant Genetic Resources

The CBD adopts an equivocal attitude to the role of intellectual property rights in the area of plant genetic resources. Article 16(3) of the CBD in providing for the access of developing countries to biotechnology, requires that where such technology is subject to patents or other intellectual property rights, such access shall be "provided on terms which recognise and are consistent with the adequate and effective protection of intellectual property rights". On the other hand, Article 16(5) of the CBD "recognising that patents and other intellectual property rights may have an influence on the implementation of this Convention, shall co-operate in this regard subject to international law in order to ensure that such rights are supportive of and do not run counter to its objectives".

Parallelling the formulation of the Convention on Biological Diversity, were the negotiations of the Uruguay Round of the General Agreement on Tariffs and Trade. Attempts by the World Intellectual Property Organisation to revise the Paris Convention on Industrial Property, 1883, which deals with the international patents, industrial designs and trade marks regime, had foundered on the irreconcilability of the position of developing countries and industrialised countries on the compulsory licensing of patents.[21] For this and other reasons, the United States proposed that the GATT formulate legislative norms for intellectual property protection and that it require the introduction of a range of mechanisms for the enforcement of intellectual property rights.[22] The resultant Agreement on Trade Related Aspects of Intellectual Property Rights (TRIPS) was annexed as a condition of membership to the Agreement Establishing the World Trade Organisation (WTO).[23] Article 27.3 of the TRIPS Agreement permits signatories to exclude from patentability "plants and animals other than microorganisms, and essentially biological processes for the production of plants or animals, other than non-biological and microbiological processes". However, the provision requires that "Members shall provide for the protection of plant varieties either by patents or by an effective *sui generis* system or by any combination thereof". Article 65.2 permits developing countries a period of five years for compliance with TRIPs commencing from the date of entry into force of the WTO Agreement, in April 1994. Least developed countries are permitted an additional five years for the implementation of TRIPS.

---

[21] See M. Blakeney, *Legal Aspects f the Transfer of Technology to Developing Countries*, (ESC, Oxford, 1989). 98 *et seq.*

[22] See Blakeney, "Intellectual Property in World Trade" [1995] 1 *Int'l Trade Law & Regulation* 76.

[23] See M. Blakeney, *Trade Related Aspects of Intellectual Property Rights: A Concise Guide to the TRIPS Agreement*, (London, Sweet & Maxwell, 1996).

In all probability, to comply with this TRIPS obligation, countries will introduce legislation based on the International Convention for the Protection of New Varieties of Plants (UPOV), which was amended in March 1991. The UPOV Convention provides for the registration and grant of intellectual property rights[24] in relation to new, distinct, stable and uniform plant varieties. Article 6 of the UPOV Convention deems a variety to be new if at the date of filing the application, "propagating or harvested material of the variety has not been sold or otherwise disposed of, for purposes of exploitation of the variety" earlier than one year within the date of filing the application in the territory of the contracting party, or earlier than four years, or in the case of trees and vines, earlier than six years in a territory of a non-contracting party. This formulation of novelty, which is much more liberal than the requirement of novelty under patent law, facilitates the acquisition of plant variety rights in relation to germplasm.

4. FAO Global System for the Conservation and Utilisation of Plant Genetic Resources for Food and Agriculture

In 1983 the FAO Conference had established the Commission on Plant Genetic Resources as a permanent intergovernmental forum to deal with questions concerning plant genetic resources. The International Undertaking on Plant Genetic Resources was adopted as the formal framework for its activities. The 1995 FAO Conference adopted Resolution 3/95 which broadened the Commission's mandate to embrace all components of biodiversity of relevance to food and agriculture. This broader mandate was reflected in the renaming of the Commission as the Commission on Genetic Resources for Food and Agriculture. The FAO considered that this would "facilitate an integrated approach to agrodiversity".[25] The statutes for the broadened Commission provide for co-operation between the FAO and other governmental and non-governmental bodies, in particular the Conference of the Parties to the Biodiversity Convention. The Commission was specifically required to co-operate with the CBD in the area of genetic resources of relevance to food and agriculture. In the discharge of its mandate, the Commission has co-ordinated the development of the *Global System for the Conservation and Utilisation of Plant Genetic Resources for Food and Agriculture*. The objectives of the Global System are "to ensure the safe conservation and promote the availability and sustainable utilisation of plant genetic

---

[24] The scope of these rights is defined in Art. 14 of the UPOV Convention, to include the authorisation of the production, conditioning for propagation, sale, export, import or stocking of the variety for these purposes.

[25] FAO, *Progress Report on the FAO Global System for the Conservation and Utilisation of Plan Genetic Resources for Food and Agriculture*, UNEP/CBD/COP/3/15, published on the Internet at http://web.icppgr.fao.org/CPGR/COP/cop3gs.html.

resources by providing a flexible framework for sharing the burdens and benefits".[26] The Global System mediated through the International Undertaking on Plant Genetic Resources comprises three elements. The first element consists of voluntary codes of conduct for plant germplasm collecting and transfer and on biotechnology, as well as the 1994 FAO/CGIAR Agreement on Genebanks. The second element is a "Global Mechanism" comprising A World Information and Early Warning System, networks of *ex situ* and *in situ* and on farm collections and crop specific networks. The third element consists of three global instruments: an inventory of the "State of the Worlds Plant Genetic Resources", a "Global Plan of Action on Plant Genetic Resources" and the "International Fund for the Implementation of Farmers' Rights".

4.1 International Undertaking on Plant Genetic Resources

(a) Introduction

In 1983 the Conference of the FAO adopted the International Undertaking on Plant Genetic Resources (the Undertaking) as a non-legally binding instrument. The Undertaking provides for the exploration and collection of genetic resources (Article 3), for conservation *in situ* and *ex situ* (Article 4), for the availability of plant genetic resources (Article 5), for international co-operation in conservation, exchange and plant breeding (Article 6), for international co-ordination of genebank collections and information systems (Article 7) and for funding (Article 8). By September 1996 the Undertaking had attracted the subscription of some 111 countries, excluding the USA.[27]

(b) The International Undertaking and Plant Breeder's Rights

The Undertaking was originally predicated on the principle that plant genetic resources should be freely exchanged as a "heritage of mankind" and should be preserved through international conservation efforts. In subsequent years the principle of free exchange was gradually narrowed. In November 1989 the 25th Session of the FAO Conference adopted two resolutions providing an "agreed interpretation" that plant breeders' rights were not incompatible with the Undertaking. [28] The acknowledgment of plant variety rights obviously benefitted industrialised countries, which were active in seed production. In exchange for this concession, developing countries won endorsement of the concept of "farmers' rights". This was a moral

---

[26] *ibid.* para. 6.

[27] FAO, "Global Participation in the Development of Major Components of the Global System for the Conservation and Utilisation of Plant Genetic resources" (September 1996), http://193.43.36.7/waice...GP/AGPS/PGR/globapp1.htm.

[28] Resolutions 4/89 and 5/89 adopted by FAO Conference, 25th Sess., Rome, November 11–29, 1989.

commitment by the industrialised commitment to reward "the past present and future contributions of farmers in conserving, improving and making available plant genetic resources particularly those in centers of origin/diversity. These rights are vested in the International Community, as trustee for present and future generations of farmers."[29]

A further narrowing of the free-flow principle occurred at the 26th Session of the FAO Conference in November 1991 which in Resolution 3/91, while reaffirming that plant genetic resources were the common heritage of mankind, subordinated it to "the sovereignty of states over their plant genetic resources".

(c) The International Undertaking and the CBD

In November 1993 the 27th Session of the FAO Conference unanimously adopted Resolution 7/93 calling for The Commission to undertake "the adaptation of the International Undertaking on Plant Genetic Resources in harmony with the Convention on Biological Diversity" which had been concluded by the Rio Earth Summit the previous year. The Resolution instructed the Commission to consider "the issue of access on mutually agreed terms to plant genetic resources including *ex situ* collections not addressed by the Convention" and "for the realisation of Farmers' Rights".[30] Negotiating Texts have been considered by the Commission in a series of sessions between 1994 and 1997. Its 1997 sessions have prepared a simplified draft text concentrating on Articles 3 (scope), 11 (availability of plant genetic resources) and 12 (Farmers' Rights).[31]

The draft text was considered in a negotiating session between June 8 and 12, 1998. The negotiation divided on North-South lines, in which the South conceived of access to the genetic resources of developing countries in terms of an exchange of nature for debt and maintained the right of farmers to save, exchange and enhance seed as a traditional right.[32] Malaysia, speaking on behalf of the developing economies of Asia, "emphasised that the revision of the International Undertaking had to recognise (i) facilitated access, (ii) benefit sharing, (iii) Farmers' Rights and (iv) the international fund as inseparable components of equal importance".[33] The E.U. and European states proposed the establishment of "a mechanism to promote and better channel the flow of funds from available sources" to developing countries and economies in transition.[34] This was supported in principle by the countries of the North American Region, Japan and the Republic of Korea.

[29] Resolution 5/89, *ibid.*

[30] CGRFA, "Revision of the Undertaking. Issues for Consideration in Stage II: Access to Plant Genetic Resources and Farmers' Rights", http://web.icppgr.fao.org/cpgr6.1/CPGR6.1–6.html.

[31] See http://web.icppgr.fao.org/cpgr/cpgr6.1/e/CPGR6.1–6.html.

[32] See FAO, *Report of the Fifth Extraordinary Session of the Commission on Genetic Resources for Food and Agriculture,* Rome, June 8–12, 1998.

[33] *ibid.,* para. 33.

[34] *ibid.,* para. 16.

(d) Farmers' Rights

The concept of Farmer's Rights was formulated in 1989, in the context of the renegotiation of the International Undertaking, as a basis for recognising and rewarding the contribution of farmers to the conservation and management of plant genetic resources. Farmers' Rights were defined in a Resolution of the FAO Conference[35] as:

> . . . rights arising from the past, present and future contribution of farmers in conserving, improving and making available plant genetic resources, particularly those in centres of origin/diversity. These rights are vested in the International Community, as trustee for present and future generations of farmers, for the purpose of ensuring full benefits to farmers, and supporting the continuation of their contributions.

Farmers' rights were intended to promote a more equitable relation between the providers and users of germplasm by creating a basis for farmers to share in the benefits derived from the germplasm which they had developed and conserved over time.[36] An International Fund for Plant Genetic Resources was proposed in a Resolution of 1991 as a means of implementing Farmers' Rights. This Fund will support plant genetic conservation and utilisation programmes, particularly in the developing countries.

Farmers' Rights are conceived of as a "retrospective equity,"[37] primarily as the recognition of the moral obligation, rather than an economic incentive. Its implementation is uncertain, although suggestions have been made in India for a seed tax, where the revenue yield will be distributed through a Community Gene Fund.[38]

4. The Intellectual Property Rights of Indigenous Peoples in Plant Genetic Resources

Outside the traditional international intellectual property conventions there are a number of international instruments which have incidentally addressed the intellectual property rights of indigenous peoples. The *International Covenant on Civil and Political Rights 1966,* provides that:

---

[35] Annex II, Resolution 5/89 adopted by FAO Conference, 25th Sess., Rome, November 11–29 1989.
[36] Glowka, n.5 *above,* p. 6.
[37] Brush, "Whose knowledge, whose genes, whose rights?", in S.B. Brush, and D. Stabinsky (eds), *Valuing Indigenous Knowledge:Indigenous Peoples and Intellectual Property Rights,* (Island Press, Washington DC), p. 12.
[38] M.S. Swaminathan and V. Hoon, *Methodoligies for Recognising the Role of Informed Innovation in the Conservation and Utilisation of Plant Genetic Resources,* (CRSARD Proceedings, no. 9, Madras, 1994).

> In those states in which ethnic, religious or linguistic minorities exist, persons belonging to such minorities shall not be deprived of the right, in community with other members of their group, to enjoy their own culture, to profess and practice their own religion or to use their own language.

It has been argued that failing to protect indigenous art from misappropriation would constitute a breach of the Covenant.[39]

The International Labour Organisation (ILO) Convention No. 169 concerning Indigenous and Tribal Peoples in Independent Countries, which entered into force on September 5, 1991 called attention to the distinctive contribution of indigenous peoples to cultural diversity and affirmed the right of indigenous peoples to self-identification. This right to self identification has been argued to include the rights of indigenous peoples to "intangible cultural, scientific and intellectual resources".[40]

One of the results of the United Nations International Year for the World's Indigenous Peoples, was the promulgation of a *Draft Declaration on the Rights of Indigenous Peoples*. The *Draft Declaration* was formulated by the Working Group on Indigenous Populations (WGIP), which had been established the United Nations Economic and Social Council in May 1982.[41] The task of the WGIP was to review developments pertaining to the promotion and protection of human rights and fundamental freedoms of indigenous peoples, giving particular attention to the evolution of standards concerning the rights of indigenous peoples. Article 12 of the *Draft Declaration* recognised the right of indigenous peoples to "practice and revitalise their cultural traditions and customs", including the right

> . . . to maintain, protect and develop the past, present and future manifestations of their cultures, such as . . . artefacts, designs, ceremonies, technologies and visual and performing arts and literature, as well as the right to the restitution of cultural, intellectual, religious and spiritual property taken without their free and informed consent or in violation of their laws, traditions and customs.

Article 29 recognised the entitlement of indigenous peoples "to the full ownership, control and protection of their cultural and intellectual property". This article also asserted the right of indigenous peoples "to special measures to control, develop and protect their . . . cultural manifestations, including . . . oral traditions, literatures, designs and visual and performing arts."

---

[39] See Wright, n.2 *above*, 151.
[40] Posey, "Indigenous Peoples and Traditional Resource Rights: A Basis for Equitable Relationships?", *Workshop on Indigenous Peoples and Traditional Resource Rights* (Oxford, June 28, 1995), p. 5.
[41] ECOSOC Res. 1982/34, May 7, 1982.

The growing self-realisation of indigenous peoples that the international recognition of their intellectual property rights in their cultural expressions would depend upon their own efforts has resulted in the development of international solidarity through international conferences of indigenous peoples which have promulgated intellectual property declarations which have formulated norms for the protection of their cultural expressions and traditional medical knowledge.[42]

A significant initiative during the UN International Year for the World's Indigenous Peoples was the First International Conference on the Cultural and Intellectual Property Rights of Indigenous Peoples which was convened by the Nine Tribes of Mataatua in the Bay of Plenty Region of Aotearoa, New Zealand in June 1993. The resultant *Mataatua Declaration on the Cultural and Intellectual Property Rights of Indigenous Peoples* insisted that the protection of the rights of indigenous peoples in their traditional knowledge was an aspect of the right of indigenous people to self determination. The *Mataatua Declaration* recommended in Article 1 that in the development of policies and practices, indigenous peoples should:

1.1 Define for themselves their own intellectual and cultural property.
1.2 Note that existing protection mechanisms are insufficient for the protection of Indigenous Peoples Intellectual and Cultural Property Rights.
1.3 Develop a code of ethics which external users must observe when recording (visual, audio, written) their traditional and customary knowledge.
1.4 Prioritise the establishment of indigenous education, research and training centres to promote their knowledge of customary environmental and cultural practices.
[. . .]
1.6 Develop and maintain their traditional practices and sanctions for the protection, preservation and revitalisation of their traditional intellectual and cultural properties.
[. . .]
1.8 Establish an appropriate body with appropriate mechanisms to:
  (a) preserve and monitor the commercialism or otherwise of indigenous cultural properties in the public domain;
  (b) generally advise and encourage indigenous peoples to take steps to protect their cultural heritage;
  (c) allow a mandatory consultative process with respect to any new legislation affecting indigenous peoples cultural and intellectual property rights.
1.9 Establish international indigenous information centres and networks.

[42] See Appendix 1 for a full list of Indigenous Peoples' Declarations.

The *Mataatua* Declaration in Article 2.1 recommended that in the development of policies and practices, states and national and international agencies "should recognise that indigenous peoples are the guardians of their customary knowledge and have the right to protect and control dissemination of that knowledge." In Article 2.2 it urged the recognition that "indigenous peoples also have the right to create new knowledge based on cultural traditions". The insufficiency of existing protection mechanisms was asserted in Article 2.3. Article 2.5 provided for the development

> . . . in full co-operation with indigenous peoples an additional cultural and intellectual property rights regime incorporating the following:
>
> — collective (as well as individual) ownership and origin-retroactive coverage of historical as well as contemporary works;
> — protection against debasement of culturally significant items;
> — co-operative rather than competitive framework;
> — first beneficiaries to be the direct descendants of the traditional guardians of that knowledge;
> — multi-generational coverage span.

The conference delegates recommended that the UN incorporated the *Mataatua Declaration* be incorporated in its Study on Cultural and Intellectual Property of Indigenous Peoples.

The statement issued by the International Consultation on Intellectual Property Rights and Biodiversity organised by the Co-ordinating Body of the Indigenous Peoples of the Amazon Basin (COICA), held at Santa Cruz de la Sierra, Bolivia, in September 1994 reiterated the assertion of the *Mataatua Declaration* that

> All aspects of the issue of intellectual property (determination of access to natural resources, control of the knowledge or cultural heritage of peoples, control of the use of their resources and regulation of the terms of exploitation) are aspects of self determination.

The COICA statement was extremely critical of the current intellectual property regime. Article 8 declared that

> Prevailing intellectual property systems reflect a conception and practice that is:
>
> — colonialist, in that the instruments of the developed countries are imposed in order to appropriate the resources of indigenous peoples;

— racist, in that it belittles and minimises the value of our knowledge systems;
— usurpatory, in that it is essentially a practice of theft.

The COICA statement in Article 9 pointed to the danger of distortion to indigenous systems in adjusting them to the prevailing intellectual property regime. The statement formulated short and medium term strategies to deal with these problems. In the short term it identified intellectual property principles and mechanisms which were either inimical to or useful for indigenous peoples. For example, Article 12 recognised that "there are some formulas that could be used to enhance the value of our products (brand names, appellations of origin), but on the understanding that these are only marketing possibilities, not entailing monopolies of the product or of collective knowledge".

The statement in Article 14 proposed the design of a protection and recognition system in the short and medium term of mechanisms which "will prevent appropriation of our resources and knowledge". These would include "appropriate mechanisms for maintaining and ensuring rights of indigenous peoples to deny indiscriminate access to the resources of our communities or peoples and making it possible to contest patents or other exclusive rights to what is essentially indigenous".

Although the COICA statement was largely concerned with indigenous peoples rights in biodiversity,[43] it called for the training of indigenous leaders in aspects of intellectual property.

In the Pacific region these initiatives were advanced through the South Pacific Regional Consultation on Indigenous Peoples' Knowledge and Intellectual Property Rights, held in Suva, Fiji in April 1995. The Final statement issued by the Regional Consultation declared "the right of indigenous peoples of the Pacific to self-governance and independence of our lands, territories and resources as the basis for the preservation of indigenous peoples' knowledge". Article 7 urged the strengthening of indigenous networks and encouraged the UN and regional donors to "continue and support discussions on indigenous peoples' knowledge and intellectual property rights". Article 8 pointed out the importance of strengthening "the capacities of indigenous peoples to maintain their oral traditions, and encourage initiatives by indigenous peoples to record their knowledge in a permanent form according to their customary access procedures".

Finally, the Final statement urged "universities, churches, governments, non-governmental organisations and other institutions to reconsider their roles in the expropriation of indigenous peoples' knowledge and resources and to assist in their return to their rightful owners".

[43] See Blakeney, "Bioprospecting and the Protection of Traditional Medical Knowledge", *Symposium on Intellectual Property Protection for the Arts and Cultural Expression of Aboriginal and Torres Strait Islander Peoples*, Perth, October 1, 1996.

A recent study by Cultural Survival Canada has identified the following "twenty shared principles" which have been affirmed by the declarations of Indigenous Peoples.[44]

1. Primacy of aboriginal rights and the right of self-determination.
2. Indigenous peoples maintain the right of self-definition as indigenous peoples.
3. Indigenous peoples are inseparable from their territories and all the constituitive parts of these territories.
4. Indigenous peoples' biodiversity stewardship must be recognised as a living tradition, subject to continuing adaptation, change and innovation.
5. Indigenous peoples' historical and contemporary contributions to global biodiversity stewardship must be recognised.
6. Customary or natural law is a vital part of the protection, transmission and regulation of knowledge and biodiversity at the community level.
7. All rights of indigenous peoples embodied in common and constitutional law, international agreements and multilateral policy statements must be respected.
8. No agreement pertaining to the conservation of biodiversity and dissemination of indigenous knowledge can extinguish indigenous peoples' sovereign rights.
9. The granting of commercial patents over living things and their constituent parts is contrary to indigenous peoples' customary laws, beliefs and worldviews.
10. Corporate-driven intellectual property rights regimes are unacceptable to indigenous peoples and antagonistic to their practices of biodiversity stewardship.
11. Reparation is required for knowledge and biodiversity lost or destroyed through outside interventions.
12. Indigenous peoples' rights pertaining to knowledge and biodiversity are collectively held.
13. There can be no participation and consent without the involvement of both indigenous men and indigenous women.
14. The right of consent includes the right to refuse.
15. Consent can not be freely granted under conditions of political, economic or social coercion or in the absence of effective mechanisms to protect indigenous peoples' rights.
16. Biological resources taken from indigenous peoples without proper consent must be repatriated.
17. Indigenous peoples have the right to full disclosure about any investigation or use of their knowledge or resources.

[44] Cultural Survival Canada, *Towards Biodiversity Righjts: The Biodiversity Convention and Indigenous Peoples,* Discussion Paper, June 1996, http://www.cscanada.org/~csc/text/CBD3.htm.

18. What is equitable will be determined by indigenous peoples themselves.
19. No benefit sharing agreement, whether agreed to by individuals and communities or imposed by external forces, can extinguish or reduce the inherent rights of indigenous peoples.
20. The need for indigenous peoples' organisations to monitor and oversee benefit sharing agreements.

5. Traditional Resource Rights

The absence of specific mechanisms to protect the rights of indigenous peoples to their genetic materials and traditional knowledge within the CBD or the various international intellectual property conventions has generated the suggestion for the creation of a *sui generis* system to meet this requirement. Traditional Resource Rights (TRRs) have been posited, principally emanating from the work of Darrell A. Posey and Graham Dutfield,[45] as "a process and framework to develop multiple, locally-appropriate systems and 'solutions' that reflect the diversity of contexts where *sui generis* systems are required".[46] "Traditional resources" include tangible and intangible assets and attributes deemed to be of value (spiritual, aesthetic, cultural, economic) to indigenous and local communities.[47] TRRs are described as "an integrated rights concept that recognises the inextricable link between cultural and biological diversity" delineating a constellation of "overlapping and mutually supporting bundles of rights" which "can be used for protection, compensation and conservation".[48] TRRs are constructed around four processes:

> (1) identifying 'bundles of rights' expressed in moral and ethical principles; (2) recognising rapidly evolving "soft law" influenced by customary practice and legally non-binding instruments, declarations and covenants; (3) harmonising existing legally-binding international agreements. . . and (4) "equitising" to provide marginalised indigenous, traditional, and local communities with favourable conditions to influence all levels and aspects of policy planning and implementation.[49]

Grounded in human rights discourse, TRRs are viewed as "more holistic than intellectual property rights".[50] Among the perceived

[45] See the publications of the Programme for Traditional Resource Rights, The Oxford Centre for the Environment, Ethics and Society, Mansfield College, University of Oxford.
[46] D.A. Posey, *Traditional Resource Rights. International Instruments for Protection and Compensation for Indigenous Peoples and Local Communities* (IUCN, Gland, 1996) xiii.
[47] *ibid.* 15.
[48] D.A. Posey and G. Dutfield, *Beyond Intellectual Property: Toward Traditional Resource Rights for Indigenous Peoples and Local Communities* (IDRC, Ottawa, 1996) p. 4.
[49] Posey, n.45 *above*.
[50] Glowka, n.5 *above*, 39.

inadequacies of conventional intellectual property law in protecting the traditional medical knowledge of indigenous peoples are:

(a) the inability of the law to recognise communal intellectual property interests, this model does not fit with the custodianship principle among indigenous peoples[51];
(b) the requirement of patent law and copyright law of a specific act of invention or authorship, among indigenous peoples traditional medical knowledge may be attributed to ancestor spirits and shared communally[52];
(c) the limitation of conventional intellectual property law to protecting expressions of information in material form, compared with the diverse knowledge systems of indigenous peoples which are often transmitted orally;
(d) the incentive philosophy of conventional intellectual property law which encourages access to and exploitation of knowledge may often be in tension with the practice of indigenous peoples to preserve access to sacred knowledge to initiates[53];
(e) the limited periods for which conventional intellectual property rights are granted, before knowledge is placed in the public domain, may conflict with the sacred requirement of indigenous peoples that certain matters cannot lose their confidential status[54]; and
(f) the expense and difficulty of securing intellectual property rights has been suggested as a factor explaining the relative disadvantage of indigenous peoples relative to mutinational corporations seeking to exploit the biological knowledge of those peoples.[55]

The obligation, in Article 27.3(b) of the TRIPS Agreement, for nations to provide for "the protection of plant varieties by patents *or by an effective sui generis system* or by any combination thereof" (emphasis added) has generated the suggestion that a sui generis system might include a system which subordinates intellectual property laws to human rights, respect for cultural heritage and the protection of cultural and biological diversity.

[51] See Blakeney, "Communal Intellectual Property Rights", (1998) *World Intellectual Property Law Journal*.
[52] See Blakeney, "Protection of Traditional Medical Knowledge of Indigenous Peoples" [1997] 19 *European Intellectual Property Review* 298.
[53] See Blakeney, "Protecting Expressions of Aboriginal Folklore under Copyright Law" [1995] 17 *European Intellectual Property Law* 442.
[54] See Brush, "Indigenous Knowledge of Biological Resources and Intellectual Property Rights: The Role of Anthropology", (1993) 95 *American Anthropologist* 653; Yano, "Protection of the Ethnobiological Knowledge of Indigenous Peoples", (1993) 41 *UCLA Law Rev.* 443; Gupta, "Ethical Dilemmas of Prospecting Biodiversity" (1995) 5 *Eubios, Jnl of Asian and Int'l Bioethics* 40.
[55] See Mead, "Misappropriation of Indigenous Knowledge: The Next Wave of Colonisation" (1994) 3 *Otago Bioethics Report* 4; V. Shiva, *Biodiversity Conservation: Whose Resource? Whose Knowledge* (Indian National Trust for Art and Cultural Heritage, New Delhi, 1994).

6. Other *Sui Generis* Systems for the Protection of Indigenous Knowledge

A number of suggestions have been made to accommodate the protection of the knowledge of indigenous peoples within the existing intellectual property system. Gadgil and Devasia[56] proposed the inclusion of the owners of source materials in patents resulting from the utilisation of those materials. This would require the participation of those owners in any patent licensing arrangements. A problem with this proposal is the focus upon ownership, rather than knowledge, which is often alien to an indigenous culture. Additionally, as is indicated in a number of the chapters below, ownership of natural resources will often be in the hands of persons other than the relevant indigenous group.

Gollin suggests that through access legislation, a fee is paid to the person or group that discovered or traditionally used a species.[57] This idea is elaborated by Lesser who proposes a registry of traditional uses of genetic materials, requiring a description of the genetic materials in sufficient detail to permit their identification.[58] It is suggested that enforcement of this proposal is through national access legislation which requires that a commercial use agreement is negotiated with the owners of indigenous knowledge and the state.

---

[56] Gadgil and Devasia, "Intellectual Property Rights and Biological Resources: Specifying Geographical Origins and Prior Knowledge of Uses" (1995) 69 *Current Science* 637.

[57] Gollin, "An Intellectual Property Rights Framework for Biodiversity Prospecting" in Reid, n.17 *above*, 159–197.

[58] See W. Lesser, *Sustainable Use of Genetic Resources Under the Convention on Biological Diversity. Exploring access and Benefit Sharing Issues* (CAB International, Wallingford, 1998) 127–135.

2. Biodiversity Prospecting and the Equitable Remuneration of Ethnobiological Knowledge; Reconciling Industry and Indigenous Interests

Martine de Koning

Studied in Utrecht and took an MBA at the University of Florida. After graduation she taught and researched intellectual property rights in Australia at the Universities of New South Wales and Melbourne. Since June 1997 she has worked with Kennedy van der Laan, a law firm in Amsterdam, practising in the areas of IP and IT law. In addition to publishing in the area of the harmonisation of intellectual property laws in Asia under the influence of GATT-TRIPS, WIPO and APEC, she has published articles on the Rio Convention.

Biodiversity Prospecting and the Equitable Remuneration of Ethnobiological Knowledge: Reconciling Industry and Indigenous Interests*

Introduction

Indigenous cultural heritage,[1] crucial for indigenous people's integrity, identity and self-determination, increasingly represents potential for commercial exploitation.[2] An unprecedented interest in indigenous visual and performing arts is one of the most notable cultural developments of the last decade.[3] Extensive misuse of indigenous works of art has been made.[4] Piracy of both contemporary and ancient works has taken place.

Simultaneously, other aspects of indigenous folklore[5] and identity have been explored for their commercial value. A trend has developed among biotechnology and pharmaceutical companies to explore indigenous medical[6] or ethnobotanical knowledge of flora and fauna to discover drugs and suitable genetic resources for genetic engineering.[7] Even human tissue of indigenous peoples has been used for these purposes by the biotechnology industry.[8]

This paper critically analyses the need and the legal regimes for the intellectual property protection of indigenous medical knowledge, thereby defining the terminology, identifying relevant specifics of

---

* Conference Paper Delivered at the International Conference on Artistic & Cultural Expressions, Traditional Knowledge, and Protection of Heritage, Brisbane, presented by the Australian Folklore Association at the University of Queensland, September 27–29, 1996.

[1] For the purposes of this paper all aspects of "indigenous cultural heritage" will be covered by the broad designation "folklore".

[2] See S. McCullough, "Indigenous Art Judges Get the Picture", *The Australian*, August 23, 1996, p.16.

[3] http://www.liberal.org.au/policy/arts/art3.html#1, pp. 1-5.

[4] *Milpurruru v. Indofurn PTY Ltd*, (1995) 30 *Intellectual Property Reports* 209.

[5] "Folklore" is used in this paper in a broad sense and covers all tangible and intangible aspects of indigenous arts, religion, knowledge and heritage. Both contemporary expressions and ancient property are comprised.

[6] I prefer the term "ethnobiological" knowledge, for reasons that will be explained in the section on the definitional context and the role of ethnobiological knowledge in biodiversity prospecting situations.

[7] M. Dolan, "Drug Companies Turn to Nature for New Medicines", *LA Times*, May 22, 1992, A32, A33; S.R. King, "The Source of Our Cures", *Cultural Survival Quarterly*, Summer 1991, pp. 19–21.

[8] "Human Genome Project"; See also *Patents Amendment Bill, Sched. 1 (Second Reading Speech)*: "A Bill To Amend the Patents Bill" by Senator N. Stott Despoja), June 1996; See also *Moore v. Regents of the University of California*, 793 P. 2d 479 (Cal 1990), cert. denied, 499 U.S. 936 (1991); See also M.T. Danforth, "Cells, Sales and Royalties: The Patients Right to a Portion of the Profits", (1988) 6 *Yale Law and Policy Review* 179.

biodiversity prospecting situations and the various industry and indigenous interests, and suggesting solutions based on an examination of the rationales of the Western intellectual property (IP) regimes and the evaluation of the intrinsic value and the nature of ethnobiological knowledge in this context.

Definitional Questions Regarding the Subject Matter of Ethnobiological Knowledge

Legal and botanical literature deals to a limited extent with the definition of traditional medical knowledge. The use of terminology is inconsistent and it is essential for the purposes of this paper to clarify the definitional context. Medical knowledge is a very broad term, comprising indigenous or "tribal" peoples' knowledge, farmers' or "rural" traditional knowledge and regionally-bound traditional knowledge about the "healing" or otherwise — for the pharmaceutical industry — useful function of flora and fauna.

In American literature particularly, "ethnobiological knowledge" is a frequently used phrase. I prefer this term, because it has a well defined scope for legal purposes and little meaning outside of that context. Several connotations should be noted:

Ethnobiological knowledge in a broad sense represents all indigenous knowledge of the ecosystems historically and/or presently surrounding peoples. The indigenous peoples not only utilise the natural resources in that ecosystem, but also interact with that system in a sustainable manner. Their behaviour often influences and preserves the system. The system is there not only to feed, and generally support them: they are an essential element in that ecosystem.

The UNCED Documents, in particular the Rio Convention regarding the preservation of biodiversity,[9] specifically acknowledge the interrelationship between biodiversity and cultural diversity. The international framework for the preservation of biodiversity deals with intellectual property protection, indigenous roles in management of resources and indigenous human rights in this context only to a very limited extent. No definition of "indigenous peoples", "medical/ethnobiological knowledge" or comparable subject matter is formulated in the documents. The scope of member countries' obligations regarding the intellectual property protection of ethnobiological knowledge under the Earth Summit and comparable international Conventions remains disputed, and the texts of the treaties leave authority for implementation in domestic law to the member countries.

Regardless of the lack of international consensus on the definitional context of the role of ethnobiological knowledge in biodiversity prospecting, several remarks are valuable.

[9] An in depth discussion of the international legal framework dealing with medical knowledge and indigenous peoples rights and obligations regarding biodiversity largely falls beyond the scope of this paper. The Earth Summit, Rio Convention Preamble and Arts. 8(j), 10(c), 17(2), 18(4) and follow-up UNCED documents are particularly relevant.

Ethnobiological knowledge should be distinguished from ethnobotanical knowledge for two reasons. Ethnobotanical knowledge tends to be limited to knowledge of various plants or micro-organisms, rather than expand to the knowledge of ecosystems and their functioning. Secondly, ethnobiological knowledge objectively represents the knowledge of indigenous peoples. Ethnobotanical knowledge refers to the descriptions of knowledge of plants made by Western researchers during or after contact with, or observation, of indigenous peoples. Ethnobotanical knowledge thus is an interpretation of indigenous knowledge rather than an objective description.

Furthermore, it should be acknowledged that ethnobiological knowledge itself is not a homogeneous body of knowledge. Indigenous communities and peoples throughout the world do not lead the same traditional or modern urbanised lifestyles and have dissimilar cultural values. Attempts to define the term "indigenous peoples" often result in essentialising and marginalising indigenous peoples and threaten to limit the scope of protection of international treaties dealing with indigenous interests. Similarly, ethnobiological knowledge of different communities is largely dissimilar. Particularly geographically "close" communities hold some common or substantially similar knowledge. The conceptual, traditional or ritual context in which the ethnobiological knowledge is embodied might nevertheless be completely different.

The distinction between ethnobiological knowledge that cannot be used and understood beyond its local/traditional/communal context and ethnobiological knowledge that can be utilised beyond its context is also important in this respect. Finally, the distinction between knowledge that has commercial value, and knowledge that lacks commercial value in the latter category is relevant.[10] It follows automatically that knowledge that cannot be utilised beyond its communal context has little or no commercial value, as concepts of private property and profits do not play a dominant role in traditional indigenous communal life. The fact that the knowledge has no commercial value in Western society does not render it useless, as the importance of indigenous knowledge in its communal context for the preservation of ecosystems and to enhance sustainable development should be recognised. The link between cultural and biological diversity in a broad sense is undisputed.[11] Indigenous peoples' involvement at all levels of conservation activities is generally considered to maximise the profitability of non-commercially profitable ethnobiological knowledge.

[10] *Traditional Related Knowledge and the Convention on Biological Diversity*, contribution by the Executive Secretary to the Preparation of the Report of the Secretary General for Programme Element 1.3 of the Intergovernmental Panel on Forests, Subsidiary Body on Scientific, Technical and Technological Advice, Second Meeting September 2–6, 1996, http://www.iisd.ca/li...v/sbstta/sb2inf3.html, p. 15.

[11] *Knowledge, Innovations and Practices of Indigenous and Local Communities*, note by the Secretariat, Subsidiary Body on Scientific, Technical, and Technological Advice, Second Meeting, September 2–6, 1996, Montreal, http://www.iisd.ca/lii...div/sbstta/sb207.html, p. 3.

For the purposes of this paper nevertheless, ethnobiological knowledge should be defined in a narrow sense as indigenous knowledge of ecosystems, plants, species and micro-organisms that can be utilised beyond its local context and that have commercial value. It is this type of ethnobiological knowledge that is used by biodiversity prospectors, rendering huge commercial profits from the development of drugs and pharmaceuticals in home countries. By utilising *objectively and "fairly" acquired* ethnobiological knowledge with the *informed consent* of the indigenous owners of the knowledge, thereby respecting *indigenous customary laws*, the biodiversity prospecting industry would make important steps towards a satisfying reconciliation of indigenous and industry interests.

In addition, I would like to take the opportunity to criticise the widespread assumption that indigenous customary laws lack concepts of intellectual property and definitions of traditional folklore in general and ethnobiological knowledge in particular. Many indications exist that substantially similar notions of intangible property function in indigenous normative frameworks. Anthropological research and indigenous voices on this matter have just begun to attract academic, but still lack governmental, attention, as the need to protect the intellectual aspects of cultural aspects only surfaced in the last decade. More clarity might be provided by the anthropological profession in collaboration with indigenous peoples in the near future.[12] Meanwhile, it is unjust to assume that Western legal regimes should override any indigenous claims to intangible property rights in folklore on basis of the fact that indigenous customary law seems to fail to provide for an alternative regime. A similar, prematurely drawn assumption in Land Rights matters has caused irreparable pain, expense and delay in the self-determination of indigenous peoples.[13]

The problems of finding a workable definition of ethnobiological knowledge for legal and practical purposes have surfaced, but we are only at the beginning of the negotiations with indigenous peoples that will be necessary to find a consensual agreement on this for further development of the debate's crucially important point.[14]

---

[12] It is particularly important to realise that whatever conclusion is reached by anthropologists and lawyers on this point, it only deals with part of the problem; the Western legalistic legitimisation of policies affecting indigenous peoples. Real issues are the societal need and objective justification for achieving appropriate protection of indigenous folklore, thereby stimulating the arts movement, cultural diversity, biodiversity preservation and self determination and autonomy for indigenous peoples.

[13] See also, M. de Koning, "The Intellectual Property Protection of Indigenous Folklore is a Conditional Requirement for the Exercise of Aboriginal Funding Cuts", a submission to the Federal Government on file with the author.

[14] The Rio Convention is often criticised for delivering uncertainty because it failed to appropriately define IP, transfer of technology and indigenous rights. The U.S. was extremely reluctant to sign the Convention, I would argue precisely for the reason that vague provisions imply broader scope of the provisions of the Convention than was meant by the parties.

The Lack of Equitable Remuneration for Indigenous Intangible Property; The Problemacy of Protecting Ethnobiological Knowledge in Current Domestic and International IP Regimes

Only in very rare cases do indigenous peoples receive remunerations for their role in the process of developing of pharmaceutical products from genetic engineering and biodiversity prospecting.[15] This result is not surprising because at present, the legal regimes dealing with intellectual property protection of indigenous folklore fail to protect indigenous interests adequately. The Anglo-American and European intellectual property regimes, of which the Australian regime is derived, require specific sets of conditions to be satisfied before protection can be enjoyed; a range of specific conditions apply for categories of different subject matter; originality, novelty, manner of manufacture, secrecy, confidential relationship, registration, and other requirements also apply.[16] Aspects of indigenous folklore in general rarely fulfil the requirements for IP protection.

On international level, a considerable level of harmonisation of IP laws is achieved, but none of the (internationally binding)[17] treaties deal explicitly with the IP protection of indigenous interests in folklore nor ethnobiological knowledge.[18]

It is valuable nevertheless to observe that due to the increased globalisation and the process of harmonisation of laws better international frameworks for IP protection and enforcement mechanisms such as the WTO dispute resolution mechanisms have been adopted.[19] The increased level of international IP protection might directly deliver some positive results for indigenous interests. The adoption of trade secret law for example could well provide for an example in this respect.[20]

---

[15] See M.J. Huft, "Comment: Indigenous Peoples and Drug Discovery Research: A Question of Intellectual Property Rights", (1995) 89 *Northwestern University Law Review*, Summer, 1678.

[16] See M. Blakeney, "Bioprospecting and the Protection of Traditional Medical Knowledge", paper presented at the *International Conference on Folklore, Traditional Knowledge, and Protection of Culture and Heritage,* presented by the Australian Folklore Association at the University of Queensland, September 27–29, 1996.

[17] I refer here to internationally binding or in other words internationally enforceable treaties (it should be noted that the extent to which these are internationally enforceable is often limited as well), as opposed to (non enforceable) Declarations of NGO's, lobby groups or minority groups; Examples Indigenous Peoples Declarations on Folklore; See for example M Blakeney, "Bioprospecting and the Protection of Traditional Medical Knowledge", paper presented at the Conference, September 27–29, 1996.

[18] TRIPS (GATT/WTO) fails to deal with indigenous IP; the Rio Convention, and other more biodiversity-orientated treaties provide for indigenous interest protection, but fail to give clarity on the correct interpretation in general, and of the implications for IP rights of indigenous peoples in particular; see the Rio Convention Art. 8(j) for example.

[19] The Rio Convention, TRIPS and WIPO treaties can be mentioned as examples.

[20] TRIPS, Art. 39.

Particularly in the Asian and South American region, the level of IP protection has increased both on legislative and enforcement level. It is also a fact that still, although unsatisfactorily, indigenous rights in an IP context have a history of slightly better protection in North American and European countries than in Asia and South America.[21] In many Asian, African and South American countries, the existence of indigenous minority groups is simply denied or considered irrelevant for policy-making purposes. The protection of folklore in those countries often takes the shape of protecting national commercial interests by economic protectionist policies against imports of Western cultural or artistic products such as films, and the enhancement of nationalism and domestic cultural awareness in general. Usually, no particular considerations are given to the protection of indigenous or "tribal" peoples.[22] It is to be hoped that some positive influence from the better international communication on the harmonisation of IP laws and the availability of global enforcement mechanisms will result in the global protection of indigenous intangible property interests.

Concrete efforts to conclude unambiguous international obligations protecting indigenous intangible property interests (instead of side-mentioning, optional protocols and implied duties for member countries) in biodiversity and conservation treaties, will be essential to realise the potential offered by the global political tendencies to include on the global trade agenda environmental issues, indigenous interests and the crucial role of indigenous peoples in sustainable development and resource management. Indigenous human rights regarding the protection of heritage in general and ethnobiological knowledge in particular should be dealt with explicitly, thus avoiding the international tendency to focus on commercial interests. The need for sustainable development including indigenous duties and the role of indigenous peoples in the process has surfaced, but what is often overlooked is the importance of granting indigenous IP rights which directly render equitable remuneration and enhance the empowerment of indigenous people for their role in the process of sustainable development and utilisation of genetic resources.

An important hurdle to overcome is the fact that ethnobiological knowledge as an aspect of folklore can be said to be generally

---

[21] I am by no means arguing that the level of protection of indigenous interests in Western countries is satisfactory, nor that Western values and legal regimes should be transplanted in Asian and South American regions, thereby reenforcing colonial attitudes. At present, most indigenous peoples live in former communist or developing countries. These countries also comprise the largest part of pristine wetlands, rainforests and other biodiversity rich land. The slow increase of global awareness of indigenous and environmental policy issues could serve the function of encouraging former communist or developing countries to rethink their policies dealing with folklore and indigenous interests. Suitable policies and structures could then be developed and formulated from sources and studies within those countries based on collaboration with all other countries in the world facing similar dilemmas.

[22] "Tribal peoples" is a term often used by Asian or South American countries that refuse to recognise the existence of indigenous minority groups. The term refers to minority groups leading traditional lifestyles in isolation from the majority population.

neglected in academic legal research on the IP protection of folklore. The misuse of artistic expressions is more visible in society and considerable progress has been made to accommodate indigenous interests regarding contemporary arts in the Copyright and Designs area. Indigenous paintings, sculptures, music recordings, etc. seem to have attracted at least limited public attention and levels of legal protection via reasonably favourable court attitudes, particularly regarding individual, contemporary visual and performing arts expressions. Ethnobiological knowledge in comparison is largely left unprotected, and until quite recently had not been addressed by policy-makers and academia. The reasons for this are complex, but an attempt will be made here to identify them.

Ethnobiological knowledge provides for a much larger challenge to the IP laws than other forms of indigenous folklore, perceivedly due to the specifics of the patent (and trade secret) regimes. Products developed with the help of traditional knowledge are usually protected by patent law, but indigenous peoples hardly ever receive equitable remuneration for their input. The patent regime can be said to be stricter in nature and scope and protection is more expensive and time consuming to achieve in comparison with for example the copyright regime. The patent regime requires novelty, utility and applicability in industry, and an inventive step (state of the art). On top of these, the "natural substances" exception applies in virtually all indigenous attempts to patent their knowledge. A joint inventor position can be legally upheld in exceptional cases, but the enforcement of such rights in practice often proves difficult, if not impossible, due to industry attitudes. Trade secrets have to be "secret", with the result that because of the fact that most ethnobiological knowledge has entered the public domain,[23] for that reason legal protection is denied. The copyright regime, in contrast, presents originality, material form and several other hurdles to indigenous folklore, but no registration is required, and the originality requirement seems to be more easily satisfied than the novelty/inventive step and secrecy requirements. Copyright protection itself also offers little to ethnobiological knowledge, because oral traditions are not protected.[24]

Legal analyses of why the specific IP regime requirements fail to grant ethnobiological knowledge legal protection have been presented

[23] Most ethnobiological knowledge is of non-contemporary nature which already severely challenges most IP regime requirements for protection, and has been collected and published in some form or the other by anthropologists, historians, botanists and other researchers or observers.

[24] Influences of "civil law", which protects oral expressions and offers moral rights protection to creators, might bring about changes in the common law world on this point in the near future due to increased harmonisation of IP laws; Berne Convention, TRIPs, etc.; See also *Copyright Act Amendments, Proposed Provisions Implementing Government Decisions For Reform,* (Exposure Draft and Commentary), February 1996; See also "Moral Rights for Our Creators", August 29, 1996, http://www.dca.gov.au/mediarel/archive/media—file; and see http://www.liberal.org.au/policy/arts/art3.htm#l.

in various papers throughout the proceedings of this Conference. More and more media attention is drawn to the matter as well. A crucial point that in my opinion has been neglected in the debate on this topic both on domestic and international level is the determinative role that the specifics of the *process of biodiversity prospecting* rather than the *characteristics and the nature of ethnobiological knowledge* play in delivering this unfortunate and unsatisfactory lack of legal protection. This paper argues that a close analysis of the characteristics and the nature of ethnobiological knowledge in the context of the rationales for and aspects of the current functioning of the IP regimes on domestic and international level legitimise/justify the legal protection of ethnobiological knowledge.

The Process of Biodiversity Prospecting

Ethnobiological knowledge severely challenges the IP laws because traditional knowledge is acquired and used by commerce in a less visible way than indigenous works of art or designs. Most research takes place in the laboratories of home countries, where indigenous peoples have no access. Patenting of the end product, or protection by trade secret law, and the inflow of profits from the monopoly situation resulting from IP protection also takes place in the home countries. It is difficult to determine the quantity, the nature and the origin of the traditional knowledge of indigenous peoples that is used during research procedures in home country laboratories. Often, direct contact between the pharmaceutical companies and indigenous peoples is established. Extensive ethnobotanical research is nevertheless also virtually always a complementary source and sometimes the only source of information for bioprospectors.

Traditional knowledge serves an important function in the selection and the process of collecting samples of genetic resources. The indigenous involvement is often limited to the initial phase of R&D only.[25] The role of ethnobiological knowledge in the development of the end product is nevertheless significant. Without it, the biotechnology industry would have to use a "hit or miss" approach. Considering the amount of species, micro-organisms and plants on our planet, the extra expenses and time involved in R&D without the use of ethnobiological knowledge is obvious.

Most indigenous peoples lack a sufficient understanding of IP regimes, and the negotiation skills to bargain for more favourable terms for the exchanges of information. Even when the indigenous people approached for co-operation in bioprospecting activities understand the opportunities given by their possession of ethnobiological

[25] *cf.* Debate over Native Title Amendments; Indigenous involvement at the three stages of mining prospecting and digging.

knowledge, the overwhelming power, expertise and skills of pharmaceutical companies and Governments (overseas and host countries') is generally sufficient to convince indigenous people to co-operate on their terms.

The conclusion that results from the evaluation is that the in essence "hidden" nature of biodiversity prospecting processes contributes to the practical hurdles for the eligibility of ethnobiological knowledge for IP protection in the present legal systems. The process makes it virtually impossible for indigenous people to prove their significant input in the process of biodiversity prospecting and R&D on genetic resources. The fact that Westerners usually keep written records of all steps taken in the process of biodiversity propecting and R&D, and that this is uncommon practice for indigenous peoples only disadvantages indigenous peoples in their quest to receive equitable remuneration for providing ethnobiological knowledge to bioprospectors.

The misuse of ethnobiological knowledge and unethical conduct by biotechnology or pharmaceutical firms in dealing with indigenous people during biodiversity prospecting activities thus falls mostly beyond the scope of the intellectual property regimes. In addition, few or no other avenues seem to be available to indigenous peoples in this respect as well.[26] The establishment of IP rights for ethnobiological knowledge would significantly empower indigenous peoples during the bargaining procedures and during the exercise of biodiversity prospecting activities.

The Characteristics and the Nature of Ethnobiological Knowledge; Indigenous Property Subject Matters

In order to determine whether the IP regimes should in fact protect indigenous folklore and in case this question is answered positively, how protection for ethnobiological knowledge should be achieved within the current legal systems, a legal analysis of the nature and intrinsic value of various aspects of indigenous folklore has to be made. Ethnobiological knowledge is part of the indigenous cultural heritage, and it should be examined with respect to its interrelatedness with other forms of indigenous folklore.[27] A definitional analysis of ethnobiological knowledge for both Anglo-American and indigenous customary law is crucial. If the two legal regimes can be reconciled, much progress has been made towards a more equitable dealing with indigenous folklore in general and ethnobiological knowledge in particular.

---

[26] See Code of Conduct, Research Ethics Conference, September 1996 (M. Tehan, University of Melbourne).

[27] See M.C. Suchman, "Invention and Ritual: Notes on the Interrelation of Magic and Intellectual Property in Preliterate Societies" [1989] 89 *Columbia Law Review* 1264.

The Western[28] legal regimes (unsatisfactorily) force several distinctions upon indigenous folkloristic subject matter.[29–30] It is submitted that during the process of dividing folkloristic expressions and information up into sections in order to neatly fit the Western legal pigeonhole system, many of its unique characteristics are lost or easily overlooked. The special function of indigenous folklore is dependent upon its coherent existence and dynamic (non static) nature.

A significant distinction is between tangible and intangible aspects of folklore. To indigenous peoples this distinction is not relevant, as material and spiritual aspects are interrelated, and material property and commercial profits do not play a dominating role in communal life. In the Western Regime, only intangible property is eligible for IP protection. The tangible indigenous objects, land and sites/places are dealt with by real property laws bounded by Cultural Heritage Protection and Repatriation of Artefacts laws and regulations. This distinction fails to recognise the indigenous approach to worship the interrelationship between tangible and intangible property, and the intellectual, non physical value of tangible aspects of folklore. For the aims of the IP framework, indigenous intangible property is separated from aspects that relate to tangible property. The outcome of the IP framework is thus unsatisfactory.

The distinction between tangible "real" and "personal" indigenous property is for the purposes of the evaluation of the possibilities for the protection of ethnobiological knowledge less relevant, but will be mentioned here for its value in analogy studies.[31] Real property ownership and access rights disputes are based on the *Mabo* decision[32] and the Native Title Act.[33] The protection of indigenous interests in real property developed in a complex, but increasingly promising way. It is noteworthy, that proposals to amend the Native Title Act,[34] will most probably result in a decreased scope for indigenous rights protection, particularly where the right to bargain in mining negotiations and pastoral licensing situations are at stake.[35] Indigenous personal property has come a long way as well. The protection of indigenous ancient cultural artefacts, and the repatriation of such items to the communities where they were taken from during and after the settlement is an interesting area for study. It is striking how Western legal concepts deal

---

[28] "Western" is defined for the purposes of this paper as representing Anglo-American and North European lifestyles, culture and legal and organisational systems.

[29–30] See Fig. 1.

[31] See subheading "The societal Implications of the Adoption of Particular Regimes for the Protection of Ethnobiological Knowledge; Balancing Industry and Indigenous Interests".

[32] *Mabo* (1992) 175 *Commonwealth Reports* 1.

[33] Native Title Act 1993 (Cth).

[34] L. Taylor, "Native Title Dialogue Breaks Down", *The Financial Review*, September 3, 1996, p. 2; see *Special Seminar on Native Title in Australia, 1992-1996*, held at the University of Melbourne on August 20, 1996, by G. Myers of Murdoch Law School and the Director of Legal Research Unit of the Native Title Tribunal.

[35] A. Ridgeway, "ATSIC Cuts Make Job Hard", *The Financial Review*, Letters, 26 August 1996, p. 18.

with personal property in an entirely different manner in comparison with real property. It seems at this stage, that the objective protection of artefacts, as of value for all mankind, seems to prevail in Western countries over the importance of such personal property for the self determination of indigenous peoples and their function in communal life.

The distinction between contemporary and non contemporary indigenous subject matters should be mentioned. Contemporary acquired indigenous real and personal property is adequately protected. Contemporary intangible property such as works of visual and performing arts by indigenous artists are protected by the Copyright laws and other IP regimes, although many have argued that the protection is insufficient because it fails to protect for example communal interests and copying of indigenous dot painting "style".

Non contemporary ancestry/ancient folklore from tangible ("personal" or "real") and intangible origin, are treated dissimilarly by Western legal regimes. Intangible non contemporary property such as ethnobiological knowledge and religious aspects of the "Dreaming" lack IP protection. Only tangible non-contemporary linkages to real and personal folkloristic property are recognised by Western laws for Native Title and repatriation purposes. The link has to be continuous over time and virtually undisputed. The difficulties with delivering evidence of such links is obvious, and the undesirable societal results for "urban" indigenous peoples are clear.

The conclusion that should be drawn here is that intangible property is only protected if it is of contemporary nature, as the IP regimes have originality, novelty or confidentiality requirements for the various categories of subject matters. Indigenous folklore fails to supply neatly defined categories of subject matter to fit in the pigeonholes of the IP regimes, because all folklore has ancient, orally transmitted aspects incorporated in, or functioning next to or complementary with newly developed cultural heritage. Much of the cultural heritage of indigenous peoples is ancient, product of oral delivery and exchange of ideas, texts, music, dances, songs, medical and other knowledge, mythology and spirituality between members of the same and different communities. Folklore does not represent a static situation. Folklore evolves, changes, complicates and also simplifies over time. The dynamic nature of this process in combination with its to Western society hidden and unknown nature makes it extremely innovative, valuable and empowering for various groups and industry sectors in Western society.

Three categories of intangible indigenous property exist; *Artistic, Spiritual* and *Physical Property*. Artistic contemporary folklore currently enjoys probably the highest level of IP protection, although its protection can still be qualified as unsatisfactory. Artistic folklore relates to all indigenous works of visual and performing arts. Paintings, drawings, music, sculptures, dances, stories, crafts, and all techniques and style characteristics involved are the most well known examples of this type of folklore. Physical folklore refers to traditional knowledge of flora, fauna, medical knowledge, geographical knowledge, and all techniques of preparing natural substances or crafts equipment from raw materials are comprised. The third category is probably the least protected and explored by the Western legal regimes, although its significance, and interrelatedness with the other two categories is striking. Spiritual folklore is representative of all aspects of indigenous religion, mythology, rites, traditions, superstition, customs, habits and normative frameworks and customary laws. It should be noted that it might be argued that normative frameworks and customary laws in combination with communal organisational and decision making structures should be placed in an umbrella category. The norms in indigenous communities are based on and at all times consistent with all three aspects of folklore. A suitable example can be mentioned here. Ethnobiological knowledge and traditional knowledge about ecosystems and the implications of human interactions in those systems are essentially physical folklore, but an important part of spirituality and customary laws encertain that the community lives in consistency with that knowledge and thus on a sustainable basis with the ecosystems. Artistic expressions play at the same time an important role in spirituality customs and rites.

In conclusion, indigenous customary laws recognise the interrelatedness of land, people and culture. The Western legal regimes not surprisingly lack the potential to accommodate indigenous interests in cultural heritage because the system was developed in and built for the Western societal environment. As research shows, indigenous concepts of law and societal order were designated to function in a community based societal environment with dissimilar concepts of property, public and individual rights, obligations, and responsibilities. In order to accommodate indigenous customary law and general interests in the protection of folkloristic property, it is submitted that the pigeonhole system should be replaced by a system that acknowledges the sliding scale between tangible and intangible, contemporary and non-contemporary property where indigenous property is at stake.[36–38]

Balancing Industry and Indigenous Interests; Examining the Societal Need and Objective Justifications for the Protection of Ethnobiological Knowledge

Commercial interests, societal and equity considerations have to be weighed against each other as part of the analyses of the need and justifications for the legal protection of ethnobiological knowledge. Due

[36–38] For concrete proposals regarding suitable legislation and their political feasibility see the longer research paper; M. de Koning, "Biodiversity Prospecting and the Equitable Remuneration of Ethnobiological Knowledge; Reconciling Industry and Indigenous Interests".

to the weaker bargaining position of indigenous peoples because of their lack of knowledge of the legal system and lack of economic power, a true balance of interests has never taken place in practice.[39]

Many justifications and legal rationales exist to protect ethnobiological knowledge and societal and equity advantages result from such protection. Similar to all other subject matter of IP regimes, the commercial value of the intellectual product, in combination with its originality, its novelty and utility to society or identification/authenticity connotation renders it its suitability for protection against misuse, thus generating exclusive monopolistic exercise rights. These objective arguments justify at least a limited indigenous share in the profits made by the industry.

The commercial value of ethnobiological knowledge is beyond doubt. It can also be argued that folklore falls within the scope of most of the other criteria. The protection thus sought for folklore is hardly too broad or unlimited. The boundaries of the benefits of the exclusivity for indigenous peoples are already determined by the relative weak position of creators, authors and small inventors in the Anglo-American IP framework, and the broader arts management and industry context.

Equitable remuneration of indigenous peoples stimulates the preservation of traditional knowledge and encourages innovation through the development of new ethnobiological knowledge in indigenous communities. It also provides for an incentive for indigenous peoples to publish or disclose the information, thus increasing its availability to industry for the benefit of all mankind. These advantages of equitable remuneration are significantly similar to the universal justifications of the existence of the IP laws in modern society.

The Societal Implications of the Adoption of Particular Regimes for the Protection of Ethnobiological Knowledge; Balancing Industry and Indigenous Interests by Analogous Reasoning

In order to examine what possible avenues exist to protect ethnobiological knowledge, and what societal implications the adoption of these avenues will have, evaluations can be made of experiences with clashes of industry and indigenous interests in the real property and "personal" property field. The legal regimes covering these areas have been dealing with clashes of industry and indigenous interests for a relatively longer time and therefore are more advanced.

Real property laws are relevant in this respect. The Native Title Property and Access Rights Controversy as brought forward by mining enterprising, has direct significance for clashes of interests in access

[39] Reference can be made here to the North versus South (Industrialised v. LDC) Intellectual Property Dilemma and Implications for Indigenous Minority Groups in Industrialised Countries.

rights to genetic resources found on indigenous territory. In Australia, the Crown (States) owns all natural resources found within its territory.[40] Negotiations with indigenous groups in mining prospecting and mining industry conduct in Australia and overseas provide for illuminating material.[41] The Native Title Act, Cultural Heritage Protection Act of Sacred/Secret Sites and Paths and the *Mabo* decision are relevant for the exploration of the likelihood of the legal expansion of their applicability to questions over access to genetic resources on land owned by indigenous peoples, or land that has a Native Title claim resting upon it, or land hat has a special sacret meaning to indigenous peoples.

The importance of mining prospecting situations goes even further than access rights to genetic resources. The Native Title Act, *Mabo* decision and other case law are relevant for the determination of the question whether ethnobiological knowledge qualifies for IP protection, either directly,[42] or reasoning by analogy.

The option of *direct applicability* has been researched by academia, and although some valuable arguments can be found in favour of such an extensive interpretation of the relevant law, the results are marginal, and at present probably politically not feasible to exercise. I would argue that *broader reasoning by analogy* provides for a larger field of research, and it will thus probably deliver stronger arguments in favour of IP protection of ethnobiological knowledge. Another advantage of this type of research is that it is more likely truly to reflect indigenous views, as their opinions and actions in practice are evaluated and weighted, rather than derived from court decisions, which reflect indigenous individual (one-off) and judge-made interpretations of indigenous opinions. The advantages of analogical reasoning furthermore surface quite clearly, when it is considered that most Native Title disputes in mining eventually are resolved through formal and informal negotiations resulting in a private agreements. The interpretation of the literal text of the Native Title Act and *Mabo* decision often plays a minor role compared to the factual influence exercised by particular negotiators, the economic power of the parties and the particular interests of lobby groups at both sides. The advantages of analogy studies of particular mining prospecting negotiation processes therefore would provide for more insight into the actual situation in the field,

[40] See H. Fourmile, "The Application of the Convention on Biological Diversity with Regard to the Exercise of Indigenous People's Natural Resource Rights under Australia's Commonwealth, State and Territory Laws: Queensland — A Case Study", paper presented at the Science & Other Knowledge Traditions Conference, August 23–27, 1996, Cairns Campus of the James Cook University of North Queensland.

[41] M. Gordon, "A Lesson in the Art of Lobbying", *The Australian*, August 27, 1996, p. 27; S. Emerson, J. Short and K. Meade, "Borbidge to Accelerate Law on Zinc Mine Talks", *The Australian*, July 10, 1996, p. 2.

[42] See S. Gray, "Vampires Around the Campfire: Indigenous Intellectual Property Rights and Australian Patent Law", paper presented at the International Conference on Artistic & Cultural Expressions, Traditional Knowledge and Protection of Heritage, Brisbane, by the Australian Folklore Association at the University of Queensland September 27–29, 1996.

and to determine what boundaries should be drawn by the law in order to adequately shape the bargaining situations for biodiversity prospecting. I would like to submit therefore that analogical research on a practical level is more suitable than any legal research on a theoretical level, whether focussing on extensive interpretations or analogy bound. Eventally both practical and theoretical level research should become complementary in the phase of drafting new legislation to deal with the problemacy of ethnobiological knowledge.

Personal property law, covering ownership of objects such as cultural artefacts, cultural artefacts protection and repatriation is relevant for two reasons. The first reason is that it is part of the pigeonhole system, and part of the whole of folkloristic subject matter. The second reason is that it is the only legal regime dealing with repatriation processes. It is doubtful if intangible property in ethnobiological knowledge which has already entered the public domain can realistically be "repatriated," but in my opinion it is an interesting field for analogical studies.

Some U.S. states have enacted repatriation legislation dealing with cultural artefacts, which illustrates the increasing need to adopt Federal legislative action on the repatriation of artefacts in Australia. The practice of museums in Australia and overseas in dealing with repatriation claims provides for much insight in the context and pitfalls of the process. Most repatriation processes happen on basis of negotiations with indigenous communities, resulting in private contracting, rather than directly based on the legal regimes. More theoretical studies will be necessary to examine the feasibility of repatriation processes for ethnobiological knowledge in the public domain.

Although no consensus between government, industry and indigenous parties has been reached in real and "personal" property fields as well, much can be learnt from comparative analyses of reasoning in the negotiations between the parties. It is nevertheless noteworthy that the challenges of indigenous interests by biodiversity prospecting are unique and significantly different from a large part of the tangible property issues.

Are There Solutions at the Horizon?

Although analogy studies can prove helpful in the policy development regarding indigenous intangible property protection, the real challenge posed by ethnobiological knowledge is how it can be protected within the intangible property framework.[43] The way in which the IP regime deals with artistic folklore is to a certain extent representative of the wider aspects of legal protection of folklore and provides for a promising field for research,[44] that might deliver suggestions for the

[43] See L.I. Yano, "Comment: Protection of Ethnobiological Knowledge of Indigenous Peoples" (1993) 41 *UCLA Law Review* 443.

[44] See for example K. Puri, "Cultural Ownership & Intellectual Property Rights Post Mabo: Putting Ideas Into Action", paper on file with the author.

direct applicability of the IP regime to achieve protection of ethnobiological knowledge.

Other options, particularly to accommodate indigenous interests on a temporary or short term basis might be more suitable/feasible. A positive link between legislation dealing with access to genetic resources and patent law is an example of enhancement of benefit sharing while respecting the current scope and pigeonhole system of the IP regimes. Another advantage of this approach is that it directly addresses the problemacy of protecting indigenous integrity and other interests during biodiversity prospecting processes.[45] An interesting suggestion for the enhanced protection of indigenous interests in biodiversity prospecting situations is the encouragement of:

> *Benefit sharing by making the validity of IP rights dependent upon the applicant providing full and frank disclosure of the sources of the material used to develop the product. It can be encouraged further by requiring the applicant to warrant that they have adhered to the access regulations of the relevant country or that they have observed an industry code of conduct such as the FAO's International Code of Conduct for Plant Germplasm Collecting and Transfer. This could also help overcome monitoring and enforcement problems. Enforcement and administration costs could be defrayed by establishing regional patent offices which have a fast track quasi-judicial review procedure, such as the dispute resolution mechanism adopted by the WIPO in 1994.*[46]

It is at this level where international organisations such as WIPO,[47] TRIPs and the WTO provide for the necessary organisational back up, thus stimulating the achievement of an adequate protection of indigenous interests beyond the literal texts of the treaties.

Eventually, a satisfying legal regime should be developed to accommodate indigenous interests in the protection of ethnobiological knowledge that fits the wider context of the societal need to protect all aspects of indigenous folklore. One of the main guidelines that will determine whether the developed regime will function adequately, refers to the recognition of the interrelatedness of tangible, intangible, contemporary and ancient aspects of folklore in indigenous customary law. This part of the development towards a satisfying protection of indigenous interests in ethnobiological knowledge heavily builds upon

---

[45] See the distinction that was drawn between the *process of biodiversity prospecting* and the *characteristics and the nature of ethnobiological knowledge* at the end of subheading, "The Lack of Equitable Remuneration for Indigenous Intangible Property; The Problemacy of protecting Ethnobiological Knowledge in Current Domestic and International IP Regimes".

[46] *Knowledge, Innovations and Practices of Indigenous and Local Communities,* note by the Secretariat, Subsidiary Body on Scientific, Technical, and Technological Advice, Second Meeting, September 2–6, 1996, Montreal, http://www.iisd.ca/lii...div/sbstta/sb207.html, p. 20.

[47] Note that WIPO was involved in earlier attempts to address biodiversity prospecting and the equitable remuneration of indigenous peoples; UNESCO-WIPO Model Provisions Tunis 1976 and 1985.

the outcome of the evaluation of the nature and intrinsic value of ethnobiological knowledge. It is at this stage difficult to determine whether ethnobiological knowledge objectively qualifies for a place in the IP framework.

Largely due to the fact that the current IP framework and the political developments do not seem to be favouring the expansion of protected subject matter in favour of the protection of ethnobiological knowledge, *sui generis* protection will be the most viable option for satisfactory protection of indigenous interests in ethnobiological knowledge in the long term. Protection in a *sui generis* framework also provides for a much wider opportunity to apply indigenous customary law concepts and normative principles. Extensive research on ethnobiological knowledge will have an important task in the preparatory phase for the adoption of *sui generis* legislative protection. Particularly definitional problems will have to be solved and a refined subject matter model for indigenous folklore will have to be structured before such law can be successfully drafted. Whether or not all folklore should be protected under one umbrella, or that a range of different folkloristic subject matters can be distinguished that should be protected in specific *sui generis* regimes is an important aspect of the problemacy to be resolved.

It is at the level of drafting *sui generis* protection for ethnobiological knowledge where WIPO should play an initiating role, and maintain a prominent forum for further developments. WIPO should be actively involved in the exercise of drafting Model Provisions. The difficulty of accomodating indigenous interests in ethnobiological knowledge and the specifics of protecting indigenous integrity and interests during biodiversity prospecting activities, is of a universal nature and much can be gained from the communication and exchange of information between the various countries facing the need for legislative action.

3. Legal And Economic Considerations of Bioprospecting

Dr Uma Suthersanen

Currently a Lecturer in Intellectual Property at Queen Mary & Westfield College, University of London, she has published articles on various aspects of intellectual property law, including the legal-economic perspective of functionality, the categorisation of intellectual property regimes, and design protection. Her research interests include: international copyright law and the economic and social rationales of intellectual property protection.

Legal and Economic Considerations of Bio-Prospecting

Hardin's thesis on the tragedy of the commons posited that man was apparently locked into a system whereby all men pursued their self interest in a society that believed in the freedom of the commons.[1] It follows that this continuous economic growth must eventually lead to an exhaustion of environmental resources.[2] Nevertheless, we are reassured that the impending Armageddon can be thwarted as long as economic growth and development is made compatible with the preservation of the environmental commons. This compatibility will be achieved if institutional intervention and technical progress are focused so that resources are continuously directed towards environmental improvement.[3] Essentially, a market failure, on the scale of Hardin's tragedy of the commons, will result unless the allocation of resources is re-directed to sectors of the economy which are devoted to the environment and which will fulfil the goals of preserving and maintaining the planet's resources.

Thus, the *zeitgeist* of the turn of the century is that of environmentally-concerned economics, with economic incentives being required to direct private and public market players towards the goal of environmental conservation and maintenance.[4] This paper concentrates on the implications of this reasoning in relation to the bio-prospecting of biological resources. One clear assumption is that we have to classify biological resources as economic goods, and address the next issue on the agenda, which is that of valuation. Biological resources must be ascribed a market value, and the best means by which this can be done would be the propertisation of such resources, be they organic or informational. Adjacent is the argument, already implemented in some countries, that all bio-prospecting activities in relation to such resources will have to reflect the true market price either by means of licenses, permits or taxes.

---

[1] G. Hardin, "*The Tragedy of the Commons*" (1968) 162 *Science* 1243, at 1244.

[2] This is also termed as endogenous growth with an exhaustible natural resource, see Dasgupta and Heal, "The optimal depletion of exhaustible resources", in (1974) *Review of Economic Studies* 3.

[3] Hardin's premise is that environmental resources, though finite are renewable and regenerable, partly due to the assimilative capacity of the environment to absorb pollution and wastes, and partly due to the ability of technical progress to substitute pollution reducing and waste recycling production and to regenerate the resources.

[4] Indeed, some commentators have gone further to hold that economic interests are indeed subordinate to those of environmental and conservation interests, despite the losses incurred by market players such as shareholders or consumers. See M. Sagoff, *The Economy of the Earth: Philosophy, Law and the Environment* (Cambridge Univ. Press, 1988), at pp. 69, 100, 219–220 (holding the view that neo-classical obsessions with efficiency and wealth maximisation, coupled with individual choice, are pursuits of hedonists. This view instead proposes that after basic needs are met, any further consumption serves no purpose.).

Institutionalising Environmental Economics

From the narrow perspective of a purist, the rationale for the conservation of bio-diversity is simple, uncomplicated by economic or property considerations.[5] The planet's resources are exhaustible matter and must be preserved from potential threats such as deforestation, the destruction of wetlands and coral reefs, and human activity (such as hunting, collecting, habitat destruction and the modification of ecosystems to industrial or agrarian units). The rationale for conserving bio-diversity is even more clear: it provides the actual and potential source of biological resources, it contributes to the maintenance of the biosphere in a condition which supports human and other life, and finally, it is worth maintaining for non-scientific reasons of ethical and aesthetic value, sometimes referred to as "biophilia".[6] This vision concludes that countries which are blessed with biological resources should sustain them, for the well-being of us all.

However, the question of conservation of biological diversity and resources raises many considerations. First, two main causes can be ascribed to this depletion: intrinsic pressures such as population growths, biomass resource depletion, agriculture and food security and deforestation[7]; and extrinsic pressures such as bio-prospecting activities. Conservation cannot be placed above the need for developing countries to industrialise further to reach the same status as developed countries.

Secondly, the global market for biological resources is concentrated geographically, both in terms of production and consumption. More than 50 per cent of the world's bio-diversity resources are held in a dozen of the more lesser-developed states of the world. However, the consumption of such resources lies outside their borders,[8] together with any accompanying profits. Thus, while developing countries produce most of the genetic resources for new products, the primary gainers are industries located in the developed countries which are

---

[5] Biological diversity refers to three distinct types of diversity: genetic diversity — the variation of genes within a species; species diversity — the variety of species within a region; and ecosystem diversity — the variety of ecosystems within a region. Thus, the Convention on Biological Diversity defines biological diversity as the "variability among living organisms from all sources including, inter alia, terrestrial, marine and other aquatic ecosystems and the ecological complexes of which they are part; this includes diversity within species, between species and of ecosystems." Article 2, Convention on Biological Diversity, June 5, 1992 (hereinafter CBD).

[6] The term was coined by E.O Wilson, in "Biophilia and the Conservation Ethic", in S. Kellert & E.O. Wilson (eds.), *The Biophilia Hypothesis*, (Island Press, 1993). See also R. Leaky & R. Lewin, *The Sixth Extinction: Biodiversity and its Survival* (Widenfeld & Nicolson, 1995) chapter 8.

[7] For a fuller account of depletion caused by such intrinsic pressures, see P.S. Ramakrishnan, "Lessons from the Earth Summit: Protecting and Managing Biodiversity in the Topics", in N. Dore & T. Mount, (eds.), *Global Environmental Economics: Equity and the Limits to Markets*, (Blackwell, 1999) at pp. 241–246.

[8] In the area of pharmaceuticals alone, 70% of consumption derives from the developed countries, with 20% going to developing countries. B. Aylward, "The role of plant screening and plant supply in biodiversity conservation, drug development and health care.", in T. Swanson (ed.) *Intellectual Property Rights and Biodiversity Conservation* (CUP, 1995).

estimated to see anything between a US$ 20 billion to US$ 100 billion return on such goods by the year 2000.[9]

As aptly summarised by one commentator:

> Two thirds of all existing species are found in the developing countries, but it is private corporations in industrial nations which own bio-technical tools to exploit these resources. Already, there is fierce competition among companies in Europe, the United states and Japan for this industry, currently worth $4 billion but expected to grow to $40/$50 billion by the end of the decade. Profits will go to those holding patents and to the governments that make those patents possible. . . . Chemical industries, biotech companies and governments in the industrialised world defend the intellectual property law which compensates private enterprises for the risks and expenses involved in research and development.[10]

By applying the "polluter pays" principle,[11] the conclusion is that the developed countries cannot continue their present environmentally unsound patterns of living, with wasteful use of resources, unsound consumption patterns and destructive modes of production. The argument proceeds that responsibilities for biological conservation and sustainable use of resources must be allocated in light of those responsible for excessive consumption and production:[12] this is generally directed towards the conglomerate of developed states, including Japan, European Union member states and the United states. Furthermore, the preservation of biological diversity entails heavy costs and can only occur for the benefit of the developed countries with a reciprocal transfer of bio-technology, capital and other technical infrastructure.

Intellectual property rights, in relation to bio-prospecting activities, feature as one of the more controversial issues as they are perceived as serving the basis by which revenue is harnessed through licensing and other fees, thus, not only widening the existing gap between the developing and developed countries, but dissipating any burden of

---

[9] The importance of biological resources is evidenced by the OECD forecast that the market for biotechnological products in the year 2000 will reach US$ 100 billion, with 90% of marketable, patented and approved new chemical entities come from eight countries — the United States, Japan, United Kingdom, Switzerland and four other European countries. OECD, *Biotechnology: Economic and Wider Impacts* (OECD, 1989) p. 21.

[10] A.O. Adede, *Towards a Convention on Biological Diversity*, presented at the Chicago Earth Summit, April 24, 1992, cited in C. Mensah, "The Role of the developing countries", in L. Campiglio, *et al*, (eds.), *The Environment After Rio: International Law and Economics*, Graham & Trotman, 1994, p. 47.

[11] For an exposition of the principle, see D. Pearce & R. Turner, *Economics of Natural Resources and the Environment* (Harvard Wheatsheaf, 1990) pp. 175–176.

[12] Within the international context, the principle of "common but differentiated responsibilities" has been offered to cajole the developed countries into accepting the larger responsibility in the task of conserving, protecting and restoring the environmental health and integrity of the ecosystem. See Principles 7 and 9, Rio Declaration.

environmental costs and responsibilities.[13] Furthermore, the nature of bio-prospecting and its impact on the economies of the host countries has become more contentious in recent years due to the synergy of three factors: advances in technology, a nascent environmentally conscious society, and legislative impetus towards the commodification of the environmental resources.

Technology and the Apotheosis of the Environment

Developments in biotechnology and genetic engineering techniques has increased the potential value of bio-prospecting for biological resources. Scientific advances now enable us to isolate, identify and synthesise plants and animals which can provide a rich source of new starting materials, not just for the drug market, but for other industries such as colourants and perfumes.[14] Major sectors for biotechnology application include pharmaceutical, agriculture, forestry, foods and chemicals, with predicted areas of growth in biosensor, bioelectronic and biochip products.[15] Much of the organism-based exploitation for the production of medicines, dyes, pesticides and flavourings derives from secondary compounds or secondary metabolites, which are generally held to be responsible for the chemical diversity in organisms, especially in plants and micro-organisms.[16]

Ironically, with the rise of bio-technologically produced goods, there is a growing abhorence and intolerance for such artificial manufactures, with a growing consumer clamour for "natural products". Thus, the advent of biotechnological and genetic engineering has produced a bifurcated response: the veneration of the environment and an eco-aware consumer society. The scepticism that fills the late twentieth century man as to our technological progress reflects that of early nineteenth century naturalists, that man's every action disrupts the equilibrium that exists within the environment. We are exhorted to accept that an elaborate web of interrelationships between organisms and their natural environment, both living and nonliving, exists. Mankind cannot continue the path of industrial and bio-technological progress without realising that all ecological interactions affect nature and the mechanisms of evolutionary change. We are exposed constantly to fascinating data on the over-exploitation of plant and animal

[13] An alternative argument is that patent rights confer major benefits on the proprietor, but exploitation of the invention could entail a possible endangering of biological diversity and social damage to the less developed world. See *Plant Genetic Systems,* (Case T–356/93, [1995] E.P.O.R. 357.

[14] L. Fellows & A. Scofield, "Chemical Diversity in Plants", p. 37 in *Biodiversity Conservation, op. cit.*

[15] OECD, *Biotechnology: Economic and Wider Impacts, op.cit.*, p. 21.

[16] L. Fellows & A. Scofield, "Chemical diversity in plants", p.19 and B. Aylward, "Role of Plant Screening", pp. 102–103, in *Biodiversity Conservation, op.cit.*

species, or the rate of habitat loss.[17] There are even ecological laws [collectively known as Commoner's Ecology Laws] which, by following the maxim "Nature knows best", posit the following revelations: everything is connected to everything else; everything must go somewhere; nature knows best; and there is no such thing as a free lunch. The first two rules have been utilised to some extent to argue against interfering with any life cycle or natural process, including the rise of use of chemicals, pollution, the extraction of materials, and the over exploitation of biological resources — all of which leave a devastating and long-lasting impact on the environment, and ultimately the planet.[18]

Admittedly, technologically induced disasters, such as the Chernobyl nuclear reactor explosion and the Bhopal leak, have done much to foster this view.[19] Not only does nature know best, but the traditional knowledge nurtured and maintained by peoples who have turned their backs on our hedonistic lifestyles has taken on a new reverence. The current societal concern over the environment has been further fuelled by an increasing institutional push to amalgamate environmental policies with those of economics and trade.

Commodification of Biological Resources

This decade has established trade as a vital living force of nation states. The conclusion of the Uruguay GATT talks with the World Trade Agreement, and its consequent impact have convinced us of the power of the barter-exchange dichotomy to influence global social, environmental and economic policies. Developing nations have quietly viewed the major trading nations haggle over the quotas regarding bananas, acknowledging the value of extending the adage "land is a commodity" to the philosophy "biological resources, including indigenous folklore and traditional knowledge" are commodities to be bartered.

The growing awareness that an economic paradigm had to be forged which implicitly accepted environmental concerns was reflected in the issuance of the Brundtland Report and the Valdez Principles. The 1987 Brundtland Report[20] identified various strategic imperatives including the conservation and enhancement of a resource base, and advocated merging environment and economics in decision making,[21] concentrating on the problems derived from the current high levels of

---

17 Estimates for the rate of extinction of species vary from 5 million to 30 million, with only 1.4 million named or described. See generally, The World Commission on Environment and Development Report, *Our Common Future* (OUP, 1987), chapter 6 (hereinafter the Brundtland Report).

18 Analysed in C. Meyers, "An introduction to environmental thought: some sources and some criticisms", in (1975) 50 *Indiana Law Journal* 426.

19 *Brundtland Report*, chapter 1.

20 n.12.

21 *Brundtland Report, op.cit.*, pp. 49, 57–60, 62–65.

consumption, the correlated pressures on resources in developing countries and the task of managing the global commons. The Report did more than pave the way for global environmental treaties such as the Convention on Biological Diversity; it further legitimised environmental and conservation as international economic issues.[22] Further impetus to incorporate environmental principles into economic forecasting and policies came from the 1989 Valdez disaster which spilled 10.92 million gallons of crude oil into Prince William Sound, Alaska. The result was the formulation of the *Valdez Principles*.[23] These principles re-formulate but do not depart from known ecological maxims: the protection of the biosphere by eliminating the release of pollutants; safeguarding habitats; sustainable use of natural resources including the preservation of biodiversity; and the marketing of safe product and services that minimise adverse environmental impacts.

This, in turn, led to the United Nations Conference on Environment and Development held in Rio de Janeiro in 1992, from which arose, *inter alia*, the Convention on Biological Diversity.[24] The CBD itself stands as a legal-economic instrument. Though its primary aim is the preservation of the earth's genetic pool and diverse species by providing guidelines for the sustainable use of natural resources, it also sets out three economically interesting premises. First, economic and social development and poverty eradication are the first and overriding priorities of developing countries.[25] The second principle is that nations have sovereignty over their genetic resources, however, this must be read in light of the right of such countries to redress their economic hardship.[26] Finally, the Convention adopts a "fair and equitable

[22] *Brundtland Report, op.cit.*, chapter 3. Legislative concerns as to the environment are not indigenous to the twentieth century. Early forest conservation laws emanated in England in the sixteenth century; however, rather than on altruistic grounds, such laws were promulgated in an effort to prevent poaching and exploitation in the forests ear-marked for royal hunts. See, D. Coquillette, "Mosses From an Old Manse: Another Look at Some Historic Property Cases About the Environment", (1979) 64 *Cornell Law Review* 761, at 804.

[23] The principles were issued by CERES (Coalition for Environmentally Responsible Economies) — a group of money managers, brokers, bankers, analysts and other social investors together with environmental groups. See Note, "The Valdez Principles: A Corporate Self-Governance Code on Environmental Conduct", (1989) 2 *Geo. International Environmental Law Review* 237.

[24] Three non-binding instruments were adopted: the Rio Declaration on Environment and Development; a non-legally Binding authoritative Statement of Principles for a Global Consensus on the Management, Conservation and Sustainable Development of All types of Forest; and Agenda 21. Two treaties were also opened for signature: The Convention on Biological Diversity; the UN Framework Convention on Climate Change. The latter identified two major environmental and economical priorities. First, the protection and conservation of various environmental media, *i.e.* combating climatic change, ozone depletion; the protection of land resources; halting deforestation; conservation of biological diversity; protection of freshwater resources; and protection of oceans and seas and marine living resources. Secondly, mechanisms had to be established for the regulation of particular activities or products of human technological and industrial innovation which were considered to be harmful to the environment, including international trade and agricultural practice. See, in general, P. Sands, *Principles of International Environmental Law*, Volume 1 (Manchester University Press, Manchester, New York, 1995), p. 10 *et seq*.

[25] Premise 18, CBD.

[26] Premise 4, CBD.

sharing" principle.[27] The issue of ethno-botanical knowledge is implicitly recognised in that the notion of bio-diversity preservation appears to extend beyond the eco-system and its living organisms to include ecological, cultural and aesthetic aspects. Thus, the "fair and equitable doctrine" should be read with the preamble's vague legitimisation of the idea that *any* use of ethno-biological knowledge should be compensated for.[28]

Armed with these principles, the developing countries have a new power at hand: the control of bio-prospecting activities within these countries. Moreover, this control is to be driven by the countries' own economic goals and policies since the Convention leaves it open for states to pursue developmental policies which are detrimental and ultimately unsustainable by its implicit acceptance of "development first, environment later" policy. Indeed, the driving force of the Rio Convention appears not so much to be conservation, but the efficient allocation of economic resources and the conservation of the environment, as a by-product of the general re-orientation of the world economy, especially in light of its references to access to genetic resources, transfer of relevant technologies and funding of sustainability.[29]

Thus, the growing consensus has emerged for a re-orientation of our economic and legal institutional policies towards more environmentally friendly regimes. The concerns are not limited to the plight of developing countries, but has also motivated major developed regions such as the European Union to issue environmental policies which highlight the principle that future development must be based on the principle of sustainable development and the prudent and rational use of natural resources, and that the environment must be integrated into the definition and implementation of all other economic and social policies, including trade, industry and agriculture.[30] Nevertheless, the 1994 report on "Europe and the Forest", commissioned by the European Parliament holds a pessimistic note, which somewhat echoes the

[27] Art. 15(7). Extending the "fair and equitable" doctrine are Arts 16–19 of the Convention which principally call for developed countries to facilitate the access and transfer of technologies to those nations who provide the genetic resources, including the transfer of intellectual property related information and technology.

[28] Premise 12, CBD. ("Recognising the close and traditional dependence of many indigenous and local communities embodying traditional lifestyles on biological resources, and the desirability of sharing equitably benefits arising from the use of traditional knowledge, innovations and practices relevant to the conservation of biological diversity and the sustainable use of its components".)

[29] Principle 16 of the Rio Declaration: "National authorities should endeavour to promote the internalisation of environmental costs and the use of economic instruments, taking into account the approach that the polluter should, in principle, bear the cost of pollution, with due regard to the public interest and without distorting international trade and investment." See also A. Boyle, "The Convention on Biological Diversity", p. 126, in *The Environment after Rio, op.cit.*

[30] Arts. 130R–130T, Single European Act. See also European Commission, *The European Union and the Environment*, Office for Official Publications of the European Communities, EN 1997, p. 8; A. Marin, "E.C. Environmental Policy", in A. Agraa, (ed.) *The Economics of the European Community* (Harvester Wheatsheaf, 1994), pp. 401–404.

forthcoming discussion on the Herculean task one faces in attempting to grapple with the notion of biological resources as economic goods:

> Due to the lack of a reliable and recognised method of standardisation (and thus an objective basis for negotiation) only a logic of group pressure or an inspired and visionary political willingness can, in a generally unfavourable climate, invert the trend of keeping forest problems on the periphery. Until now, the European forestry sector has neither generated nor given rise to one or the other. The membership of Sweden and Finland may perhaps alter the situation. A true Life economy (policy) which would include the forest heritage, has yet to be created. In a society where, in the absence of a regulatory system, preference is systematically given to having rather than to being — and having in material terms as opposed to immaterial — it is important to define a specific economic and financial logic, thus guaranteeing survival. Beyond statements of good intention, the conflict between development and the environment tends to make people forget that wood sales today constitute the least expensive tool available to local governments for financing forest management programmes. Even if it is often insufficient (and increasingly so) to rely purely on market demands to finance all the necessary expenses: mountain forests, semi-urban forests, unusual or fragile ecosystems, etc.[31]

Prospecting Biological Resources

Bio-prospecting Activities

A wide definition of bio-prospecting is the search for valuable wild genetic resources found in wild plants, animals and micro-organisms. The main output is to gather enough resources so as to enable the successful development of new products including drugs, crops, industrial products and consumer products.[32] The increase in bio-prospecting activities is two-fold. First, the biotechnological landscape has altered considerably since its inception from a purely laboratory-based activity to the active prospecting for useful information in plants, animals and insects, the latter activity being concentrated in areas rich in biodiversity material. Successful and profitable gains have accompanied the discovery of some chemical compounds, such as the detection of *taxol*, an anti-cancer drug, in the fungus of yew tree Montana. Secondly, the continued improvement and advance of biotechnology ensures that bio-prospecting activities will continue to increase.

[31] "Europe and the Forest", Vol. 3, 1997, http://www.europarl.eu.int/dg4/wkdocs/forest/en/eurfo.htm.
[32] J. Adair, "The bio-prospecting question: should the United States charge biotechnology companies for commercial use of public wild genetic resources?" (1997) 24 *Ecology Law & Quarterly* 132, at p. 140.

Biological Resources: Organic and Informational

The CBD defines "biological resources" as including "genetic resources, organisms or parts thereof, populations, or any other biotic component of ecosystems with actual or potential use or value for humanity."[33] The notion of biotic components is wide enough to include resources deriving from human activities, as well.[34] If we approach the nature of biological resources in this wider sense, we can see that prospected resources can be grouped into two categories: organic resources and informational resources. Thus, on the one hand, bio-prospecting can be viewed as being solely concerned with the harvesting of the tangible, organic material, for either making a product directly or for the chemical, genetic or other information provided by the organic material. The notion of "organic resources" can encompass not only plants and their chemical diversity, but also microbial diversity,[35] and marine and species diversity.[36]

On the other hand, bio-prospecting also extracts and exploits informational resources. Such resources can be available in the tangible organic resource form of the chemical or genetic knowledge stored within the plant or animal, both in the *phenotype* (the observable characteristics of individual plants and animals) and in the *genotype* (the genetic composition of the plant or animal). A second source of informational resources are established gene banks, seed banks, databases or compilations of information.[37] A final type of informational resource is human-cultivated information concerning the use or maintenance of organic resources. A fair amount of such resources may be protectable under copyright or *sui generis* database rights, if they fulfil the requisite criteria. A further, more controversial, informational source is the indigenous or tribal or cultural knowledge, collectively referred to here as ethno-botanical knowledge.

---

[33] Art. 2, CBD.

[34] A biotic environment is part of any organism's environment that consists of other living organisms, including other competitors, predators or symbionts. Man is classified as a living organism, belonging under the *Animalia* kingdom to the *Chordata* phylum. *A Concise Dictionary of Biology* (OUP, 1990).

[35] Microbial diversity is the source of natural chemical products evidenced by the discovery of penicillin and anti-biotics; they differ from plant or animal species in that the source of such microbes lies in a scoop of soil or material. Furthermore, such microorganisms can be cultured under laboratory conditions, unlike other organisms where additional samples or collections may be required from the origin site, and where it may be difficult to synthesise the naturally available plant chemical.

[36] B. Aylward, "Role of plant screening", in *Biodiversity Conservation, op. cit.*, pp. 104–105. For instance, the INBio/Merck partnership includes the right of Merck to investigate the chemical properties of plant, microbial and insect species, discussed below. However, marine prospecting has not been, as yet, exploited to the same extent of plants due to high operational costs such as deep sea exploration to gather sea fauna, marine macroorganisms and microorganisms.

[37] Thus, for example, there are currently two projects on course to catalogue detailed information as to the living organisms in North America: the "Flora of North America", which details the range and distribution of every plant in North America; and the more recently created "National Biological Survey", which will catalogue all living organisms in the United States. J. Adair, *op. cit.*, at p. 156.

Ethno-botanical knowledge is considered as a conveyor of experience based on the direct dependence on natural systems. The phenomenon of harvesting ethno-botanical knowledge is not new, and has often been anchored to some sort of economic extraction and production cycle. Early colonial expeditions yielded the discovery of chocolate, tobacco, maize and potatoes as a result of ethno-botanical knowledge. The field of "ethno-botany", introduced in the nineteenth century, was promoted as a socio-economic cause, which would eventually offer valuable information on methods of husbanding resources, the distribution of plant species, trade routes, and new lines of manufacture. Equally ancient is the subsequent use and result of such ethno-botanical knowledge: the identification of an organic resource, the synthesis and production of it in different climates, and the marketing and consumption of such fruits of this indigenous knowledge.[38]

Current bio-prospecting activities continue to benefit from ethno-botanical information. The chemical arsenals of plants represent 300 million years of evolution of ecologically active compounds and industries do need any information which can convert this organic resources into a form which can be used in a market economy. Undoubtedly, the hit rate of finding useful organic information is linked to use of such organisms in traditional or indigenous medicine.[39] The clamour for the economic recognition and valuation of ethno-botanical knowledge is unsurprising. Host countries have not been part of the production/consumption chain of past discoveries which have resulted from screening ethno-botanical leads such as Etoposide used for chemotherapeutic agents,[40] oil of evening primrose,[41] and the Vinca alkaloids used for treating leukaemia, Hodgkin's disease and other cancer-related ailments.[42] Furthermore, an integrated economic regime is increasingly being sought which will pay for the maintenance and conservation of ethno-botanical knowledge.[43] Economic incentives are

[38] J. Sheldon & M. Balick, "Ethnobotany and the search for balance between use and conservation", pp. 55–56, in *Biodiversity Conservation, op. cit.*

[39] Sheldon & Balick, *op. cit.*, pp. 58–59. The authors claim that 25% of all medical drugs are either based or linked directly to traditional medicine use. Furthermore, only 6% of random collections of plant samples show activity as opposed to 25% of ethnobotanical collections. Further anecdotal evidence shows that a hit rate of 80% or more can be achieved where the screening of plants is limited to species used as medicine by indigenous communities.

[40] It is synthesised from a chemical in the May apple (*Podophyllum peltatum*) and has been used by native Americans for centuries as an ameliorate for wart problems. Etoposide is currently used in the treatment of small cell lung and testicular cancer, and is estimated to have a world market value of US$ 500 million.

[41] Extracted from the *Oenothera* species, it is used by Native Americans for skin problems, and is currently marketed for eczema and pre-menstrual syndrome.

[42] The Vinca alkoids originated from the traditional medicinal use of the weed *Catharanthus roseus*, a Madagascan periwinkle, which led to the drugs, Vincristine (VCR) and Vinblastine (VLB). The drugs have an estimated global sales of $100 million.

[43] The indigenous approach to ecosystem management is based on detailed knowledge of plant use and biology which can further provide an invaluable long-term model for sustainable use, especially since traditional resource management consciously fosters genetic diversity within the species as compared with the modern propensity for monoculture agriculture. See Statement of

thus required which promote such direct experience and dependence on diversity. This in turn calls for the assignment of economic values, not only to the natural organic resources, but also to the informational resources and to the communities that propagate and use such resources, *i.e.* two distinct and different economic animals. Organic resources are rivalrous and excludable albeit finite and potentially exhaustible; whilst, informational resources are non-rivalrous and non-excludable.

BIOLOGICAL RESOURCES

- **Rivalrous, excludable, potentially exhaustible**
  - Organic Resources
    - Plants, animals and other organisms
- **Non-rivalrous and non-excludable**
  - Informational Resources
    - Genetic information from organic resources
    - Other types of human-derived information, including ethno-botanical information
    - Bio-diversity databanks, records, and other fixed sources of informational

Economic Considerations of Bio-Prospecting

Collectively, institutional anguish over the degradation of the biosphere has led to the magical solution of "sustainable development", *i.e.* development that meets the needs of the present without compromising the ability of future generations to meet their own needs.[44] Sustainable development involves two disparate questions: what are the essential needs of the present generation; and what limitations should be imposed by institutions on exploitation which strain the environment's ability to meet present and future needs.

Principles and Guidelines for the Protection of the Heritage of Indigenous People, in D. Posey, *Traditional Resource Rights* (IUCN, 1996), at pp. 86–91, calling for the protection of, *inter alia*, all scientific, agricultural, technical and ecological knowledge of indigenous peoples.

[44] *Our Common Future, op. cit.*, chapter 2. See also Rio Declaration, principle 27, and Agenda 21, chapter 39.

Neo-classical Economics and Sustainable Growth

The notion of "sustainability" is not a novel feature in economic thought. An early recitation of the concept was offered by Hicks in his discourse *Value and Capital*:

> The purpose of income calculations in practical affairs is to give people an indication of the amount which they can consume without impoverishing themselves. Following out this idea, it would seem that we ought to define a man's income as the maximum value which he can consume during a week, and still expect to be as well off at the end of the week as he was at the beginning. Thus, when a person saves, he plans to be better off in the future; when he lives beyond his income, he plans to be worse of.[45]

Therefore, a key purpose of income accounting is to predict patterns of economic activity and resource use in the long term with detailed asset and liability accounts. Equally, in ecological terms, progressing towards a sustainable environment requires an account of all costs and liabilities, to be balanced against the activities of both individuals and societies. One possible means by which we can solve the "who pays" question is simply to re-define the eco-system as a market and realise its potential economic functions[46]: the supply of resources, the assimilation of waste, the provision of direct utility and the life support system.[47] Focusing solely on resources, it follows that renewable resources should be used at rates less than or equal to their re-generation rate; while, non-renewable resources are only used at rates corresponding to the rates at which technological substitutes can be developed. Thus, when we consider sustainable development in neo-classical terms, it merely means that the maximisation of the net economic benefits be obtained while maintaining the services and quality of resources over time.[48] This, however, is more simply said than done. The following analysis follows the several approaches by which the simple tenet of "maximisation versus sustainability" is purportedly to be achieved, and the difficulties which some of these approachs give rise to.

Effective resource allocation

It has been posited that a wide range of issues which arise from the extraction and use of biological resources can be analysed by utilising

---

[45] J.R. Hicks, *Value and Capital* (OUP, 1946), p. 172.
[46] An ecosystem comprises of populations and communities of organisms and the physical environment associated with it.
[47] H. Daly, "Elements of Environmental Macroeconomics in Ecological Economics, in R. Constanza, (ed.), *The Science and Management of Sustainability* (1991), pp. 44–45.
[48] H. Daly, *ibid.*

the market system. Thus, the neo-classical market economist sees man as a rational being who seeks two goals: wealth maximisation and equilibrium. Both of these goals are arrived at by utilising the golden criterion of "resource allocative efficiency" whereby resources are allocated in such a manner as to maximise the public good by providing the amount and mix of goods and services that consumers desire. Optimal efficiency in allocation or Pareto optimal is reached when there can be no possible reallocation or change so as to make one individual better off without making someone else (in his own estimation) worse off. The pricing of the goods provides the necessary fulcrum by which an equilibrium is reached. And, after all, what are biological resources but one set of factors of production, similar to labour or capital.

However, it is almost impossible to obtain a Pareto-efficient outcome as four major assumptions are built into the equation[49] : perfect competition; good information about supply, demand and price; the absence of externalities or public goods; and the presence of private rights and a perfect enforcement of such rights.[50] The problem of attempting to reach an equilibrium of efficient allocation of biological resources lies not only in the interaction between organic and informational resources, but also in the fact that organic resources themselves are subject to different considerations, depending on the nature of the resource.

Appropriable resources

Some natural resources can be classified as appropriable resources, whereby the economic value of such resources can be captured. Thus, vast tracts of land can be cordoned off and anyone desiring to develop or harvest the land can either purchase either the land or the products on it. However, the problems with such notions are numerous, and it is not always certain that a competitive and unregulated market is the right regime. First, are biological resources to be categorised definitely as private or public goods? Secondly, market transactions between the owner of the land or the fruits thereof and the putative purchaser exclude external diseconomies that are formed such as over-use of the resource, non-renewable practices and the depletion of resources for

[49] Due to the restrictive application of the Pareto criterion, the alternative criterion of "Kaldor-Hicks efficiency" is often used (and often confused with Pareto efficiency or the Posnerian wealth maximisation criterion). The alternative Kaldor-Hicks theory is that any change within an economy that favours *some individuals* at the expense of others will constitute an improvement, if the gains to the winners exceed the losses to the losers. All the above principles owe much, in this author's view, to the school of utilitarianism. See, J.S. Mill, *Utilitarianism* (Collins, 1962), Chapter 2, p. 257.

[50] For a further account, see N. Mercuro & S. Medema, *Economics and the Law: From Posner to Post-Modernism* (Princeton University Press, 1997), p. 15 *et seq.*; R. Cooter and T. Ulen, *Law and Economics* (Addison-Wesley Longman, 1996), p. 12 *et seq.*; and P. Samuelson and W. Nordhaus, *Economics* (15th ed., McGraw-Hill Inc., 1995) p. 746.

future generations. Thus, one study shows that market-based economies can flounder due to the differences in the extent of property rights conferred on such resources between the developed and developing countries. This, in turn, can lead to a pattern of international trade in which the developing countries export environmentally intensive goods, at prices below social costs, and prospect resources beyond Pareto efficiency.[51] We return to the basic theorem that the developed nations over consume, and that externalities are not captured but instead are dissipated over the global commons. Most studies show that deforestation and overuse of land occurs with the purpose of transforming forests for agricultural use to support consumption in the international market, the latter often an esoteric reference to developed countries.[52] Overuse of biological resource is partly aided by institutional policies such as those of the World Bank which emphasises exports of agricultural cash crops as a foundation for development aid. A case in point is that of Mexico which is located partly in the North American ecosystem and partly in the Neo Tropical Zone of Latin America. Despite its 1986 Forestry Law, regarded by many as a glowing piece of environmental legislation, it enacted a further law which provided no ecological limitations in order to turn Mexico's protected forests into commercial plantations — a legislative policy which coincided with Mexico's economic policy of making the country attractive to foreign capital and with its acceptance of a World Bank loan aimed at opening up the rich forests of Chihuahua and Durango in northern Mexico.[53]

If we turn our attention to informational resources, the value of such resources are almost always inappropriable, leading to externalities.

Inappropriable Resources and Public Goods

Most biological resources have a vexing habit of being inappropriable resources whereby use of the resource is free to the individual but costly to society. In the case of organic resources, part of the problem lies also in the fact that they are non-renewable where species extinction results.[54] Furthermore, such resources, especially informational resources, are also public goods whereby the benefits of such resources are spread among entire communities, irrespective of the individual's desire to purchase the good.[55]

[51] G. Chichilnisky, "North-South Trade, Property Rights and the Dynamics of the Environment", pp. 206–233.
[52] See, in general, *The Environment After Rio*, *op. cit.*
[53] A. Szekely, "The Legal Protection of the World's Forests after Rio '92", pp. 69 *et seq.* in *The Environment After Rio*, *op. cit.*
[54] However, not all economists consider biological resources as being non-renewable. See, for instance, Samuelson & Nordhaus, *op. cit.*, p. 342.
[55] Samuelson & Nordhaus, *op. cit.*, p. 347 (organic resources); Landes & Posner, W. Landes & R. Posner, "An Economic Analysis of Copyright Law" (1989) 18 J. Leg. Stud. 325, at 326 (informational resources).

Public goods are defined by two characteristics: non-excludability (*i.e.* one cannot practically exclude people from using it) and non-rivalrous consumption (*i.e.* the use of the good by one does not limit or leave less for the other to use). This characteristic is alternatively applied to define free goods, *i.e.* those goods which exist in large quantities and whose stock is not diminished by use such as sand or air. In such circumstances, the market price of free goods is zero as there is no scarcity in such goods and no corresponding need to ration them among the consumers.[56] However, as with all environmental concerns, such notions are increasingly suspect if we consider the *potential* externalities that can be caused by excessive deforestation of tropical forests, which in turn, has lead to an increase in the global carbon dioxide concentration.[57]

The problem with a public good is that if it is only regulated by the exigencies of market forces, where non-excludability and non-rivalry can flourish, the result is that externalities build up.[58] Externalities, in ecological terms, refer to the use of resources without cost to the user, but at a cost to others or where the activities of one person affects the welfare of other persons who have no direct control over those activities, *i.e.* situations when the effect of production or consumption of goods imposes costs or benefits on others which are not reflected in the prices charged for the goods and services being provided. Such costs would include[59]: the costs of remediation and reinstatement of the environment; compensatory measures (such as victims' damages); ecological damage to the environment, to the ecological system; costs of pollution charges; degradation of resources and informational goods.

How do we internalise such the costs? The correction of the imbalance to market conditions caused by externalities and the production of public goods justifies state intervention; but it is not at all clear in what form such intervention should take in the case of organic and informational resources. There are several possible solutions: institutional regulation of the public goods in the form of permits; public subsidies or taxes (for example, in the payment of subsidies to companies to eliminate environmental hazards); and private property rights.

[56] S. Pejovich, "Towards an Economic Theory of the Creation and Specification of Property Rights", in A. Ogus & C.G. Veljanovski (eds) *Readings in the Economics of Law and Regulation* (Clarendon Press, 1984), p. 53. For the view of intellectual property as a free good, see OECD Report, *Competition Policy and Intellectual Property Rights* (OECD, 1989), p. 12; K. Arrow, "Welfare Economics and Inventive Activity", in *The Rate and Direction of Inventive Activity* (National Bureau of Economic Research, 1962), pp. 617–18.

[57] C. Clegg & D. Mackean, *op. cit.*, p. 82; and *Our Common Future, op. cit.*, p. 33.

[58] Externalities usually arise where property rights (or conversely, liabilities) cannot be clearly assigned, see OECD, *Glossary of Industrial Organisation Economics, Competition Law and Policy Terms* (OECD, 1991).

[59] H. Smets, "The Polluter Pays Principle in the Early 1990s", in *The Environment after Rio, op. cit.* p. 134.

Regulatory Taxes and Permits

The solution whereby public goods can be regulated with respect to environmental costs is sometimes referred to as "green taxes", though it is not always clear which aspect of environmental problems are being solved.[60] This approach is commonly employed to solve air quality degradation. The reasoning is thus: the air is polluted as nobody owns the air; manufacturers' production costs do not encompass the cost of discharging pollution into the air; however, a private market solution whereby a society bands together to pay the producer to reduce pollution is not a viable solution as the transaction costs of forming such a group are prohibitive. The alternative solution is to establish market price indicators which call for the establishment of taxes, *i.e.* by pricing the resource. Thus, the United states does tacitly acknowledge the notion that "resources are economic goods", to be bought and sold in the open market, with the implementation of its legislative program which promotes the purchase and sale of rights to emit certain kinds of pollution.[61] However, the price must not be so high as to exceed "effects cost", *i.e.* the economic value assigned to the harm which is to be avoided by the proposed prevention expenditure.[62] In bio-prospecting terms, any charging of use of resource should then be equal to the "effects costs", *i.e.* the costs of preventing the depletion of resources, and/or the costs of maintaining such resources.

Bio-prospecting Permits

A variation on the above is to attempt to amortise any resulting externalities by instituting a regime of economic incentive systems such as taxation and compensation programmes. This has largely been

---

[60] For a quixotic view of environmental property in the 21st century, see P. Krugman "White collars turn blue", *The New York Times Magazine*, September 9, 1996, suggesting that income taxes can be eventually abolished due to its substitution by environmental taxation.

[61] The role of economic theory to (a) recognise environmental resources as economic goods, and (b) to acknowledge the vast range of externalities caused, has been part of United States psyche since the 1960s, especially with the publication of Rachel Carson's *The Silent Spring* (1962) wherein she attacked the widespread use of DDT and other chemical pesticides and insecticides as they entered the food chain, and ultimately affected the entire ecosystem. These concepts are enshrined in the United States National Environmental Policy Act 1969 (NEPA) which proposes the following potentially wide goals: fulfilling the responsibilities of each generation as trustee of the environment for succeeding generations; assuring for all Americans safe, healthful, productive and aesthetically and culturally pleasing surroundings, and attain the widest range of beneficial use of the environment without degradation, risk or health or safety, or other undesirable and unintended consequences.

[62] This rationale springs from Pigou who postulated that externalities can be removed by using corrective taxes to modify the prices for goods in existing markets, so that all costs are correctly priced, and paid for. Pigou notes that when interrelations of various private persons who are affected are highly complex, the government may find it necessary to exercise some means of authoritative control for example, over land or sea. See A.C. Pigou, *The Economics of Welfare* (1932), especially pp. 192 *et seq.*

advocated, in more ambiguous terms, by the CBD.[63] One method is to ascribe a value to either a resource, or to the bio-prospecting activity, and to regulate it by utilising the marketable permit model. This has worked in certain countries in respect of pollution control whereby the regulator sets a ceiling on the amount of pollution allowed for a whole industry, and issues permits, or credits to individual firms for their share in that amount.[64] Permits can be auctioned off and those who acquire permits pay the regulator for the privilege.[65]

However, the application of the model on bio-prospecting of biological resources raises several considerations. The first concern is that a ceiling on the total units of resources that can be used, or the total units of bio-prospecting activity that can take place has to be determined — a task that may not be scientifically certain. However, this can be tackled in two ways. First, flexibility can be built into the scheme and the total figure may be revised annually according to changing conditions and scientific evidence. Secondly, the communal owner can issue freely marketable permits equal in number to the resource units or bio-prospecting units permitted. The scheme is attractive in that it emulates a property rights system, especially where tradable permits are subject to registration, with a fixed duration period which may be renewed.[66] The governmental role would be limited to defining such rights, to ensuring market exchanges occur and to enforcing those bargains.[67] Thus, the regime follows the classical notion of efficient allocation of rights (or duties).

However, such a permit system may not work in relation to depletion of bio-diversity as externalities such as future evolutionary growth or harm may not be quantifiable in any meaningful way, even where the ceiling on the amount of viable bio-prospecting activity is adjusted annually. There is once again the problem we face regarding the information currently existing as to ecological systems. Furthermore, the assumption is that areas where resources are held lend themselves to policing, and in turn, that the country or territory in question will have adequate monitoring and enforcement systems. Another cause for concern lies in the potential failure to internalise further externalities such as trans-boundary environmental damage where the over-prospecting of resources in one state causes harmful effects in another state. Finally, while such reasoning may work in relation to organic resources, the prospect of estimating a ceiling on the

---

[63] See, in particular, Arts. 8 and 11, CBD.

[64] The system is mainly in use in the United States, and in Australia in respect of fishing rights. F. Cairncross, *Green, Inc.*, (Earthscan, 1995), pp. 68–73.

[65] For a further discussion on marketable permits, see Stewart, "Controlling environmental risks through economic incentives", (1988) 13 *Columbia Journal of Environmental Law* 153 (supporting the scheme); J. Mintz, "Economic reform of environmental protection: a brief comment on a recent debate", (1991) 15 *Harvard Environmental Law Review* 149, at 156 *et seq.* (criticising this regime).

[66] Short, but renewable, term permits have been incorporated in New South Wales, Australia in respect of fisheries, Cairncross, p. 71.

[67] C. Meyers, *op.cit.*, p. 453.

amount of available knowledge, and pricing each unit of knowledge, is tantamount to creating a new currency.[68]

Property Rights and Externalities

By adopting the Coasian approach, externalities can be removed by the correct allocation of property.[69] In the case of air pollution, it has been suggested that one can create property interest in pollution rights.[70] In the case of resources, the neo-classicist would argue that bargaining, consumer choice and social welfare would all be best enhanced by the creation of property interests in resources. Then, we can stand back and admire the ability of the market to allocate the priced resource. In the alternative, if there are no enforceable private property rights in the resource, then the cost to an individual of using an additional unit of resource as an input of production would be low or nil, since the cost would only reflect the private cost of the prospector instead of reflecting the full impact on the society of the use of the resource.[71]

Oblivious to their instinctive distrust of neo-classical economics, the property argument is ironically espoused by many environmentalists and naturalists who feel that bio-prospecting activities should not only be priced, but priced optimally. It is assumed that a corrective balance of the market is achieved through the creation and enforcement of rights in the organic and informational resource. The creation of such rights need not necessarily exclude the role of the government. Where voluntary exchanges cannot be effected due to high costs or practical impossibilities, it may be necessary to involve governmental authority, especially where it is technically difficult to identify the victims of the externality in question or to exact the correctional measure such as appropriating compensation or taxes. However, to push the scenario further, the creation of private property rights in genetic resources and in the ethno-biological information would also propose that the priced resource be sold to the highest bidder. The neo-classicist, above all, would wish that social and global resources be organised so that all consumer preferences are validated and individual freedom to choose is upheld. This can even include a choice which ultimately leads to the destruction of Pacific Yews to enable more anti-cancer drugs to be marketed, especially where a synthetic substitute market is unavailable.

---

[68] This is not to say that quasi-permit schemes do not exist in relation to informational sources, such as collective licensing arrangements in relation to broadcasting, newspapers or art works. However, such schemes derive and exist on property rights.

[69] R.H. Coase, "The Problem of Social Cost", (1960) J. Law & Econ. 1; H. Demsetz, "Toward a Theory of Property Rights", (1967) 57 *American Economics Review* 347, at 348.

[70] C. Meyers, *op. cit.*, p. 449.

[71] Thus, industrial societies tend to use less resources by privatising their organic and informational resources and by enforcing such rights clearly. Dasgupta and Heal, *Economic Theory and Exhaustible Resources* (CUP, 1979), chapter 3. For an analysis as to the determination of entitlement rights of "commons" and the efficiency criterion, see D. Farber, "Environmentalism, Economics and the Public Interest", (1989) 41 *Stanford Law Review* 1021.

Leaving aside the question of informational resources (which we deal with in assessing the intellectual property rights regime), is it feasible to confer proprietary rights on organic resources?

Organic Resources

Apparently, yes especially in light of the official sanction under the CBD that natural resources are *not* to be considered the common property of all mankind.[72] A second quandary appears: should ownership be public or private, within the national territories? One predominant economic rationale is that *res communes* are subject to overuse. Furthermore, such forms of ownership are less economically optimal due to inefficiencies of production, market disequilibrium, lack of incentives for growth, and high administrative decision making.[73] But, would not these disqualifications only apply in territories which have adopted a more industrial economy and culture, as opposed to the territories peopled by indigenous tribes, where the prevailing ethos is supposedly sustainable growth and management? There is much to be said as to classifying such resources as *res communes*, with the resources being held in trust for the public.[74]

Much of the forestry in developing countries, such as Honduras and Cameroon, are either considered nationalised state property or common property to be exploited, whereas there is much less exploitation and consumption of forestry in developed countries as more lies in private hands or are subject to taxation through property rights or permits.[75] Indeed, if we are influenced by Friedman's withering response as to the question of state or private ownership of national parks,[76] we would easily conclude that private parties are the more responsive to externalities than public owners.

One oft-cited example of using quasi-state property rights to steer bio-prospecting arrangements is the step taken by Costa Rica to rationalise its country's biological resources. The basic rationale is that of generating information while balancing biodiversity, taking into account the range of potential users of biodiversity and information. With this in mind, a private, non-profit, public interest organisation was formed — the Costa Rica Institute of Biodiversity (INBio) whereby

---

72 Art. 3, CBD.

73 H. Demsetz, "Toward a theory of property rights", (1967) 57 *American Economics Review*, 347, promoting the notion that common property is generally subject to overuse and over exploitation. For a critique on this view, see J. Grunebaum, *Private Ownership* (Routledge & Kegan Paul, 1987), pp. 158–168.

74 For a discussion on classical categorisation of property and environmental resources, see D. Coquillette, *op. cit.*, pp. 801 *et seq.*

75 The latter means is examined below.

76 M. Friedman, *Capitalism and Freedom* (Univ. Chicago Press, 1962), p. 31. ("If the public wants this kind of an activity enough to pay for it, private enterprises will have every incentive to provide such parks. And, of course, there are many private enterprises of this nature now in existence. I cannot myself conjure up any neighbourhood effects or import monopoly effects that would justify governmental activity in this area.").

all organic resources are placed under the aegis of the institute which engages in the collection and cataloguing of biodiversity samples, and finally in marketing these to scientific and commercial users. The first bio-prospecting agreement was with Merck & Co. whereby Merck pays US$ 1.135 million every two years and receives an unknown quantity of specimen of Costa Rica's plants and insects, and the right to analyse these resources for possible commercial use. If the company discovers a marketable product based on the information obtained, it will retain all intellectual property rights but will pay INBio a royalty.[77] 50 per cent of the INBio share in future royalties will be invested in Costa Rican conservation, with the remainder of the research budget supporting *in situ* scientific infrastructure, such as the sustainable use of biodiversity. Merck obtains a six-month to 2-year grace period, wherein INBio will not supply identical resources to another party.[78]

Other countries have also implemented the property model but along different lines.[79] Thus, countries such as Ecuador, Venezuela, Bolivia and Brazil, instead of granting permits for bio-prospecting activities, have allocated bio-resource rich land in the Amazon Basin, to its indigenous Indian population.[80]

Is this the way forward for all bio-prospecting activities? As a model, the Costa Rica-Merck agreement appears to have solved the question of "who pays".[81] The host country of the resources obtain a share of the profits of any products made from the use of resources, while the bio-prospector retains all intellectual property rights. It is almost tempting to imagine that such costs will eventually pass on to the consumer of the resource-based goods, thus ensuring a truly equitable distribution of costs.

However, several issues arise. First, a mechanism whereby extensive information capturing is required may lead to regulatory capture. Will the host country or host institute be open to regulatory capture? Although, in most cases, it is probably the state or a private statutory monopoly which will be the most viable owner of the biological

[77] The details of the royalty figure remain confidential, though estimates range between one to 40%. A. Lerch, "Property Rights and Biodiversity", (1998) 6 *European Journal of Law & Economics* 285, at 293.

[78] A. Lerch, *op. cit.*, pp. 292–293; INBio URL: http://www.inbio.ac.cr/.

[79] For further examples, see W. Reid, "The Economic Realities of Biodiversity", (1993-94) *Issues in Science and Technology* 48.

[80] G. Chichilnisky, *op. cit.*, p. 226.

[81] An analogous model is that of Shaman Pharmaceuticals which relies extensively on the fieldwork of internationally recognised ethno-botanists, indigenous peoples and shamans in the tropical regions of Asia, Africa and Latin America. It channels some of the profits it makes from its bio-prospecting activities to the local region whose knowledge had provided the key hints and relevant plants. Shaman institutes this mechanism through a parallel non-profit making company called "Healing Forest Conservancy" for the needs and rights of indigenous communities. However, two points should be noted. First, the scheme is voluntary on the part of Shaman; secondly, the valuation of the knowledge is left to the discretion of the bio-prospector. For further details, see D.E. Bierer, T.J. Carlson, S.R. King, "Shaman Pharmaceuticals: Integrating Indigenous Knowledge, Tropical Medicinal Plants, Medicine, Modern Science and Reciprocity into a Novel Drug Discovery Approach", http://www.netsci.org/Science/Special/feature11.html.

resources, officials who manage the resources are open to other persuasions to allow resources to go through without proper regulatory check. A second problem is that of enforcement costs. A popular perspective is that a global system of property rights, regulation of bio-prospecting activities and the consequent enforcement costs would be inefficient as the transaction costs would be too high. However, this leads us to conclude rather lamely that the current situation of an largely unregulated, polluted, over-exploited world is optimal and all for the best.[82] The final problem is the valuation of resources — an issue we return to.

Are property rights of local users of biological resources the key to regulating bio-prospecting? Perhaps, in the short term, one may be able to implement a taxation/permit scheme; however, in the longer term, such a scheme may only work when property rights on resources are in place. Irrespective of some illogicalities, we can still attempt to apply the rationale in the context of organic resources. However, informational resources raise other problems.

Informational Resources

The propertisation of informational resources is not new, and many rationales have been put forth based on their characteristic of being public goods. Many informational resources are protectable if they fall within any of the current intellectual property categories such as copyright or patent laws. Thus, informational bases may be protected as copyright literary works in most countries in the European Union or in the United states; more over, there is the possibility of gaining *sui generis* database protection under the European Union member states. However, there are still certain types of informational resources which escape the intellectual property penumbra and one such type is ethno-botanical information or indigenous knowledge relating to plant and medical use. This lack of protection for such informational resources have led to criticism of the Western biased intellectual property laws which act antagonistically towards developing countries' creative and innovational works.[83] The perception that such resources should be conferred property rights is further boosted by Article 8(j) of the CBD which proposes the following ambiguous policy, that each nation should

> respect, preserve and maintain knowledge, innovations and practices of indigenous and local communities embodying traditional lifestyles relevant for the conservation and sustainable use of

[82] E. Mishan, "Pangloss on Pollution", (1971) 73 Swed J. Econ. 1 (satirising the views of Voltaire's Pangloss in relation to the regulation of the environment).

[83] See generally, T. Swanson, *Biodiversity in Conservation, op.cit.*; M-W. Hoe, *Genetic Engineering: Dream or Nightmare?* (Gateway Books, 1998), chapters 1 and 2.

biological diversity and promote their wider application with the approval and involvement of the holders of such knowledge, innovations and practices and encourage the equitable sharing of the benefits arising from the utilisation of such knowledge, innovations and practices.[84]

There are several factors at work here. First, it is true that most intellectual property laws do not, *per se*, allow the protection of wild organic or genetic resources.[85] However patent law, on occasion, has extended its scope to grant protection to discoveries relating to such resources for example in the distillation of a new compound or a new use of a compound,[86] which in turn, will also indirectly propertise the chemical or genetic resource within. The problem with this is that not only do some of these inventions tend to be discovered and developed outside the boundaries of territories which hold the genetic resources, but the inventions can also enable a known indigenous compound or medicine to be synthesised and manufactured in a more industrially efficient manner. The furore thus arises when it is perceived that a patent is being granted to known indigenous uses or methods, and indirectly control over the organic resource itself is imposed.[87] Secondly, part of the problem of non-protection of ethno-botanical knowledge can be ameliorated by the fixation and/or publication of the knowledge, either as discrete works or by way of a compilation in the form of a database. This may not stop the actual use of the knowledge contained therein, but it may provide a means to price and market the

---

[84] Countries acknowledging protection for the knowledge, innovations and practices of indigenous and local communities include the Andean Pact countries (Art. 50(d), Andean Pact Decision 391); Fiji (s.254(6)(a), Sustainable Development Bill); Philippines (Implementation Regulations of Executive Order).

[85] For a detailed account of property protection in organic resources, see I. Cooper, *Biotechnology and the Law* (West Group), Volume 2, paras 11.02–11.03; for a perspective on the very real problem of determining protection of organic resources, especially at an international level, see M. Blakeney, "Intellectual Property Rights in the Genetic Resources of International Agricultural Research Institutes — Some Recent Problems", (1998) 1 B.S.L.R. 3.

[86] See generally, J. Strauss, "The Rio Biodiversity Convention and Intellectual Property", (1993) 24 I.I.C. 602; R.A. Sedjo, "Property Rights, Genetic Resources, and Biotechnological Change", (1992) 35 *Journal of Law and Economics* 199.

[87] Such a furore was caused over the W.R. Grace patents over the extraction and stabilisation of the neem compound. The objections was based on the fact that the compound had been used in its extracted form for countless years in India, and that the stabilisation technique was already a known process in India., which environmentalists. For an account of the objections, see V. Shiva, "The neem tree — a case history of biopiracy", http://www.southside.org.sg/souths/twn/title/pir-ch.htm. For the petition to the United States PTO listing the reasons why the inventions were not novel or inventive, and for an abbreviated list of the Patent numbers, see http://www.southside.org.sg/souths/twn/title/neem-ch.htm. For the text of the 14 patents issued to Grace, see the United States PTO databases at http://164.195.100.11/netahtml/srchnum.htm.

The issue is difficult, partly due to the United States concept of relative novelty, whereby certain material publications and use will be disregarded within a certain time period before the priority date, see D. Chisum, *Patents*, Matthew Bender, paras 3.04–3.07.

information to interested parties.[88] A further means by which an economic rent can be recouped from informational resources which do not come within the traditional intellectual property framework, is by attaching the right to use or access the knowledge to the tangible resource. Thus, in Peru, the Aguaruna people of the Peruvian Amazon have entered into a bio-prospecting arrangement with the United states International Co-operative Biodiversity Group, two Peruvian universities and Searle & Co. (the pharmaceutical division of Monsanto), whereby use of biological resources is linked to a know-how licence for medicinal knowledge.[89]

Economic Parameters of Intellectual Property

There is a view that all useful knowledge should be protected. One can turn to Machlup's work on valuation of knowledge and examine his example of the transmission of the results of a baseball game to explain valuable knowledge:

> This activity will be regarded as production [. . .] if those who telephone or otherwise transmit the report could have done something else with their time (something they or someone else would appreciate) and if some of those who receive the report would "give something" to hear it (either because their curiosity is thereby satisfied or because they are in any other way "enriched" or "gratified" by receiving or having received the information). The communicators of this information would not be called production in an economic sense if its transmitters did it for the fun of it without sacrifice of otherwise employable time and effort, and if its receivers were not totally uninterested and no third party were interested in the transmitters' giving, and the receivers' getting, the information.[90]

Machlup's view of knowledge can be disturbing from the perspective of an intellectual property theorist, especially since courts have used this rationale to condone dubious instances of the propertisation of knowledge. Thus, in *Franklin v. Giddins*[91] the court proceeded to confer a quasi-proprietary right on the owner of the tangible resource, holding that when the defendant stole budwood from the plaintiff's orchard, he had obtained a trade secret. However, the courts were not valuing

[88] To some extent, this has begun in India with the creation of "people's biodiversity registers" which are databases of knowledge on plants, animals and local conservation practices. Other schemes, to attempt to mould ethno-biological knowledge, include translating such knowledge into trade secrets (Ecuador) and instituting know-how licence practices (Peru). See L. Glowka, *A Guide to Designing Legal Frameworks to Determine Access to Genetic Resources* (IUCN, 1998), p. 40.
[89] *ibid.*, pp.41–42.
[90] F. Machlup, *The Production and Distribution of Knowledge in the United States* (Princeton Univ. Press, 1962) p. 36.
[91] 1978 Qd. R. 72.

the property in the tangible resource but rather the plaintiff's knowledge:

> The secret was the technique of propagating Franklin Early White nectarines using budwood from the plaintiff's orchard, where the plaintiff guarded it by exercising general surveillance over fruit pickers and visitors. . . . The "information" which the genetic structure of the wood represented was of substantial commercial value, much time and effort had been expended by the plaintiff and it could not be duplicated by anybody whatsoever."[92]

Ethno-botanical knowledge as "Information Services"

If we wholeheartedly embrace the above, the propertisation of knowledge follows the reasoning that if one holds knowledge valuable enough for another to want to appropriate it, because the latter will be enriched or gratified, then this is but a step away from the notion that "what is worth *using or appropriating* is worth protecting."[93]

One can perhaps view ethno-botanical knowledge rendered by indigenous groups as a professional service. Indeed, the commoditication of organic resources has spawned a new information industry: bio-prospecting brokers.[94] One such example is Biotics Ltd, a private company which supplies the pharmaceutical industries with biological samples and materials. Its main role is to act as an intermediary between sellers and buyers of biological materials, which can either be supplied on a random selection basis or based on ethno-botanical information. Biotics Ltd attempt to include a term in their standard contracts that a share of royalties be contributed to bio-diversity related projects in the host resource country.

The analogy can go one step further with the resource-rich country or the holders of ethno-botanical knowledge playing the role of professional service industries which specialise in producing and selling the resources. In some categories of resources, it may be necessary for existing property rights to enforce payment of such services, but in others, are such services that different from those such as legal, engineering, financial or medical services? Each of the later industries involves the accumulation and conveyance of informational resources from one generation to another. There are no specific property rights over their accumulated knowledge; however, as Machlup points out, they have aggregated this information which is of value to the general recipient. It may be that the market value of these

---

[92] *ibid.* p. 82.
[93] Of course, intellectual property rights are instituted on this very premise, calling upon Arrow's information paradox that information is not marketable until revealed, but upon marketing the tangible product, the information will invariably be revealed, thus rendering it less valuable.
[94] A. Sedjo, *op. cit.*, p. 209.

resources are too high, in which case, competitive forces may step in to turn the potential recipient of the information to another information resource, *i.e.* another lawyer or doctor.[95]

Nevertheless, many still argue for "traditional resource rights"[96] whilst others call for an expansion of intellectual property rights for ethno-biological knowledge.

"Informational Resource Rights"

An interesting example of the latter is the "informational resource rights" proposal, offered as a sub-set of the existing intellectual property rights system.[97] The proposal purports to represent "an extension of this idea for compensating intangible services into realms other than those deriving from human capital investments." The scheme is attractive in its simplicity. "Biodiversity reserves" would be established, such reserves being restricted to uses compatible with biodiversity prospecting. It appears that the system would be open to individuals, groups of peoples, or states. Any discovery within such areas would be made subject to internationally recognised exclusive rights on registration with a centralised office, analogous to a patent office; the registration office would also function as an examining office, with the role of determining the scope of monopoly rights. When such a programme is established, the potentially useful life forms should be registered, together with a list of the range of chemical, genetic and other characteristics first identified within the species. The registration/examination office would have to determine whether an award should be made to the programme, and what characteristics of the life form (chemical, genetic, entire organism) should be subject to exclusive rights. This question will be necessarily dependent on the believed usefulness of the natural habitat being conserved and the optimal scope of a right which will be required to generate a reasonable return to the investment. The length of the award is a separate, institutional issue which is to be determined by the costliness of the selection process. If an award is made, any subsequent development of the product which incorporates a chemical combination within the scope defined must take a licence. Thus, a constant source of funding for natural habitat conservation could be maintained.

Necessity of Intellectual Commons

Several issues arise from the "informational resources rights" proposal, which, to a certain extent, apply to most proposals which attempt to

[95] J. Grunebaum, *op. cit.*, pp.192-193, arguing that professional persons cannot acquire property rights due to subsidisation of their education or training, coupled with their duty to help others.
[96] D. Posey, *op. cit.*, pp. 13–19.
[97] T. Swanson, "The appropriation of evolution's values: an institutional analysis of intellectual property regimes and biodiversity conservation", pp. 166 *et seq.*, in *Biodiversity Conservation*, *op. cit.*

capture the rent on information goods. In respect of informational resources, one economic response to such goods is justifiable state intervention in the creation and enforcement of intellectual property rights in such resources, thus internalising the externality in the most efficient means by which to secure beneficial industrial progress at the minimum cost.[98] Nevertheless, any net economic benefit derived by society from the initial allocation of rights in informational goods to the creator will be proportional to the charge or hindrance placed on their use by other market actors. Inherent in the economic efficiency and reward/incentive doctrines of intellectual property protection is the equally important tenet that harm to society will result if there is no secure barrier in place to ensure that the benefits to society are not outweighed by the cost.

Where informational goods are concerned, and this includes a variety of goods such as inventions, cultural property, brand names and ethno-biological knowledge, the allocation of resources must necessarily correspond to the costs to be suffered by other market actors. Unlike organic and tangible resources, there is a greater need for other market actors, including private individuals, to make use of such informational goods for the development of society, in general. Thus, intellectual property rights cannot merely be viewed in a holistic manner as rewards or incentives to be doled out to all creators of knowledge or other informational resources. They also behave as restrictions on others' freedom and are impositions of duties. In the case of ethno-biological knowledge, the rationales can also rest on more utilitarian grounds as burdens are being placed on other indigenous groups who adopt the collective societal lifestyle, for the sake of the greater social good. The instinct among legal theorists is that intellectual property rights must construct a living space consisting of "public domain materials" or "intellectual commons" and this view is as strong[99] as that held by developing countries that any conservation of resources must go hand in hand with "environmental space", *i.e.* the space necessary to pollute in order to develop.[1]

The "intellectual commons" is a wide, nebulous area but it is an amalgamation of the following types of intangible matter: ideas; abstract matter, commonplace or standardised matter, discoveries,

---

[98] H. Demsetz, *op. cit.*, p. 348; F.M. Scherer & D. Ross, *Industrial Market Structure and Economic Performance* (Houghton Mifflin, 1990), p. 682; K. Dam, "The Economic Underpinnings of Patent Law", (1994) 23 J. Leg. Stud. 247. However, for a sceptical view of the role played by the intellectual property system in industrial progress, see, D. Vaver, "Some Agnostic Thoughts on Intellectual Property", (1991) 6 I.P.J. 125, pp. 126–127; A. Plant, "Economic Theory Concerning Patents for Inventions" (1934) 1 *Economica* 30, at 42–44; F. Machlup, *An Economic Review of the Patent System*, Study of the Sub-committee on Patent, Trademarks and Copyright of the Committee on the Judiciary, 85th Congress, 2nd Session, Study No. 15, pp. 78–80.

[99] For proponents of this view, see J. Waldron, "From Authors to Copies: Individual Rights and Social Values in Intellectual Property", (1993) 68 Chi-Kent L. R. 842, at 842–844, 862; J. McCarthy, *McCarthy on Trade Marks and Unfair Competition* (Matthew Bender, 1988), para. 1.01[2].

[1] C. Mensah, *op. cit.*, p. 38.

principles of construction, or methods; and it is argued here, that traditional and ancient ethno-biological knowledge comes within this category. There are various reasons offered for the exclusion of such subject matter. First, if such subject matter are protected, the ultimate race would be to develop ideas or discoveries and to protect them, with less investment in the actual development of ideas. This, in turn, would lead to increased rent seeking behaviour, with a subsequent decrease in the dissemination of such matter. Secondly, if subject matter, such as a well-established means of extracting a plant-based chemical compound, is protected, the cost of actually creating subsequent works will increase. A subsequent creator would have to invest time and effort to work around the original idea or even incur licensing costs to obtain rights to the first idea. Thirdly, the administrative costs of defining rights in ethno-biological and other indigenous knowledge would increase. Courts would have to define the specific type of knowledge protected and the boundaries of protection. Hence, the accepted exclusion of ideas from copyright laws, or the exclusion of scientific discoveries and theories from patent laws. Any attempt to protect such subject matter would incur high transaction costs.[2]

In addition to the above, there are other concerns. In relation to ethno-botanical information, there is an assumption that traditional uses of plants or other living organisms are naturally demarcated by geographical or ethnographic boundaries. What if a particular type of knowledge in relation to one plant is widespread among several tribes or peoples? Will the right be conferred on the first group to come forward to claim the property, or on all the groups. Secondly, will there be any criterion of protection such as proven record of historical and societal use? If not, it remains open for any inventor to avoid the stricter patent regime, in favour of the more lenient "informational resource right". Thirdly, the question of duration is not addressed, and in sympathy, it must be acknowledged as being almost impossible to define an "efficient" or "just" period of duration. One model for a *sui generis* system to protect "the innovations and intellectual knowledge of local communities" proposes a perpetual and non-extinguishable right, with ownership vesting in the community.[3] One admits to finding it difficult to argue that perpetual and non-extinguishable rights are not a known concept within the present intellectual property rights regime, in the face of the strong *droits moraux* in France; nevertheless, such rights only accrue upon a work fulfilling certain

[2] See especially W. Landes & R. Posner, "An Economic Analysis of Copyright Law", (1989) 18 J. Leg. Stud. 325 (copyright); S. Cheung, "Property Rights and Invention", in J. Palmer and R. Zerbe Jr. (eds), Research in Law and Economics: The Economics of Patents and Copyrights (JAI Press, London, 1986), pp. 14–15 (patent).

[3] The proposal is a Third World Network proposal. For its views, and a detailed listing of the proposal, see N. Singh, *In Defence of Local Community Knowledge and Biodiversity: A Conceptual Framework and the Essential Elements of a Rights Regime* (Third World Network: 1996).

criteria, including creativity.[4] It may be that in many instance in the past, intellectual property law has allowed unprecedented claims to be made to subject matter which should correctly have remained in the intellectual commons. However, this is no reason to further diminish an already denuded intellectual commons.[5]

Valuation of Organic and Informational Resources

Irrespective of whether the property or regulatory taxation/permit approach is adopted, all these mechanisms call for some means by which pricing of the goods derived from biological resources can be determined. If the pricing or valuation of the resource fails to achieve the optimal equilibrium, leading to an overuse of a resource, then no amount of tinkering with property rights, or other regulatory means would result in equitable or fair sharing of responsibilities. Valuation is problematic as it will be difficult to obtain the correct information as to the scarcity of the initial organic resource, or by-products of such a genetic resource.[6]

Distinct or Continuous Valuation?

It is difficult to maintain discrete solutions for the different types of resources as they tend towards a continuous economic transaction. The problem with the "valuation of biological resources" theorem is the difficulty in appropriating the correct rent price, and in some cases, trying to merely appropriate something at all. Market failure is often due to resource allocation failure caused by bio-prospecting fees being set at levels too low to reflect the true costs of maintaining the organic resources and promoting informational resources. For example, the maintenance and promotion of biological resources by indigenous group "A" may be valued at the price of training the peoples of the group, providing technical support, providing a trust fund and a scholarship programme for the peoples, and a grant back or royalty free licences over products developed, and fees for the collection of

---

[4] Adopting the dualist concept of copyright, France accords a term of life and 70 years *post mortem auctoris* in relation to economic rights; however, authors have perpetual and inalienable moral rights in respect of protecting the paternity and integrity of their work. See JAL Sterling, *World Copyright Law* (Sweet & Maxwell, 1998), paras 6.02–6.04; 7.06–7.07; 8.08.

[5] See also, Crucible Group Report, *People, Plants and Patents* (IDRC, 1994), pp. 49–52, acknowledging that national innovation strategies for conserving resources and encouraging local formal and informal inventive human genius (*i.e.* ethno-botanical knowledge) do not necessarily require intellectual property rights. "The critical challenge is not how to monopolise innovation but how to bring about cooperation between the two broad systems of innovation and between public and private innovators. The world cannot afford the luxury of barriers, cutting off the ideas of one from the ideas of the other."

[6] Indeed, an objection always levelled at traditional neo-classical economics is that the over-emphasis on the "efficiency" criterion tends to overuse reservoirs of raw materials and non-economic objects. See, for example, K. Boulding, "The Economics of the Coming Spaceship Earth", in *Environmental Quality in a Growing Economy*, H. Jarrett (ed.), (1971).

resources. But are these sufficient? It has been highlighted that in the Merck-Costa Rica agreement, the payment of US$ 1.135 million may cover short term cost advantages, but not in terms of further development of the Costa Rica's own research and biotechnological industry.[7]

Further exogenous factors may also have to be included, such as the developmental and economic aims of the country in which indigenous group "A" live in, for example, the possibility of relocation of settlers and developers into the region habitated by the group.[8] Thus, Brazilian governmental policies often lead to the uprooting of traditional peoples and economies from the Amazon region in order to subsidise the economic development of the north of the country.[9] Even in relation to the bio-prospecting agreement between Merck and INBIo, the latter admits that:

> The issue of benefits accrued from bioprospecting is difficult given the inherent complexities of assigning value to the accumulated and increased knowledge of our own biodiversity, to the transfer of know-how and technology that has occurred, or to enhanced human resources capabilities among others. From an strict economic point of view, since INBio started this activity in 1991, direct financial contributions to other divisions in INBio, the Conservation Areas, MINAE and national universities exceed $2.5 million dollars.[10]

The counter problem is that of over-pricing the resource as was the case of the discovery in the 1960s of the steroid diosgenin in the *Dioscorea* species in Mexico. The diosgenin was the foundation of a lucrative contraceptive market. However, in trying to appropriate rent for the use of the diosgenin resource, the Mexican government over-priced the resources which led to companies seeking alternative synthetic substitutes.[11]

The Resource Value Time-Line

Indeed, the problem of valuation of resources, especially informational resources such as ethno-biological knowledge, arises early from the inability to classify it either as an investment or a cost, part of the

---

[7] R. Simpson & R. Sedjo, "Commercialisation of indigenous genetic resources", (1994) *Contemporary Economic Policy* 12, at 38–40.
[8] These elements constitute the know-how licence instituted between the Aguaruna peoples in Peru and bio-prospectors, L. Glowka, *A Guide to Designing Legal Frameworks to Determine Access to Genetic Resources*, *op. cit.*, p. 41.
[9] Cairncross, *op. cit.*, at p. 76.
[10] http://www.inbio.ac.cr/.
[11] D. Pearce & S. Puroshothaman, "Value of plant-based pharmaceuticals", in *Biodiversity Conservation*, *op. cit.* p. 129.

rationale being that production of knowledge varies according to its purpose. Knowledge, thus, can be conceptually viewed as a valuable production if it is made with a view to bringing forth valuable output.[12] The valuation of knowledge cannot enter the normative economics model without the realisation that a certain type of knowledge produced will eventually increase productivity of resources, whatever its nature, in the foreseeable future. In neo-classical economic terms, the free market will enhance the general welfare if all consumers have perfect information about goods and services and producers have equally perfect information about costs of production. The market failure which is so inherent in any economic analysis of the environment is the lack of information since the market price of any natural resource gives little information as to the environmental effects of producing or using the product. Simply put, where will the use of the informational resource lead to — more understanding and knowledge, or a viable product?

Part of this lies in the enormous difficulty in defining an item of information, the purchaser's lack of knowledge as to the value of the information and the interdependence amongst inventive and other productive activities.[13] For example, proposals as to how valuation of the resource may be approached include looking at the actual market value of the plants when traded, looking at the market value of the drugs of which they are the source material, or looking at the value of the drugs in terms of their life-saving properties.[14] However, all these proposals are inherently untrustworthy as offering the best means of capturing the rent for the use of the resource, and they all tend to point to the implausibility of viewing the bio-prospecting, analytical, inventive, and marketing activities as discrete concepts. Instead, the activity should be viewed as a continuous cycle of investment, production and consumption. Even doctrines such as the "polluter pays" principle implicitly value one or more of the above activities as an expense or cost of current productions, instead of viewing them as final value-ridden outputs, capable of cost reductions or product improvements in the future.[15]

One pricing model is the contingent valuation technique whereby people are surveyed as to what they are willing to pay for a benefit or what they would accept in compensation for its loss. Such calculations have been used in the United states and in Australia. In the latter case, the contingent value survey as to whether mining should be allowed on the edge of Kakadu National Park revealed that people were quite often willing to pay far more per hectare of wilderness than for land in

---

[12] F. Machlup, *op. cit.*, note 90, p. 35 *et seq.*
[13] D. Lamberton, "Intellectual Property and Trade: Economic Perspectives", (1998) 16 *Prometheus* 255, at p. 257.
[14] D. Pearce & S. Puroshothaman, *op.cit.*, p. 131.
[15] F. Machlup, *op.cit.*, note 90, pp. 38–39.

downtown Melbourne.[16] However, how much are such indications an actual measurement of the public's willingness to pay for the services? Another example is the attempt to measure the marketable value of Costa Rica's natural forest reserves whereby the marketable value of standing timber and future timber losses when the forest is cleared was adopted. This was the closest that came to approximate market values, but even this did not reflect other values such as the value a forest may have as a home for wildlife or recreation. Furthermore, marketable natural resources such as timber posed more problems since such values were dependent on global timber prices, which in the case of the Costa Rican forest reserve, exaggerated the impact of the physical loss of trees.[17] The wider notion of biological resources to include both organic and informational resources also means that there may be a bifurcated valuation of such resources. First, the organic resources may be valued at expected market prices; however, informational resources such as ethno-botanical information defy such easy pricing, though one view could be to categorise it as an informational service.

Another means by which valuation may be solved would be to actually create a market for bio-prospecting products. This, to some extent, is done with respect to organic resources sold as natural products. A pioneer was Cultural Survival, a campaigning group that has built markets in the United states, Canada and Britain for the resources of the Amazon Basin, used to make, *inter alia*, "Rainforest Crunch" for the upmarket Ben & Jerry ice cream company, and cosmetics for the Body Shop company.[18] However, this model only serves for natural resources that lend themselves to areas heavily influenced by consumer preferences and high elasticity products, as opposed to pharmaceutical or industrial products.

A final more promising model suggests the measure of the economic value of the resource with reference to the expected patent value of the eventual product. Thus,

$$CPV = a \times EPV$$

where CPV is the capturable production value, and EPV is the expected production value of a patented end-product.[19] Thus, in a study concerning the patent value of the end-product as a factor of the rate of extinction of the utilised resources, it was concluded that in the developing economies, the value of a tends to be small and the value of nil to US$ 20 per hectare of land occupied by the natural resource was

[16] F. Cairncross, *op.cit.*, pp. 25–27.

[17] Cairncross, *op.cit.*, pp. 103–104, citing the study conducted by R. Repetto, *et al.*, *Wasting Assets: Natural Resources in the National Income Accounts and Accounts Overdue: Natural Resource Depletion in Costa Rica*, (World Resources Institute, 1989).

[18] Cairncross, *op.cit.*, at p. 170.

[19] The formulation is that of J. Ruitenbeek, *Republic of Cameroon: the Korup Project* (Cameroon Ministry of Plan and Regional Development, 1989), as cited by Pearce & Puroshothaman, *op. cit.*, at p. 132.

prescribed. Even this model is subject to information assymmetry: thus, the authors have subtracted from evaluation the role played by informational resources. A final query relates to the value of the resource-based product after the expiry of patent protection.

Let us assume that bio-prospector A has obtained a plant sample due to his study of ethno-botanical practices of a local community living nearby. He discovers a new use for the compound, correlating to the ethno-botanical practice. He proceeds to expend more resources in synthesising the compound into a stable form, after which he patents the compound and submits it for clinical and regulatory testing. The drug enters the market with a competitive lead; after the expiry of the patent, other generic drugs enter the same product market. Bio-prospector A's sales drop for a period of 20–30 years, after which time, a new use of the compound is found. Sales rise dramatically.

Resource Value Time Line

Plant, soil or micro-organism gathering	Screening process, synthesis	Isolation of valuable compound, stabilisation of compound	Viable drug product	5–10 year competitive lead	Generics enter market
Using ethno-biological information			Patent applied and granted with 3 year time lag	Securing market position through trade mark	Drug relies on brand value
			Clinical trials, market trials with 5 year time lag		

In estimating the production value of a resource-based drug, should one also take into the following factors: the ability of other generic drugs to penetrate the market after the expiry of the patent, the cross-elasticity of the drug, the strength of the brand name of the leader product to maintain market share, and the ability of a known drug to enter a new phase of exploitation and value through the discovery of a new use.[20]

[20] Despite having nil patent protection, the drug Aspirin which was formulated by Bayer Pharmaceuticals in 1899 still continues to have an enviable market position, despite competition from other generic and non-generic substitutes. Bayer's success with its Aspirin drug, which is derived from *acetylsalicylic acid* and had been known since Egyptian times for its medicinal and healing properties for centuries, can not only be attributed to its brand name loyalty, but also to the continuing saga of discoveries made as to the medicinal properties of *salicyclic acid*. In the 1970s it was discovered that small doses of aspirin reduced the risk of strokes and heart attacks, while today tests are being conducted to prove the latest hypothesis that Aspirin can reduce the likelihood of cancer. See D. Pilling, "Pill of the Century", *Financial Times Weekend*, February 13–14, 1999.

Bio-prospecting harvests do not end with the synthesis of the basic plant alkaloids but can lead to much more lucrative end products; thus, previous ethno-botanical leads such as Etoposide and Vinca alkoids are leading to new product derivatives.[21] Does and can the valuation of the biological resource incorporate such factors as societal need and health, future generational benefits, and the future evolutionary paths of the eco-system?[22] The answer is clearly no, but an estimate must be made and some means of making such an estimate must be found.

Furthermore, the future of bio-prospecting in search of biological resource-based products cannot be assured in the near future. Studies do show that pharmaceutical and drug dependency on biological resources, especially plant genetic material, tend to go through cycles.[23] Thus, plant-based drug resources were thought to be exhausted in the early 20th century, but was revived in the mid-century by the discovery of the Vinca alkaloids with their anti-cancer properties. By the mid-70s, the drug industry had once again lost interest in plant genetic material, though a return was made with the advances made in purifying and analysing techniques. The current rise in interest in plant resources is also indicated by the plant screening programmes instituted by Monsanto, Smith Kline, Merch and Glaxo; while companies such as Shaman Pharmaceuticals solely concentrate on prospecting and analysing plants which have a human medicinal-use history or species whose activity is recognised in the traditional context.[24] By this, it hopes to increase their rate of success and cut investment of time and capital to prove the drug successful and to take it into the market.

Perhaps at the end of the day, the focus of economic exercises on the value of biological resources is fallacious. Instead, we should accept that biological and informational resources are unquestionably of vast value, and something that defies empirical or even normative economic valuation. As one biologist stated, "If I were one of the many exploiters and destroyers of biological diversity, I would like nothing better than for my opponents, the conservationists, to be bogged down over the

[21] A new semi-synthetic derivative of Etoposide is currently being developed, while further investigation of the Vinca alkoid drugs has led to the invention of a new structural chemical compound. The new structural chemical derivative *anhydrovinblastine* was discovered using a variation of the same synthetic process used for VCR and VLB. Human trials have already commenced with the drug which is destined for same anti-cancer drug market, but with allegedly significantly reduced toxic side effects. A patent was filed for the drug by the University of British Columbia in 1988, and is being developed and marketed by IGC Pharma. See http://www.biotech.bc.ca/bcba/igt/products/.

[22] For a discussion on such estimates, using a cost-benefits analysis, see W. Rodgers, "Benefits, Costs and Risks: Oversight of Health and Environmental Decision Making", (1980) 4 *Harvard Environmental Law Review* 191.

[23] D. Pearce & S. Puroshothaman, *op. cit.*, at pp. 129-130.

[24] This is done by tapping the expertise of traditional healers called "shamans" or medicine people, in various parts of the tropics. For an account of shamans, see N. Tobert, "Rainforest Shamans", (1998) 28 *The Ecologist* 233–239, reviewing in detail the work of anthropologist Gerardo Reichel-Dolmatoff on shamans in Colombian Indian tribes.

issue of valuing."[25] Hayek, as well, pointed out that the question of knowledge economics is not how shall we best allocate given resources, but rather it is to ask ourselves how to secure the best use of resources known to any of the member of the society, for ends whose relative importance only these individuals know. [26]

With this in mind, perhaps we should opt for the view of the botanist, Hugh Itlis who had discovered a tomato variety in the 1980s. To the issue of valuing biodiversity, he replied:

> I have no patience with the phony requests of developers, economists and humanitarians who want us biologists to "prove" with hard evidence, right here and now, the "value" of biodiversity and the "harm" of tropical deforestation. Rather, it should be for them, the sponsors of reckless destruction, to prove to the world that a plant or animal species, or an exotic ecosystem, is *not* useful and *not* ecologically significant before being permitted by society to destroy it.[27]

The Future: Homo Economicus or Homo Ecologicus?

The future prospects of combining economic and legal analysis, with environmental and conservation concerns appear doomed in light of the two disparate schools of thought. One the one hand stand the "cornucopians" who fervently believe that we are far from exhausting natural resources or the capabilities of technology, and that we can look forward to limitless economic growth and rising living standards.[28] On the other hand, stand the environmentalists and biologists who warn against mankind's suicidal behaviour in bringing about the degradation and exhaustion of almost all resources, leading to the very extinction of mankind.[29] The permeation of evolutionary and environmental theories can be worrying with their perspective of man as part of the larger eco-system whereby every action will be reflected in environmental terms. To build an economic or legal theory from these tenets leads us to conclude that all human activity must be confined to these parameters, and that environmental overload through the maximisation of production and consumption should be

[25] R. Leaky & R. Lewin, *op. cit.*, p. 135.
[26] F. Hayek, "Use of Knowledge in Society" (1945) 35 *American Economic Review* 519.
[27] R. Leaky & R. Lewin, *op. cit.*, pp. 134, 140–141. This proposal appears to be propped up by various other hypothesis which prove that ecosystems rich in species diversity are more stable and promote productivity, both in ecosystems and in agricultural systems.
[28] P. Samuelson & W. Nordhaus, *Economics*, (15th ed. McGraw-Hill, Inc., 1995), p. 338.
[29] E.O. Wilson, "Is Humanity Suicidal", *The New York Times Magazine*, May 30, 1993; R. Leaky and R. Lewin, *op. cit.*

restricted.[30] But, will it not also lead us to conclude that all production should be socially controlled, with economic policymaking being made compulsorily participatory?

On a juridical level, international economic law may be the only recourse left for the question of bio-prospecting activities in relation to organic and informational resources. International economic law refers to private transactions carried out in the context of international trade or other economic activities; it also refers to institutional regulation of economic matters. Of the various problems mentioned above, perhaps we need a more institutionalised legal approach, as evidenced by the success under the then GATT, and now WTO dispute settlement systems.[31] The benefits and harms which may entail in relation to extracting or using organic or informational resources effect are not merely national matters, to be regulated by national governments, but have a trans-border impact effecting manufacturing, distribution, and consumer trends in other regions. Many of the economic incentives, such as property, tax or subsidies which may work to curb the problems of market failure or public goods in a national context, may not work in a globalised situation. If resource-rich countries attempt to capture the economic rent for informational resources by declaring such matter to be subject to intellectual property rights, there is no guarantee that such policies can be subsequently displaced by subsidy programmes instituted by other nations. Thus, in attempting to ascribe values to biological resources, a co-ordinated global valuation exercise, instituted by a specific institutional framework, could legitimately create and maintain an effective informational process. However, a global accounting system appears impractical to impose, especially in light of the CBD's failure to institute any global informational, management or enforcement mechanism by which such indicators can be measured.[32]

---

[30] This notion of interdependency was initially developed by the British chemist and inventor James Lovelock who expanded it into the Gaia hypothesis. The theory essentially suggests that all the physical and chemical conditions of the Earth, the atmosphere and the oceans *i.e.* the entire ecosystems of the planet, are essentially interdependent, operating as a whole and inextricably linked to each other. See R. Leaky & R. Lewin, *op.cit.*, pp. 137–138; C. Clegg, *Advanced Biology* (J. Murray, 1994), p. 682. For a critical account of the Gaia notion in evolutionary biology, see G. C. Williams, "Gaia, Nature Worship and Biocentric Fallacies", (1992) 67 *Quarterly Review of Biology* 479.

[31] Since 1948, there have been some 250 cases brought before the GATT dispute system. For a greater elaboration of regulatory approaches under international economic law, see J. Jackson, "Global Economics and International Economic Law" (1998) 1 *Journal of International Economic Law* 1, 8–20.

[32] The CBD does provide that environmental impact assessments may be done, but such assessments are to be conducted within the territory of the party conducting it as opposed to trans-border assessments. Furthermore, although parties are encouraged to notify, exchange information and consult each other, the means by which this can be achieved is left to signatory parties (Art. 14). Furthermore, although there is provision for UN agencies and NGOs to have observer status, the effectiveness of any proposal will depend on political will and adequate information, especially in light of the fact that there is no provision for independent monitoring or inspection. (Art. 23(5)). Finally, there is no as to dispute settlements but merely provision for negotiations. States, in the final recourse, disputes, may submit their to the ICJ or arbitration, but this is optional. (Art. 27, and Annex 2, CBD).

On an economic level, the impression may be that the traditional concepts of wealth maximisation and efficiency have no place in a new economic order which promotes sustainable environment. The growing impetus of the eco-aware jurist or economist now decries traditional Neo-classical economic thought with its *grundnorm* of allocative efficiency and wealth maximisation, and instead claims to move towards an evolutionary based economic framework. Perhaps we should shy away from conventional neo-classical theories, and even outdated notions of intellectual property as properties tied to intangible inputs of human creativity.

More forward-looking theorists argue that the environment is a gigantic capital asset, and that economic notions must shift from optimal development to sustainable development, where the national GNPs should reflect this environmental resource. Thus, pollution costs, stocks of biological species, ethno-biological knowledge are to be regarded as "sustainable income" factors which need to be included in national and regional GNP figures.[33] Such an environmental accounting regime would attempt to adjust a country's entire national-income account to reflect what happens across the environmental resource board. Income generated by depleting natural resources may not be sustainable — in which case, the terms of a bio-prospecting license can be set with reference to the rate of depletion of resources. A logical extension of this rationale is to effect a truly global economic order which would view, as part of international economic policies, indicators of capital such as bio-diversity, resource stocks, quality of the environment, and informational resources.[34] A valid reason for this approach is that the rate and distribution of consumption between individuals across the globe varies significantly. To maintain a sustainable environment, overall development and consumption patterns must be considered by treating such factors as different goods with different prices or social values.[35] If one measures the combined global market value of resources and of capital against the costs incurred by externalities such as pollution, over-use of resources and consumption patterns, the result is a global welfare function.[36]

A final emergent is the bionomics school of thought: supposedly based on the principles of evolutionary biology,[37] whereby the economy is like an "evolving ecosystem". A modern market economy is likened to a tropical rainforest, populated by vast numbers of highly specialised organisations instead of highly specialised organisms, which

---

[33] This the project has worked in several countries such as France, Norway, Indonesia and Costa Rica, where natural resource accounting projects have been undertaken.

[34] R. Hahn & K. Richards, "The Internationalisation of Environmental Regulation", (1989) 30 *Harvard International Law Journal* 421, at 429.

[35] A. Sen, "Real National Income", 1976 *Review of Economic Studies* 19.

[36] P. Hammond, "Is there Anything New in the Concept of Sustainable Development", *The Environment after Rio, op. cit.*, pp. 190–191.

[37] See in general M. Rothschild, *Bionomics: Economy As Ecosystem* (Rei, 1995).

are all linked together in an incredibly complex web of competitive and co-operative relationships. By treating the economy like a rainforest, bionomists are extremely cautious as to government intervention or regulation, as part of the "ecologically sensitive" nature; however, these cautions are apparently to be thrown to the wind in respect of environmental policies. The new bionomic approach? Regulations should be introduced to tax price every resource and to tax the consumption of such resources, after which the "invisible hand of the biocentric market" will go to work. In other words, we return to the neo-classical model.[38]

Conclusion

This article does not presume to offer solutions. But it does try to raise questions that need asking as to the proper criteria that should be considered in evaluating the optimal means of regulating bio-prospecting activities. That biological resources are economic goods was clear by the early 1980s when it was advocated that the current production and consumption cycle of developed countries, and those aspiring to come within this hallowed club, was taking its toll on finite, potentially exhaustible earth resources, and in turn, on its biodiversity. The classification of such resources as economic goods provides a circular rationale: biodiversity must be protected because of the organic and informational resources which may lead to new types of drugs and food; and such resources must be protected if we are to find an economic rationale for preserving the biodiversity of the environment, and by extension, natural and environmental resources. In this manner, the traditional remits of real and intellectual property are being pushed wider to encompass this new creation.

Are these feasible proposals, especially in respect to the allocation of property rights to such resources? Can the problems caused by transgressing acceptable or "sustainable" environmental limits be solved, or even controlled, by traditional market mechanisms and property rights? Or will we, by commodifying the global commons end up with the commercial enclosure and privatisation of all the ecosystems and all the knowledge that make up earth's living space, both physically and intellectually?

---

[38] For a trenchant criticism on this area, see P. Krugman, "The Power of Biobabble: Pseudo-economics meets Pseudo-Evolution", http://web.mit.edu/krugman/www/bionomic.html.

4. Ethnobiological Knowledge and the Intellectual Property Rights of Indigenous Peoples in Australia

Professor Michael Blakeney

Queen Mary Intellectual Research Institute

Ethnobiological Knowledge and the Intellectual Property Rights of Indigenous Peoples in Australia

I. Genetic Resources in Australia

Australian biological diversity is considerable. It has some 44,000 species of plants of which 88 per cent occur only in Australia. L. Webb, writing in 1969, records that:

> Since World War II, a systematic survey of the Australian flora for plants of chemical and pharmacological interest has produced a voluminous chemical literature. For example, during the past 20 years, approximately 500 alkaloids were identified in Australian plants and some 200 were new.

A recent report of the Co-ordination Committee on Science and Technology of the various Australian state and Federal Government Departments noted that 90 per cent of Australian flowering plants, more than 80 per cent of its mammals, 70 per cent of terrestrial birds, 89 per cent of its reptiles, and 93 per cent of its frogs, are endemic to Australia.[1] Similarly, of the estimated 600 inshore fish species in the southern temperate zone, about 85 per cent are found only in Australia.[2]

The isolation of the Australian continent has resulted in the survival of a number of simplified plant and animal types which have been particularly suitable for genetic modification, or which have provided a valuable reservoir of characteristics for the genetic modification of non-Australian plants and animals. For example, the aridity and salinity of the continent has resulted in the development of organisms with particular resistance to these conditions.

A factor which is becoming relevant to the legal regime which may be established to control access to genetic resources in Australia, is the role of its Indigenous people in the identification and ownership of these resources.[3] This issue within Australia involves the same collision of North-South values as occurs in other parts of the world. The therapeutic properties of plants have long been known to the indigenous

---

[1] Coordination Committee on Science and Technology, *Access to Australia's Biological Resources* (AGPS, Canberra, March 1994) p. 12.

[2] *ibid.*

[3] See Blakeney, "Bioprospecting and the Protection of Traditional Medical Knowledge of Indigenous Peoples: An Australian Perspective" [1997] 6 E.I.P.R. 298.

peoples of Australia and one of the methods used to guide the selection of promising species is for ethnobotanists to search the early literature and collect plants used as medicines by indigenous Australians.

For example, in Australia, Smokebush (Genus Conospermum), which has been used by the Aborigines of Western Australia in the treatment of "old peoples'" diseases, has been found to contain Conocurvone. This substance which apparently has beneficial effects in the treatment of rheumatism and lumbago, has also been found to destroy the HIV virus in low concentrations. The Western Australian Government has licensed Amrad, a Victorian pharmaceutical company, to develop an anti-AIDS drug. Amrad has been granted an exclusive global licence by the U.S. National Cancer Institute to develop this drug. Amrad paid the Western Australian Government AU$1.5 million to secure access to Smoke-bush and related species and it has been estimated that if Conocurvone is successfully commercialised the state will be receiving royalties of AU$100 million by 2002.

An earlier example concerned the *Duboisia* plant, which was used by Aboriginal peoples in Queensland for therapeutic purposes. At the end of the last Century, a Brisbane surgeon used this knowledge to develop a substitute for atropine from the plant. *Duboisia* was also found to contain hyoscine, used as a sedative in treating motion sickness and as a "truth drug". The cultivation of *Duboisia* is currently conducted on a commercial scale in Northern New South Wales and Southern Queensland, but without any recompense to Indigenous peoples.

To facilitate the exploitation of its plant genetic resources, the Western Australian Government in 1993 introduced an amendment to the *Conservation and Land Management Act 1984* (*CALM Act*) to expand the functions of the Conservation and Land Management Department to include, subject to the direction and control of the Minister,

> to promote and encourage the use of flora for therapeutic, scientific or horticultural purposes for the good of people in this state or elsewhere, and to undertake any project or operation relating to the use of flora for such a purpose;

Pursuant to this function, the Act was amended to provide that the Minister and the Executive Director may enter an agreement with another person under which they agree to

> . . . exercise powers under the Wildlife Conservation Act and this Act to grant, issue or refuse licences or permits to take or remove forest produce or other flora in a manner that has the effect of conferring on the other person an exclusive or preferential right to take or remove forest produce or other flora referred to in the agreement from land (other than private land) referred to in the agreement.

The effect of these amendments may be to deny the use of Smokebush to the Aboriginal people who first discovered its therapeutic application. The constitutional validity of this state legislation, which appears to fly in the face of the Federal Australian Government's guarantee of native land title rights is yet to be tested. That legislation preserves native land title and associated usufructory rights from confiscation by state legislation and administrative Acts. The rights and interests comprising native title are amplified in section 223(2) of the Native Title Act 1993. The closest analogy to intellectual property rights is the reference in the sub-section to "hunting, gathering or fishing rights and interests" as being included within native title. This provision does not, at first blush, appear to include the right to exclude others from hunting, gathering or fishing, but preserves the rights of Aboriginal peoples to continue these activities in areas where native title has not been extinguished. This provision would appear to permit Aboriginal people(s) to continue to use traditional medical remedies where such remedies might have become the subject of a patent or plant variety registration.

2. The Biodiversity Convention and Australia

In June 1992 more than 150 countries signed the United Nations Convention on Biological Diversity, affirming their commitment to "the conservation of biological diversity, the sustainable use of its components and the fair and equitable sharing of the benefits arising out of the utilisation of genetic resources". The harmonisation of North-South interests is reflected in the Convention's requirement of the ensuring of "appropriate access to genetic resources and by appropriate transfer of relevant technologies, taking into account all rights over those resources and to technologies by appropriate funding". The USA delayed accession to the Convention until June 1994, until President Clinton had obtained the views of biotechnology industry representatives. Upon accession, the President issued an interpretative statement, requiring that Parties to the Convention "must ensure that access to and transfer of technology recognise and are consistent with adequate and effective protection of intellectual property rights".[4] The statement warned that the USA would strongly resist any actions "taken by Parties to the Convention that lead to inadequate levels of protection of intellectual property rights".

A problem with this approach, is that it begs the question of what are the intellectual property rights of the providers of genetic resources from which biotechnological inventions or plant varieties are fashioned. Are those rights to be assessed by reference to established principles of intellectual property law, or are those rights to enshrined in a *sui generis* regime, which is established specifically for the purpose of recognising the interests of the South?

[4] *Statement from the President of the United States transmitting the Convention on Biological Diversity*, Treaty Doc. 103–20, 103rd Congress, 1st Sess.

The Rio Earth Summit, at which the Biodiversity Convention was promulgated, identified the importance of indigenous peoples in the maintenance of biological diversity. The *Rio Declaration on Environment and Development* in Principle 22 stated that "Indigenous peoples and their communities . . . have a vital role in environmental management and development because of their knowledge and traditional practices".

The Plenary of the Rio Summit also adopted *Agenda 21* which in chapter 26 detailed the relationship which conference participants recognised between indigenous peoples and their lands. The Agenda at paragraph 26.3(a) required governments "to establish a process to empower indigenous peoples and their communities" through measures that include:

- recognition of their values, traditional knowledge and resource management practices with a view to promoting environmentally sound and sustainable development;
- enhancement of capacity- building for indigenous communities based on the adaptation and exchange of traditional experience, knowledge and resource-management practices, to ensure their sustainable development;
- establishment, where appropriate, of arrangements to strengthen the active participation of indigenous peoples and their communities in the national formulation of policies, laws and programs relating to resource management and other development processes that may affect them.

The Preamble to the Convention on Biological Diversity recognised the

> close and traditional dependence of many Indigenous and local communities embodying traditional lifestyles on biological resources, and the desirability of sharing equitably arising from the use of traditional knowledge, innovations and practices relevant to the conservation of biological diversity and sustainable use of its components.

Article 8(j) of the Convention requires each signatory

> Subject to its national legislation, respect, preserve and maintain knowledge, innovations and practices of indigenous and local communities embodying traditional lifestyles relevant for the conservation and sustainable use of biological diversity and promote their wider application with the approval and involvement of the holders of such knowledge, innovations and practices and encourage the equitable sharing of the benefits arising from the utilisation of such knowledge, innovations and practices.

In February 1992 the Commonwealth and state and Territory Governments had already signed the Intergovernmental Agreement on the Environment (IGAE) in which they formally recognised that "biological diversity is a major and valuable component of the environment and should be protected". Pursuant to this Agreement a Task Force on Biological Diversity was established by the Australia and New Zealand Environment and Conservation Council (ANZECC) to report on the implications and manner of implementation of the Convention on Biological Diversity. Pursuant to the recommendations of the Task Force, the Committee on Australian Government (COAG) in December 1992 agreed to implement a National Strategy for Ecologically Sustainable Development, one of the central objectives of which is "to protect biological diversity and maintain essential ecological processes and life support systems".[5]

A National Strategy for the Conservation of Australia's Biological Diversity was drafted by an Advisory Committee which was established for this purpose. Recommended Action 6.1.7 of the strategy highlighted the importance of the knowledge of indigenous people in enhancing knowledge and understanding of biological diversity:

> Recognise the value of traditional knowledge and practices of Aboriginal people and Torres Strait Islanders and integrate this knowledge and those practices into biological diversity research and conservation programmes by:
>
> - encouraging the recording (with the approval and involvement of the indigenous people concerned) of traditional knowledge and practices;
> - assessing their potential value for nutritional and medicinal purposes, wildlife and protected area management and other purposes; and
> - applying traditional knowledge and practices in ways which ensure the equitable sharing of the benefits arising from their use

The House of Representatives Standing Committee on Environment Recreation and the Arts in its report *Biodiversity. The Role of Protected Areas* observed that the identification of traditional practices and culture was much more than an exercise in information gathering as it raised "questions of authenticity, knowledge and power".[6]

The Committee proposed that the first dot point of Recommended Action 6.1.7 be amended to provide that indigenous communities be encouraged "to undertake or otherwise collaborate in research projects

[5] *National Strategy for Ecologically Sustainable Development*, December 1992, p. 4.

[6] House of Representatives Standing Committee on Environment, Recreation and the Arts, *Biodiversity. The Role of Protected Areas* (AGPS, Canberra, January 1993) para. 4.70.

which utilise traditional knowledge and practices in the study of biodiversity and in conservation".[7]

The Task Force on Biological Diversity, which had been established by the ANZECC, had recommended that a Commonwealth, state and Territory Working Group be established to investigate and report on the strengthening of existing controls governing access to genetic resources including legislation. This Working Group was established in February 1993 with the task of ensuring, inter alia, that Australia's national and international obligations are honoured.

To assist informed debate on these matters the Co-ordination Committee on Science and Technology (CCST) in March 1994 prepared a discussion paper *Access to Australia's Biological Resources.* This discussion paper high-lighted the significance of the ILO Convention No. 169, The Convention on Biological Diversity, Agenda 21 and the Rio Declaration on Environment and Development and the United Nations Working Group on Indigenous Populations in recognising the obligations owed to indigenous peoples for the contributions made by them in promoting environmentally sound and sustainable development.

The discussion paper observed that although only the Convention on Biological Diversity imposed legal obligation on Australia the other instruments could not be ignored with impunity.[8] It stated that:

> Together these instruments represent important manifestations of current international thinking on the subject of the rights of indigenous peoples and Australia, as part of the international community, has actively contributed in several international forums to the development of the views, ideas and ideals expressed in these instruments. Moreover, to the extent that certain common themes appear in these instruments, they reinforce each other and inevitably have the effect of exerting greater pressure upon Governments to implement the obligations contained therein.[9]

Among the common themes identified in the discussion paper were the need to:

- respect, preserve and maintain knowledge, innovations and practices of indigenous relevant to the conservation and sustainable use of biological diversity;
- promote the wider application of such knowledge, innovations and practices with the approval and involvement of indigenous peoples; and
- share equitably benefits arising from the use of traditional knowledge, innovations and practices with indigenous peoples.[10]

---

[7] *ibid.* para.4.72.
[8] Department of the Prime Minister and Cabinet, Office of the Chief Scientist, *Access to Australia's Biological Resources* (AGPS, Canberra, March 1994) p. 31.
[9] *ibid.*
[10] *ibid.* p. 32.

Among the common themes identified in the discussion paper were the need to:

- respect, preserve and maintain knowledge, innovations and practices of indigenous relevant to the conservation and sustainable use of biological diversity
- promote the wider application of such knowledge, innovations and practices with the approval and involvement of indigenous peoples; and share equitably benefits arising from the use of traditional knowledge, innovations and practices with indigenous peoples.[11]

3. Bioprospecting and the Application of Traditional Intellectual Property Doctrine in Australia

Historically, the suggestion that intellectual property rights arising from plant-derived drugs be shared with indigenous peoples, originated in the context of the suggestion by agricultural scientists working on the development of new agricultural plant varieties, that indigenous communities be compensated for the exploitation of their genetic resources.[12] This suggestion was made largely from two different perspectives. First, it was hoped to deploy intellectual property laws to protect genetic resources from extinction.[13] Secondly, it was perceived that the development of new plant varieties may involve the expropriation of the genetic resources of developing countries.[14]

A threshold problem in Australia, which reflects the conflict between North/South intellectual property concerns elsewhere, is the limited applicability of traditional intellectual property doctrine to the contribution of indigenous peoples.

Communal rights play a very significant role in ordering the affairs of indigenous peoples in Australia. Two fairly recent intellectual property cases, *Yumbulul v. Reserve Bank of Australia*[15] and *Milpurrurru v. Indofurn Pty Ltd*[16] emphasise the failure of communal interests to be recognised in intellectual property law.

Yumbulul concerned an attempt by representatives of the Galpu Clan, located in North-Eastern Australia, to prevent the reproduction by the Reserve Bank of the design of a Morning Star Pole on a commemorative banknote. The pole had been created by a member of the clan who had obtained his authority and knowledge to create the

---

[11] *ibid.* p. 32.

[12] Huft, "Indigenous Peoples and Drug Discovery Research: A question of Intellectual Property Rights" (1995) 89 Nw. U. L. R. 1678, at 1684.

[13] Sedjo, "Property Rights and the Protection of Plant Genetic Resources" in Jack R. Kloppenburg, Jr. (ed.), *Seeds and Sovereignty* (1988), p. 293.

[14] Odek, "Bio-piracy: Creating Proprietary Rights in Plant Genetic Resources" (1994) 2 J. Intell. Prop. L. 141.

[15] (1991) 21 *Intellectual Property Reports* 481.

[16] (1995) 91–116 *CCH Australian Intellectual Property Cases* 39,051.

pole through initiation and revelatory ceremonies. The Galpu asserted that the communal obligation of the artist was such that he owed an obligation to the clan to avoid prevent the design of the pole from being used in any way which was culturally offensive. Although sympathetic to this argument, the trial judge considered that the artist who had created the pole had successfully disposed of his intellectual property rights in it through a legally binding agreement, lamenting that "Australia's copyright law does not provide adequate recognition of Aboriginal community claims to regulate the reproduction and use of works which are essentially communal in origin".[17] He concluded by recommending that "the question of statutory recognition of Aboriginal communal interests in the reproduction of sacred objects is a matter for consideration by law reformers and legislators".[18]

In *Milpurrurru* the court awarded damages for breach of copyright to a number of Aboriginal artists whose designs were wrongfully reproduced on carpets. The court ruled that this was a particularly egregious breach of copyright, involving a culturally demeaning use of the infringed works. In computing the damages payable by the defendants to the individual artists whose works were infringed the court was prepared to recognise the cultural harm suffered by the individual artists However, the court considered itself unable to compensate the communities of those artists who were no longer alive, as "the statutory remedies do not recognise the infringement of ownership rights of the kind which reside under Aboriginal law in the traditional owners of the dreaming stories".[19]

Indeed a major problem, which has been identified in analysing traditional knowledge and cultural expression in conventional intellectual property terms is the observation that "indigenous peoples do not view their heritage in terms of property at all . . . but in terms of community and individual responsibility. Possessing a song, story or medical knowledge carries with it certain responsibilities to show respect to and maintain a reciprocal relationship with the human beings, animals, plants and places with which the song, story or medicine is connected".[20]

A second major problem is that the activities of ethnobiologists over the years has placed the exploitable knowledge of indigenous peoples in the public domain. Unless that knowledge was communicated in circumstances importing an obligation of confidence, it will not be protectable as confidential information.[21] Patent protection is similarly

[17] (1991) 2 *Intellectual Property Reports* 481 at 490.
[18] *ibid.* at 492.
[19] (1995) 91–116 *CCH Australian Intellectual Property Cases* 39,051 at 39,077.
[20] E.I. Daes, *Discrimination Against Indigenous Peoples: Study on the Protection of the Cultural and Intellectual Property of Indigenous Peoples* (1993), para. 26 quoted in Puri, "Cultural Ownership and Intellectual Property Rights Post-Mabo: Putting Ideas into Action", (1995) 9 *Intellectual Property Journal* 293 at 308.
[21] See *Forster v. Mountford* (1977) 14 A.L.R. 71, for a rare example.

unattainable as the publication of this ethnobiological material will often destroy its novelty.[22]

Even where the loss of novelty is not in issue, it will often be questionable whether the contribution of indigenous knowledge from which a pharmaceutical product is developed can be considered to be the sort of contribution which will allow the indigenous persons to be considered a joint inventor under patents law.

Joint inventorship typically requires that each of the joint inventors must have contributed to the inventive conception, "working toward the same end and producing an invention by their aggregate efforts".[23] It has been held that one does not become a joint inventor by being the first to observe a useful property or effect of an invention.[24] To be able to claim inventorship, there must be some demonstrable role in the final conception. The collaboration of indigenous peoples with ethnopharmacologists may be considered to be too indirect to the process of joint invention. However there are cases of collaboration where the ethnopharmacological investigators interact with the indigenous communities expressly for the purpose of discovering both the identity of medicinal plants and the conditions under which they are used to treat. In these circumstances the contribution of indigenous knowledge to the development of a plant derived drug may be an essential part of the conception.

4. The Julayinbul Statement on Indigenous Intellectual Property Rights

The use of indigenous knowledge in biotechnological patenting has led to calls by indigenous peoples for either the creation of a sui generis intellectual property regime or by the modification of existing patent and copyright laws to confer rights upon indigenous peoples in both their genetic resources and in traditional knowledge which becomes the subject of biotechnological patents.

The Rio Earth Summit of 1992 coincided with the promulgation by the United Nations of the Year of Indigenous Peoples. A number of conferences of indigenous peoples in 1992 issued declarations and statements affirming the intellectual property rights of indigenous peoples and interpreting and elaborating the intellectual property issues raised in the Biodiversity Convention.[25] Principal among these were: the Penang, Conference of February 1992 which promulgated the Charter of the Indigenous-Tribal Peoples of the Tropical Forests (CITP); the World Conference of Indigenous Peoples on Territory, Environment and Development, held at Kari-Oca, Brazil in May 1992, which

---

[22] See Huft, n.1 above at 1718.
[23] 269 F. Supp. 818 (DDC 1967).
[24] *Consolidated Aluminum Corp. v. Foseco Int'l Ltd* 10 U.S.P.Q. 2d 1143.
[25] See Blakeney, n.5 at 301–303.

issued the Indigenous Peoples Earth Charter; and the First International Conference on the Cultural and Intellectual Property Rights of Indigenous Peoples, held in the Bay of Plenty Region, New Zealand in June 1993 which issued the Mataatua Declaration on the Cultural and Intellectual Property Rights of Indigenous People. Typical of these declarations was the Declaration Reaffirming the Self-Determination and Intellectual Property Rights of the Indigenous Nations and Peoples of the Wet Tropics Rainforest Area, issued at the Julayinbul Conference on Intellectual and Cultural Property, held at Jingarrba, in the Daintree Forest region of North-Eastern Australia on November 27, 1993. Clause 5 of the Declaration asserted:

> That the intellectual property of the Indigenous Nations and Peoples of the Wet Tropics region includes and has always included the ability to discover and make what they deem appropriate use of knew knowledge derived from their total environment: such as the discovery of new genotypes and the right to control subsequent use of and access to the genetic make-up within the flora and fauna of the forests.

Additionally, the Jingarrba Conference issued the Julayinbul statement on Intellectual Property Rights. This statement affirmed the right of indigenous peoples "to define for themselves their own intellectual property". It also contained the proposition that "Aboriginal intellectual property, within Aboriginal Common Law, is an inherent inalienable right which cannot be terminated, extinguished, or taken" and that "Any use of the intellectual property Aboriginal Nations and Peoples may only be done in accordance with Aboriginal Common Law, and any unauthorised use is strictly prohibited".

Australian Indigenous Peoples' representatives also participated in the South Pacific Regional Consultation on Indigenous Peoples' Knowledge and Intellectual Property Rights, held in Suva, Fiji in April 1995. The Final statement issued by the Regional Consultation declared "the right of indigenous peoples of the Pacific to self-governance and independence of our lands, territories and resources as the basis for the preservation of indigenous peoples' knowledge". It reaffirmed "that imperialism is perpetuated through intellectual property rights systems, science and modern technology to control and exploit the lands, territories and resources of indigenous peoples". Article 1 of the Final statement sought a treaty to declare the Pacific region "a life forms patent-free zone". Article 2 called for "a moratorium on bioprospecting in the Pacific" and urged indigenous peoples not to co-operate in bioprospecting activities until appropriate protection mechanisms are in place. Article 7 urged the strengthening of indigenous networks and encouraged the UN and regional donors to "continue and support discussions on indigenous peoples' knowledge and intellectual property rights".

Finally, the Final statement urged "universities, churches, governments, non-governmental organisations and other institutions to reconsider their roles in the expropriation of indigenous peoples' knowledge and resources and to assist in their return to their rightful owners".

A direct relationship can be drawn between the communal real property rights of indigenous peoples which were recognised in *Mabo* and the communal rights of indigenous peoples in their traditional knowledge. The content of much of the traditional knowledge and spiritual beliefs of indigenous peoples involves their use of and relationship with the land. The nature and incidents of native title were defined in *Mabo* by reference to the laws and customs of Aboriginal Peoples and Torres Strait Islanders. Thus the extent to which the traditional knowledge and cultural expression of indigenous peoples is associated with the land, it becomes part of native title. This is reflected in the definition in section 223(1) of the Native Title Act 1993 which defines "native title" as "the communal, group or individual rights and interests of Aboriginal Peoples or Torres Strait Islanders in relation to land or waters" where three tests are met. First the rights and interests must be possessed under the traditional laws acknowledged and customs observed by the Aboriginal Peoples and Torres Strait Islanders. Secondly the Aboriginal Peoples or Torres Strait Islanders must, by those laws and customs have a connection with the land and waters. Thirdly, the rights and interests must be recognised by the common law of Australia.

The first two elements of this definition does not present too much of an obstacle to the recognition of the traditional knowledge and cultural expression of indigenous peoples as embraced within the concept of native title. A greater problem is the recognition of those matters by the common law of Australia.

5. Reform Proposals

The Commonwealth-State Working Group on Access to Biological Resources (CSWG) was established in 1994 to formulate a national approach on access to Australia's biological resources, to identify benefits from a national approach, to develop management principles and "to suggest mechanisms which could be used to govern access, collection, processing, development and export of Australia's indigenous biological resources"[26] In 1998 the CSWG released its discussion paper: *Managing Access to Australia's Biological Resources: Developing a Nationally Consistent Approach.*[27] As the title of the discussion paper indicates, the CSWG considered that in the face of administrative and

[26] Commonwealth-State Working Group on Access to Australia's Biological Resources, *Managing Access to Australia's Biological Resources: Developing a Nationally Consistent Approach* (AGPS, Canberra, 1998), p. 13.
[27] *ibid.*

political difficulties in securing a national policy on access to genetic resources, a nationally consistent approach on the part of states and Territories was the preferred option.[28] The CSWG promulgated 12 principles, derived from the CBD, to guide the management of access to genetic resources in Australia. These principles were:

1. Facilitate access to, and use of Australia's biological resources, in ecologically sustainable ways.
2. Foster a balanced approach to access to biological resources which promotes the conservation of biological diversity and which encourages the development of ecologically sustainable uses of biological resources for the benefit of Australia.
3. Ensure that Australia captures appropriate economic and other benefits from access to its biological resources and ensure the widest possible sharing of those benefits.
4. Ensure that administrative and regulatory practices are transparent, consistent and minimise duplication and regulation, building wherever possible on existing regulatory mechanisms.
5. Ensure continued access for Australia to biological resources in other countries for research and commercial purposes by developing an approach which Australia would be prepared to comply with if the same approach was used by other countries.
6. Be based on consultation with affected communities who should be given sufficient information to make informed decisions.
7. Be comprehensive, in terms of the coverage of biological resources on Australian territory and in waters under Australian sovereignty. . . .
8. Take into account with the interests of Aboriginal and Torres Strait Islander peoples, rural communities and rural landholders/owners.
9. Be consistent with:
   (a) Australia's responsibilities and interests in international instruments such as the Convention on Biological Diversity, the United Nations Food and Agricultural Organisation (FAO) International Undertaking on Plant Genetic Resources and the United Nations Convention on the Law of the Sea.
   (b) The Intergovernmental Agreement on the Environment
   (c) National Competition Policy and the Trade Practices Act.
10. Provide for sharing of information between the Commonwealth, states and Territories on biological resources and their conservation and management.
11. Provide adequate mechanisms for monitoring and enforcing the requirements of contracts and permits.

[28] *ibid.* p. 14.

12. Where possible, provide opportunities for active participation by Australia in all stages of the development of biological resources, including collection, screening, research and product development.[29]

As a mechanism to govern access, collection, processing, development and export of Australia's indigenous biological resources, the discussion paper proposes an multi-purpose contract system (MSC). This was proposed on the basis that it would require minimal changes to existing legislation, that it was consistent with Australia's international obligations and was flexible and cost-effective.[30] The development of a MSC to cover all aspects of access to biological resources was recommended as a means of eliminating the existing complicated system of permits. Despite its suggestion that a nationally consistent approach is preferable to a national approach, it is difficult to see the MSC device working without the exercise of national sovereignty over biological resources.

In relation to the recognition of the rights of indigenous peoples, the discussion paper rejects intellectual-property style protection in favour of bioprospecting contracts entered into prior to the divulging of traditional knowledge.[31]

In October 1994 the Australian Federal Attorney-General, the Minister for Aboriginal and Torres Strait Islander Affairs and the Minister for Communication and the Arts jointly released a discussion paper calling for submissions on the inadequacies of current intellectual property laws in their application to Indigenous arts and culture.[32] An Inter-Departmental Committee on Indigenous Arts and Cultural Expression was set up to evaluate such submissions as were made. At the beginning of 1996, the Aboriginal and Torres Strait Islander Commission (ATSIC), the governing body of Indigenous peoples in Australia, established an Indigenous Reference Group, to co-ordinate the submissions of Indigenous peoples to the reform process initiated by the Federal Government. At the same time ATSIC also established the Australian Institute of Aboriginal and Torres Strait Islander Studies (AIATSIS) to co-ordinate a project "which aims to develop practical reforms that would improve protection and ensure recognition of Indigenous Cultural and Intellectual Property."[33] In August 1997, AIATSIS issued its own discussion paper, canvassing proposals for the recognition and protection of Indigenous cultural and intellectual property.[34]

[29] *ibid.* pp. 17-18.

[30] *ibid.* p. 19.

[31] *ibid.* p. 27.

[32] *Stopping the Rip-offs: Intellectual Property Protection for Aboriginal and torres Strait Islander Peoples* (AGPS, Canberra, 1994).

[33] AIATSIS, *Our Culture, Our Future. Proposals for the recognition and protection of Indigenous cultural and intellectual property*, (AIATSIS, Sydney, 1997), p. 2.

[34] *ibid.*

The AIATSIS discussion paper refers to the possibility of the Patents Act 1990 being amended to "give Indigenous peoples rights of recognition and compensation in respect of the contribution of Indigenous knowledge from many agricultural and pharmaceutical products are developed".[35] The discussion paper also refers to suggestions for the modification of the Plant Breeders Rights Act 1994, to require applicants for the registration of a new plant variety to identify the contribution of any Indigenous people and to oblige the registration to be conditional on its consent and approval. This procedure could form the basis of a royalty arrangement.[36]

Agitation, particularly among developing countries, for an international instrument providing for the recognition of the intellectual property rights of indigenous peoples in the preservation, conservation and dissemination of global biological diversity and the protection of the cultural and intellectual property rights of indigenous peoples, precipitated a joint UNESCO/WIPO World Forum on the Protection of Folklore was convened in Phuket, Thailand in April 1997. One of the results of this Forum was the institution by WIPO in its 1998–99 biennium of fact-finding missions "to identify and explore the intellectual property needs, rights and expectations of the holders of traditional knowledge and innovations, in order to promote the contribution of the intellectual property system to their social, cultural and economic development". Australia was chosen as the first port of call for this expert mission, which visited Darwin and Sydney from June 14–18, 1998. Among the matters considered by the Expert Mission were:

- the role of intellectual property rights in the preservation, conservation and dissemination of global biological diversity;
- the intellectual property rights aspects of biotechnology; and the use of intellectual property rights in the transfer of technology under multilateral environmental agreements;
- The feasibility of establishing databases of traditional knowledge.

7. Proposed Commonwealth Biodiversity Act

In February 1998 the Commonwealth Minister for the Environment issued a Consultation Paper *Reform of Commonwealth Environment Legislation.* The Consultation Paper foreshadows three new Commonwealth Acts; an Environment Protection Act, a Biodiversity Conservation Act and new heritage legislation. These proposals arise out of an Agreement on Commonwealth/State Roles and Responsibilities for the Environment which was settled at the November 1997 meeting of the Council of Australian Governments (COAG). The central tenet of the

[35] *ibid.* 64.
[36] *ibid.*

Agreement was that "the Commonwealth should be focussed on matters of national environmental significance".[37] Consequently, the Minister announced the withdrawal of the Commonwealth "from matters of only local or state significance".[38] The question of access to biological resources was not directly identified in the COAG Agreement as a matter of national significance. The Consultation Paper refers to the unified national approach on access to biological resources which is being developed by the CSWG.

In a chapter of the Consultation Paper on the question of access it is stated that "the Commonwealth Government currently has no specific legislative ability to implement the provisions of the Convention on Biological Diversity dealing with the control of access to biological resources" and that the Biodiversity Conservation Act will provide it with that ability "by allowing regulations to be made in relation to the management of access to biological resources on Commonwealth land and in marine environments under Commonwealth control".[39] The Consultation Paper provides no hints as to the form or scope of these regulations.

The Consultation Paper infelicitously expresses the legislative ability of the Commonwealth in this area. Legislation pursuant to the external affairs power in placitum 51(xxix) of the Constitution would permit the Commonwealth to implement the access provisions of the Biodiversity Convention in full force. Indeed as the joint submission on the Consultation Paper of the Australian Conservation Foundation and others, points out on the subject of threatened species the Consultation Paper states "This provision will apply to all of Australia and its waters. It will not be restricted to Commonwealth areas".[40] The joint submission also addresses the issue of the prior informed consent of traditional and other owners as the cornerstone of access to biodiversity.[41]

[37] Sen. The Hon. Robert Hill, Commonwealth Minister for the Environment, *Reform of Commonwealth Environment Legislation* (Canberra, 1998), p. 3.
[38] Sen the Hon Robert Hill, *Environmental Law Reform — A New Era*, (Media Release, February 25, 1998), http://www.environment.gov.au/portfolio/minister/env/98/mr25feb298.html.
[39] n.44 above at 32.
[40] The Australian Conservation Foundation and Others, *Submission*, March 23, 1998, http://www.internetnorth.com/au/edonsw/policy/cthlawref.htm.
[41] *ibid.* ch.3.12.

5. Protecting and Revitalising Traditional Ecological Knowledge: Intellectual Property Rights and Community Knowledge Databases in India

Graham Dutfield

Co-ordinates the Working Group on Traditional Resource Rights at the Oxford Centre for the Environment, Ethics and Society, Mansfield College, University of Oxford. He has an M.Phil in Environment and Development from Cambridge University and has published numerous articles on traditional resource rights, conservation and bioprospecting. He has also co-written three books in this area. At present he is working on a D.Phil thesis called "The International Biotrade, Conservation and Intellectual Property Rights" at Oxford University.

Protecting and Revitalising Traditional Ecological Knowledge: Intellectual Property Rights and Community Knowledge Databases in India

1. Introduction

One of the great ironies for indigenous peoples and local communities is that while scientific and commercial interest in their ecological knowledge and resource management practices have never been greater, human cultural diversity is eroding at an accelerating rate as the world steadily becomes more biologically and culturally uniform. According to the IUCN Inter-Commission Task Force on Indigenous Peoples,[1] "cultures are dying out faster than the peoples associated with them. It has been estimated that half the world's languages — the storehouses of peoples' intellectual heritages and the framework for their unique understandings of life — will disappear within a century". According to the Task Force, the main threats include genocide, uncontrolled frontier aggression, military intimidation, extension of government control, unjust land policies, cultural modification policies, and inappropriate conservation management.

Although scientific and commercial investigation and collection of traditional knowledge and biological resources have been going on for centuries, "bioprospecting" has intensified in recent years,[2] while multilateral and bilateral donor agencies, United Nations agencies, and international environmental law have embraced the principle that traditional knowledge has a vital role in sustainable development and therefore needs protection. Indigenous peoples and local communities often welcome interest in their knowledge as long as their rights as holders of this knowledge are respected. But they condemn the "mining" or "salvaging" of their knowledge by commercial concerns and scientists that feel they have no responsibility to ensure that

---

[1] IUCN Inter-Commission Task Force on Indigenous Peoples, *Indigenous Peoples and Sustainability: Cases and Actions* (IUCN & International Books, Utrecht, 1997), p. 60.

[2] Balick, M.J. Elisabetsky, E. and Laird, S.A. (eds) *Medicinal Resources of the Tropical Forest: Biodiversity and its Importance to Human Health* (Columbia University Press, New York, 1996); D.J. Chadwick, and J. Marsh, (eds) *Ethnobotany and the Search for New Drugs* (John Wiley & Sons, Chichester), 1994; C. Joyce, *Earthly Goods: Medicine-Hunting in the Rainforest* (Little Brown and Co. New York, Toronto and London, 1994); C. Juma, *The Gene Hunters: Biotechnology and the Scramble for Seeds* (Princeton University Press, Princeton, N.J., 1989); D.A. Posey, *Indigenous Peoples and Traditional Resource Rights: A Basis for Equitable Relationships?* (Green College Centre for Environmental Policy and Understanding, Oxford, 1995); W.V. Reid, S.A. Laird, C.A. Meyer, R. Gámez, A. Sittenfeld, D.H. Janzen, M.A. Gollin & C. Juma, (eds) *Biodiversity Prospecting: Using Genetic Resources for Sustainable Development* (World Resources Institute, Washington D.C., 1993).

benefits flow back to their communities, or to help stem the erosion of their cultures. Intellectual property rights, especially patents, have been criticised by many indigenous peoples, other grassroots organisations and pro-Third World advocacy groups[3] because they are considered to *encourage* and *legitimise* "biopiracy" (the unauthorised commercial exploitation of their knowledge and biological resources). These sentiments are felt very strongly in India, where there is a particularly large number of highly vocal non-governmental organisations including farmers and local community rights advocacy groups engaged in IPR, biodiversity and food security issues.

Such criticisms of IPRs are heartfelt but not always well-informed. Nevertheless, it is undeniable that IPRs are inadequate for protecting traditional knowledge, innovations and practices, or reversing the alarming erosion of traditional systems of knowledge. Increasingly concerned scientists are calling for the documentation of such systems before they are lost forever. Some indigenous peoples' organisations are sceptical because they worry that documentation initiatives are likely to be top-down and exploitative. Their past experiences with scientists give them ample cause to feel suspicious. Nevertheless, recording traditional systems of knowledge may be indispensable as a means of ensuring that they do not disappear. Perhaps the best solution to protect and revitalise knowledge is for the communities and peoples themselves to take control over the documentation process so that their knowledge is kept *in situ* where it can continue to evolve rather than simply to be stored elsewhere in international "traditional knowledge banks".

This paper consists of five sections: (a) the growing interest in and respect for traditional knowledge; (b) the protection of traditional knowledge as an IPR issue; (c) case studies of patents and traditional knowledge; (d) the protection of IPRs and traditional rights in India; and (e) an evaluation of Indian initiatives to document traditional knowledge.

2. The Growing Status of Traditional Knowledge

Traditional ecological knowledge (sometimes referred to as "traditional environmental knowledge" or "indigenous knowledge") is defined by Johnson[4] as "a body of knowledge built by a group of people through generations living in close contact with nature. It includes a system of classification, a set of empirical observations about the local environment, and a system of self-management that governs resource use". It

[3] For example, Rural Advancement Foundation International (Canada & USA), Genetic Resources Action International (Spain and Philippines), Research Foundation for Science, Technology and Ecology (India), Kalpavriksh (India), and Cultural Survival Canada.

[4] M. Johnson, "Research on Traditional Environmental Knowledge: Its Development and Its Role". In M. Johnson (ed.) *Lore: Capturing Traditional Environmental Knowledge* (IDRC, Ottawa, 1992) p. 4.

is important to avoid the common assumption that "traditional" necessarily implies "outdated". According to a report submitted to the Secretariat of the Convention on Biological Diversity (CBD) by a Canadian indigenous peoples organisation, the Four Directions Council[5]:

> what is "traditional" about traditional knowledge is not its antiquity, but *the way it is acquired and used*. In other words, the social process of learning and sharing knowledge, which is unique to each indigenous culture, lies at the very heart of its "traditionality". Much of this knowledge is actually quite new, but it has a social meaning, and legal character, entirely unlike the knowledge indigenous people acquire from settlers and industrialised societies. (original emphasis)

Two relevant issues are hotly debated by anthropologists and continue to be controversial. The first is whether traditional knowledge and western science are clearly distinguishable or not.[6] The second issue concerns the alleged inherent environment-friendliness of traditional knowledge systems and livelihood practices. With respect to the first issue, Johnson identifies several ways that traditional ecological knowledge (TEK) is generated, recorded and transmitted different to Western scientific knowledge according to a survey of relevant academic literature.[7] Thus, traditional ecological knowledge:

- is recorded and transmitted through oral tradition
- is learned through observation and hands-on experience
- is based on the understanding that the elements of matter have a life force. All parts of the natural world are therefore infused with spirit
- does not view human life as superior to other animate and inanimate elements: all life-forms have kinship and are interdependent
- is holistic (whereas Western science is reductionist)
- is intuitive in its mode of thinking (whereas Western science is analytical)
- is mainly qualitative (whereas Western science is mainly quantitative)
- is based on data generated by resource users. As such it is more inclusive than Western science, which is collected by a specialised group of researchers who tend to be more selective and deliberate in the accumulation of facts
- is based on diachronic data (whereas Western science is largely based on synchronic data)

[5] Four Directions Council, *Forests, Indigenous Peoples and Biodiversity: Contribution of the Four Directions Council.* Submission to the Secretariat for the Convention on Biological Diversity (1996).
[6] For example see A. Agrawal, "Dismantling the Divide Between Indigenous and Scientific Knowledge". *Development and Change* 26 (1995) pp. 413–439.
[7] *op cit.* at pp. 7–8.

- is rooted in a social context that sees the world in terms of social and spiritual relations between all life-forms. In contrast, Western science is hierarchically organised and vertically compartmentalised
- derives its explanations of environmental phenomena from cumulative, collective and often spiritual experiences. Such explanations are checked, validated, and revised daily and seasonally through the annual cycle of activities.

Indigenous and traditional livelihood systems are often said to embody the concept of sustainability, but generalisations should only be made with caution. Just as some studies of subsistence and resource management practices of present-day traditional peoples have been used to support the view that a conservation ethic is a prevalent feature of such societies,[8] other anthropologists claim that in many traditional societies, this ethic is either not observed by many community members or is entirely non-existent.[9] Ellen[10] argues that many traditional societies impact minimally on the environment merely because they are often small and isolated. Redford and Stearman[11] are also sceptical of the "ecologically noble savage" hypothesis. They feel it is inappropriate to generalise about traditional communities and make broadly applicable assertions about their environmental values, and argue that expecting traditional peoples to continue using only traditional technologies and low-impact subsistence strategies places an unfair burden of responsibility on them and implicitly denies the right of such peoples to develop according to their own preferences.[12]

Nevertheless, academic studies of traditional communities provide ample evidence that the protection of traditional ecological knowledge provides significant environmental benefits as well as possible commercial applications. For example, in many forest areas, indigenous peoples

[8] *e.g.* J. Bodley, *Anthropology and Contemporary Human Problems* (Benjamin Cummings Publishing, Menlo Park, 1976); J. Clad, "Conservation and Indigenous Peoples: A Study of Convergent Interests" *Cultural Survival Quarterly* 8 (1984) pp. 68–73, C. Martin, *Keepers of the Game* (University of California Press, Berkeley, 1978); G. Reichel-Dolmatoff, "Cosmology as Ecological Analysis: A View from the Rain Forest" *Man* 11 (1976) pp. 307-318.

[9] R. Hames, R. "Wildlife Conservation in Tribal Societies". In: M.L. Oldfield, and J.B. Alcorn, (eds) *Biodiversity: Culture, Conservation, and Ecodevelopment* (Westview Press, Boulder, San Francisco and Oxford, 1991) pp. 172–199, A. Kalland, "Indigenous — Local Knowledge: Prospects and Limitations". In: Hansen, B.V. (ed.), *Arctic Environment: Report on the Seminar on Integration of Indigenous peoples Knowledge, Reykjavik, September 20–23, 1994* (Ministry for the Environment (Iceland), Ministry of the Environment (Denmark) and The Home Rule of Greenland (Denmark Office), Reykjavik and Copenhagen, 1994) pp. 150–167.

[10] R. Ellen, "What Black Elk Left Unsaid: On the Illusory Images of Green Primitivism" 2 *Anthropology Today* (1986) pp. 8–12.

[11] K.H. Redford, "The Ecologically Noble Savage". [1991] *Cultural Survival Quarterly* 15, pp. 46–48 K.H. Redford, and A.M. Stearman, "Forest-Dwelling Native Amazonians and the Conservation of Biodiversity: Interests in Common or in Collision?" (1993) 7 *Conservation Biology* 248; A.M. Stearman, "Neotropical Hunters and their Neighbors: Effects of Non-Indigenous Settlement Patterns on Three Native Bolivian Societies" in K.H. Redford and C. Padoch, (eds) *Conservation of Neotropical Forests: Building on Traditional Resource Use* (Columbia University Press, New York, 1992) pp. 108–128.

[12] Redford *op. cit.*; Kalland, *op. cit.*

plant forest gardens and manage the regeneration of bush fallows in ways which take advantage of natural processes and mimic the biodiversity of natural forests. Researchers are increasingly aware of the extent to which indigenous natural resource management can enhance biodiversity, and in this way have realised the extent of anthropogenic landscapes even within "pristine" tropical forests.[13]

Much of the world's crop diversity is in the custody of farmers who follow age-old farming and land use practices that conserve biodiversity and provide other local benefits. Among such benefits are the promotion of diet diversity, income generation, production stability, minimisation of risk, reduced insect and disease incidence, efficient use of labour, intensification of production with limited resources, and maximisation of returns under low levels of technology. These ecologically complex agricultural systems associated with centres of crop genetic diversity include traditional cultivars or "landraces" that constitute an essential part of the world's crop genetic heritage, and non-domesticated plant and animal species that serve humanity in various ways.

It is not only in terrestrial biomes that indigenous peoples conserve biodiversity. They carry out a range of practices that are effective in the conservation of coastal and marine biological diversity including such biodiversity-rich biomes as mangrove systems and coral reefs.[14]

Traditional knowledge systems are increasingly accepted as an important source of useful information in the achievement of sustainable development. Until the 1970s, development planning and conservation policies were usually based on very negative assumptions about traditional rural societies. Poor rural dwellers were generally assumed to be backward and inimical to change, and their livelihood practices, such as shifting cultivation, were thought to be at best inefficient and unproductive and at worst environmentally destructive. More enlightened attitudes towards the knowledge, skills and subsistence practices of rural communities in developing countries emerged in the 1970s, according to Adams,[15] "as part of a liberal and populist reaction against the unsuccessful technological triumphalism of rural development practice". These attitudes have become increasingly mainstream in academia and among international development and conservation agencies. A highly influential volume published in 1980 called "Indigenous Knowledge Systems and Development"[16] consisted of contributions exclusively from

---

[13] For example, see S.B. Hecht, and D.A. Posey, "Preliminary Results on Soil Management Techniques of the Kayapo Indians" (1989) *Advances in Economic Botany*, 174; D.A. Posey, "The Science of the Mebengokre" *Orion* (Summer, 1990) pp. 16–23.

[14] For examples, see K. Ruddle and R.E. Johannes, *The Traditional Knowledge and Management of Coastal Systems in Asia and the Pacific* (Jakarta, UNESCO, 1985).

[15] W.M. Adams, *Green Development: Environment and Sustainability in the Third World* (Routledge, London 1990) p. 169.

[16] D.W. Brokensha, D.M. Warren and O. Werner, (eds) *Indigenous Knowledge Systems and Development* (University Press of America, Lanham, 1980).

anthropologists and geographers. A follow-up volume published 15 years later contained contributions also from such disciplines as agronomy, soil science, entomology, agroforestry, agroecology, veterinary medicine and rural sociology. Since 1993, the Centre for International Research and Advisory Network (CIRAN) has been publishing the Indigenous Knowledge and Development Monitor for "the international community of people who are interested in indigenous knowledge". There are now 3,000 subscribers in 130 countries. CIRAN is one of a network of 35 indigenous knowledge resource centres located throughout Europe, the Americas, Africa and Asia.

Many multilateral and bilateral donor agencies including the World Bank, United Nations agencies such as FAO, UNESCO and UNEP, and several of the International Agricultural Research Centres now recognise the role of traditional knowledge in sustainable development.[17] Such recognition is often accompanied by acknowledgement of the need for bottom-up participatory development policies in place of the now discredited paternalistic and top-down strategies of the recent past.

With respect to nature conservation, international organisations like the IUCN-World Conservation Union and the World Wide Fund for Nature are far more willing than before to respect traditional knowledge and to understand that such respect must include support for the *rights* of the holders. At the first World Conservation Congress in 1996, IUCN acknowledged that "the knowledge, innovations and practices of indigenous peoples and local communities embodying traditional lifestyles are: (i) important elements of biological diversity; (ii) responsible for the conservation, selection and improvement of biodiversity elements and should therefore be valued, respected and protected; but (iii) are often used without fair compensation." WWF's "Statement of Principles on Indigenous Peoples and Conservation"[18] expressed appreciation of "the enormous contribution indigenous peoples have made to the maintenance of many of the earth's most fragile ecosystems" with regret that "the goals of conserving biodiversity and protecting and securing indigenous cultures and livelihoods have sometimes been perceived as contradictory rather than mutually reinforcing."

Awareness of the destruction of traditional knowledge systems is increasing but there is some debate concerning the most appropriate way to respond. Many academics and development workers have urged that traditional knowledge be documented. According to Johnson[19]:

---

[17] D.M. Warren, "The Interface Between and the Integration of Indigenous Knowledge Systems and Modern Technologies". Paper presented at XIII International Plant Protection Congress, The Hague, Netherlands, July 2–7, 1995.

[18] World Wide Fund for Nature International *Indigenous Peoples and Conservation: WWF Statement of Principles* (WWF, Gland, 1996).

[19] Johnson, *op cit.* at 11.

> The first and most urgent problem associated with integration [of TEK and Western science] is the rapid disappearance of TEK with the passing of the elders. Orally based knowledge systems lost in this way cannot be retrieved. It is only through documentation that the usefulness of TEK can become apparent and an improved understanding can be gained of the practices and conditions that lead to the breakdown and reestablishment of TEK management systems.

There is a tendency among some of those who advocate documenting traditional knowledge to emphasise *ex situ* rather than *in situ* conservation. Thus, Professor Ulluwishewa, Director of the Sri Lanka Resource Centre for Indigenous Knowledge, one of the above-mentioned IK resource centres, argues that the mission of each centre should *inter alia* be[20]:

- to act as a clearinghouse for collection, documentation, comparison with global knowledge systems, dissemination and utilisation of indigenous knowledge;
- to facilitate and undertake the documentation of indigenous knowledge in the areas of agriculture, fisheries, environment and natural resources management, animal health, human health, etc.; and
- to undertake research projects in order to establish the scientific validity and economic viability of indigenous technologies, and to evaluate the cost effectiveness of incorporating indigenous knowledge components in development projects.

While recording traditional knowledge before it falls out of use may often be the only way to prevent it from being lost completely there are potential dangers with archiving traditional knowledge in national and international databases to the exclusion of locally-based initiatives. First, it must be understood that traditional knowledge is not static but evolves. Storing it in *ex situ* collections fixes it temporally. Therefore, its relevance will diminish over time unless it is constantly updated. As Agrawal argues,[21] "divorced in archives from their cultural context, no knowledge can maintain its vitality or vigour". Second, such an approach may deflect attention from the far more important priority of protecting traditional knowledge *in situ* which of course requires that attention be given to the cultural, spiritual and physical well-being of the knowledge holders and their communities. Indeed, such a "solution" hardly seems an adequate way to deal with the problem that such knowledge is falling out of use in the very communities that

---

[20] R. Ulluwishewa, "Indigenous Knowledge, National IK Resoure Centres and Sustainable Development" (1993) 1(3) *Indigenous Knowledge and Development Monitor* 11 at 13.
[21] A. Agrawal, *op cit.* at 429.

generate it. This is even more true if the archives are inaccessible to the communities providing the knowledge to the archives. Third, documenting traditional knowledge is unethical *and* counter-productive if the intellectual property rights of the generators and holders of such knowledge are ignored by those doing the recording. At the 3rd International Congress of Ethnobiology which took place in Lucknow, India in 1995, the many tribal people in attendance from various parts of India confirmed that their ecological knowledge is endangered, and attributed this problem in large part to the failure of outsiders to (a) understand traditional knowledge, (b) respect its scientific basis, and (c) recognise the intellectual property rights of tribal communities and individuals. It seems paradoxical but it is often the case that traditional knowledge is respected more than the people who generate and share it. According to Akhil Gupta,[22] "natives" serve as informants and sometimes collaborate in eliciting data; significantly, they are rarely the "experts" who compile, systematise, and store the data in retrievable form".

It is perhaps out of such concerns that representatives of indigenous peoples attending the Workshop on Traditional Knowledge and Biological Diversity organised by the Secretariat of the Convention on Biological Diversity in November 1997 went so far as to call for "a moratorium on the registering of [traditional] knowledge". Fortunately, some scientific organisations are sensitive to the concerns of indigenous peoples. The International Society of Ethnobiology recently drafted a set of Guidelines for Research, Collections, Databases and Publications. According to these Guidelines no research, collection, database or publication shall be undertaken without the prior informed consent of "all potentially affected communities of indigenous peoples or traditional societies". Moreover, "no member of the International Society of Ethnobiology (ISE) or affiliated organisations of ISE shall undertake any research, collection, database or publication derived or obtained from information or materials from any community that has requested a moratorium on any relevant research, collection, database or publication."

3. IPRs and the Rights of Traditional Knowledge Holders

3.1 Are IPRs inimical to indigenous peoples' rights?

The following patent case studies illustrate various concerns about patents in the context of traditional knowledge. The turmeric case may be atypical since there was so obviously no real invention and the decision to grant the patent was clearly a mistake by the patent examiner. The system proved to be self-correcting in the sense that the

[22] A. Gupta, *Postcolonial Developments: Agriculture in the Making of Modern India* (Duke University Press, Durham & London, 1998) p. 173.

patent was revoked, yet it required the active intervention of a foreign government agency to ensure that this happened. Even the most controversial of the multiplicity of neem patents display more inventiveness, but the turmeric patent case (3.1.1) shows that patented inventions which relate closely to public domain traditional knowledge can be challenged successfully if they are considered to lack novelty and/or an inventive step (3.1.2). The quinoa patent (3.1.3) is an example of how the breadth of a patent's claims may be construed as encompassing the traditional plant varieties.

3.1.1 The turmeric patent

In March 1995, a United States patent on *Use of Turmeric in Wound Healing* was awarded to the University of Mississippi Medical Center. The claim covered "a method of promoting healing of a wound by administering turmeric to a patient afflicted with the wound", such wounds including surgical wounds and body ulcers. According to Agarwal and Narain[23] in India the powder of the turmeric plant is "a classic grandmother's remedy" which "has been applied to the scrapes and cuts of generations of children".

In mid-1996 the Council of Scientific and Industrial Research of India (CSIR) requested the U.S. Patent and Trademark Office to revoke the patent on the basis that turmeric powder is widely known about and used in India for its wound healing properties, and that a great deal of scientific research has been carried out by Indian scientists that confirms the existence of these properties. One could easily suppose that the patent was awarded because the applicant had omitted to mention related traditional use of turmeric and to cite the relevant literature. After all, there is a limit to the amount of time patent office examiners can devote to examining each application for novelty, inventive step and usefulness. However, the patent description helpfully states that: "Turmeric, a yellow powder developed from the plant *Curcurma longa,* is commonly used as a food colorant in many Indian dishes and imparts a bitter taste. . . . Although it is primarily a dietary agent, turmeric has long been used in India as a traditional medicine for the treatment of various sprains and inflammatory conditions." No method for extracting the active principle was described. Instead, the patent simply declares that "turmeric is a natural product that is readily available in the food store."

Given the admission that turmeric has long been used to treat inflammatory conditions, it is difficult to see how this patent could have passed the tests of novelty and non-obviousness during the examination.

---

[23] A. Agarwal, and S. Narain, "Pirates in the Garden of India". *New Scientist,* October 26, 1996, pp. 14–15.

This patent was revoked after the CSIR's challenge on the basis of its absence of novelty. CSIR did not succeed by proving that many Indians already use turmeric as a wound healing agent, but because it was able to provide relevant scientific literature.[24] Patent examiners in the United States are not required to accept the evidence of traditional knowledge held outside the USA as prior art (*i.e.* already known) unless it has been reported (and thereby validated) by scientists and published in learned journals or otherwise made available to the public. The inventors in fact made no explicit claim that the wound healing agent (*i.e.* the turmeric powder) was any different from the one used traditionally by Indians.

3.1.2 The neem patents

The neem tree (*Azadirachta indica*) has been the subject of at least 153 patents worldwide.[25] The inventions described in virtually all of the neem-related patents used public domain traditional knowledge as a starting point. They have aroused considerable controversy, especially in India, where most of the traditional knowledge holders are from. There have been at least two patent challenges: (1) to a European Patent Office (EPO) patent for fungicidal effects of neem oil (Patent No. 436 257 B1) owned by W. R. Grace & Co., and (2) to a U.S. patent for a storage stable azadirachtin formulation (Patent No. 5124349) also owned by W. R. Grace.[26] The challenge to the former patent has been successful insofar as the Opposition Division of the EPO in September 1997 delivered an interim judgment expressing doubt that the patent can be maintained on the basis of lack of novelty and inventive step.

3.1.3 The quinoa patent[27]

Quinoa (*Chenopodium quinoa*) is a highly nutritious drought-resistant food crop grown in the cold high-elevation regions of the Andean countries of South America. Indigenous communities in Bolivia and Peru have bred numerous varieties, including Apelawa, named after a

---

[24] According to Pradesh "[t]he [CSIR] claim had to be backed by written documentation claiming traditional wisdom. CSIR went so far as to present an ancient Sanskrit text and a paper published in 1953 in the Journal of the Indian Medical Association." Pradesh, S. *Country Study: India*. Trade and Development Centre website (1998) http://www.itd.org/issues/india6.htm.

[25] As revealed by the author's search of the European Patent Office's patent information database on November 30, 1998.

[26] J. Kocken, and G. van Roozendaal, "The Neem Tree Debate". (1997) 30 *Biotechnology and Development Monitor* 8.

[27] This case study is based on information from U.S. Patent 5304718 and the following sources: A. Bonifacio "Technical Considerations on Cytoplasmic Male Sterility in Quinoa" [unpublished paper], 1997; exchanges between S. Ward and P. Mooney on the Environment in Latin America Network e-mail listserv; and the two press releases issued by RAFI on June 19, 1997 and May 22, 1998. For a more detailed discussion of the quinoa patent see J.-A. Garí, *The Role of Democracy in the Biodiversity Issue: The Case of Quinoa* (CEDLA (Centre for Latin America Research and Documentation) Papers CEDLA, Amsterdam, 1997).

village in Bolivia. Although still a little-known food outside these countries, there is a growing demand for quinoa among health-conscious Europeans and North Americans and industrial plant breeders have started to take an interest. In order for plant breeders to produce hybrids from self-pollinating quinoa plants, the male properties of one parent must be eliminated so that plants of two different varieties do not fertilise themselves as well as each other leaving progeny that are mixtures of the hybrid and the two parental varieties. Use of male sterile plants in the breeding of hybrids can avoid the labour intensive work of removing anthers from plants. In April 1994, a United states patent was awarded for *Cytoplasmic Male Sterile Quinoa*. The patent accepts that male sterile quinoa lines have been reported in the literature but claims that "a reliable system of cytoplasmic male sterility has not been reported, and cytoplasmic male sterile plants have not heretofore been available for commercial production of quinoa hybrids".

The patent states that "the cytoplasm conferring the property of male sterility is derived from the Apelawa variety of quinoa". However, in an Internet exchange between one of the named inventors, Professor Sarah Ward, and Pat Mooney of Rural Advancement Foundation International (RAFI), the former states that she *found* the cytoplasm in question in quinoa plants of the Bolivian Apelawa variety growing in a field in Colorado, USA. The cytoplasm, she argued, does not exist in quinoa plants growing in South America but had been transferred naturally from a related weed species growing nearby (in Colorado). This was not made clear in the patent. Consequently, the failure to indicate the non-Bolivian provenance of the cytoplasm inducing male sterility or to refer to its discovery made it possible to interpret the patent very broadly in ways the inventors may not have intended. For example, the first two patent claims were for a quinoa seed of the variety Apelawa having male sterile cytoplasm and a quinoa plant produced from this quinoa seed. Although it is difficult to see how Andean farmers could be directly affected by the patent, since the existence and value of quinoa plants with the male sterility characteristic were known to many traditional cultivators, it was understandable that those farmers exporting quinoa to the United States would feel threatened by these claims. An international campaign involving RAFI and Bolivia's National Association of Quinoa Producers that called for Colorado State University to let the patent lapse was successful when in May 1998 Dr Ward admitted that it had been abandoned.

3.1.4 Conclusions

Comparing these cases shows some of the various ways that inventions may be derived from traditional knowledge and how the entitlements of traditional knowledge holders may vary as a result. In the turmeric case, the "invention" *was* the traditional use of the plant, and it is because this traditional use had been documented that the invention was ultimately deemed to lack novelty. At least some (and possibly most) of the neem-related inventions embody uses identical to those of Indian farmers but the products and/or methods of extraction are different. In such cases it can safely be assumed that the existence of relevant traditional knowledge was *a* (but not *the*) *sine qua non* for the inventions.

Even if this traditional knowledge had been held only by a small number of farmers, would this mean that their knowledge had been pirated? To be consistent, those arguing in favour would also have to agree that a temporary monopoly right to an incremental improvement is inherently exploitative of *all* people that had contributed to the state of the art (or more accurately all the states of the arts) relevant to the patent. This position is difficult to sustain on both theoretical and practical grounds. The state of the art in this case includes not only the knowledge that neem seed extracts are an effective pesticide, but also the industrial techniques that can be applied to produce neem derivatives that are in one way or another more useful than the natural product.[28] In the case of the quinoa patent, traditional knowledge was not a *sine qua non* for the invention except in the sense that the development and continued existence of quinoa varieties can be attributed to the efforts of past and present Andean peoples. The main problem with this patent is that it seems to appropriate part of the public domain by dint of the excessive breadth of what it claims rather than that it "pirates" traditional knowledge. A case can still be made for compensating the Andean farmers when their knowledge and resources are used in such patent applications, but patent law is hardly the best possible mechanism for benefit sharing given that most patented inventions are not commercially viable while many natural products may not even be IPR-protected.[29]

3.2 Can IPRs protect traditional biodiversity-related knowledge?

Only inventions that can be dated and attributed to an individual or small group of people are patentable. In traditional societies, the sources of traditional knowledge may be attributable to individuals,

[28] Having made this point, it should still be noted that two of the most controversial neem patents — U.S. patents 4,556,562 ("Stable anti-pest neem seed extract") and 5,124,349 ("Storage stable azadirachtin formulation") — both describe fairly basic chemical processes that could conceivably render the invention "obvious" to one who is skilled in the art (see Kadidal *op. cit.*).

[29] According to Leskien and Flitner: "the principle of benefit sharing certainly requires more than being integrated into IPR legislation, simply because not all applications of plant genetic resources end up being protected by an IPR. Since in many countries plant varieties and other products need to undergo an authorisation or certification procedure before they are allowed to be released, the application for such marketing authorisation could also be used as a trigger for benefit sharing." D. Leskien, and M. Flitner, *Intellectual Property Rights and Plant Genetic Resources*. Issues in Genetic Resources No. 6. (International Plant Genetic Resources Institute, Rome, 1997).

kinship or gender-based groups, or to single communities. In theory such knowledge may be patentable. However, a great deal of traditional knowledge is not traceable to a specific community or geographical area and is ineligible for patent protection. Whether widely known or not, once traditional knowledge is recorded and publicly disseminated, its use and application is beyond the control of the original knowledge providers. As we saw earlier, if a researcher investigates a piece of published traditional knowledge and then improves upon it in a practical way, the result may well become a patentable "invention" that this researcher can own.

Patents cannot be expected to accommodate the subtleties and complexities of many non-western proprietary systems. These systems are sometimes assumed to be collective or communally-based, but in fact any assumption that there exists a generic form of non-western, traditional collective intellectual rights ignores the intricacies and sheer diversity of indigenous and traditional proprietary systems.[30] Implicit in some criticisms of patents is an erroneous assumption that collective and individual *ownership* and *property rights*, including intellectual property rights, are necessarily alien concepts in all traditional societies[31] which are characterised by a strong sharing ethos. In fact, reviews of anthropological literature reveal that such concepts (or at least close equivalents to them) are quite common.[32] Any laws that aim to protect property rights, including IPRs, should not therefore be dismissed out of hand.

Critics of patents are certainly correct in asserting that the lack of economic self-sufficiency of many traditional communities, the unequal power relations between them and the corporate world, and the high cost of litigation, would make it very difficult for them to protect their IPRs through the patent system.[33] However, it is not the fault of the patent system *per se* that the main beneficiaries from the trade in products derived from genetic resources appear to be corporations located mainly in the technologically advanced countries. In the absence of a patent system, corporations would most probably still dominate this trade.

3.2.1 Conclusions

If we accept that the purpose of an IPR system is to protect the rights of knowledge holders for the public good, arguably it should be

---

[30] Four Directions Council, *op. cit.*

[31] See Biothai & Genetic Resources Action International *Road Maps to a Peoples' Sui Generis Rights Plan of Action* (Biothai and GRAIN, 1998).

[32] D.A. Cleveland, & S.C. Murray, "The World's Crop Genetic Resources and the Rights of Indigenous Farmers". (1997) 38(4) *Current Anthropology*, 477; T. Griffiths, *Indigenous Knowledge and Intellectual Property: A Preliminary Review of the Anthropological Literature*. (Unpublished paper commissioned by Working Group on Traditional Resource Rights, Oxford, 1993).

[33] Posey, *op. cit.*

possible for all those who create useful knowledge with economic value to secure its protection. To the extent that present-day IPR systems cannot protect traditional knowledge whose dissemination is beneficial to the wider community[34] *and* that has *industrial application,* these systems are failing to operate optimally in terms of their public function. It is fully understandable that the disproportionate legal treatment of commercially useful knowledge held by companies and similarly useful knowledge held by indigenous peoples, seems unjust to the latter. When large industrial concerns in new technological fields find the IPR system cannot protect their innovations, it seems that new forms of IPRs are created in response. Traditional knowledge holders, on the other hand, do not have the political influence to change the system.[35] Moreover, they are rarely successful in ensuring that their own custom-based intellectual property rights systems are observed by others.

In the absence of an adequate IPR system, other means need to be adopted urgently to ensure that traditional ecological knowledge is protected and revitalised.

4. The Politics of IPRs and Traditional Resource Rights in India

In India, there is a great deal of discussion concerning IPRs, biodiversity conservation and traditional resource rights. Ambivalence — if not hostility — towards the TRIPS Agreement is widespread, especially the section on patents. The patents on "Indian" products like neem, turmeric and, most recently, basmati rice have provoked a furore throughout India, and is indicative of the sense of frustration felt by many Indians that their biological wealth is being plundered by transnational corporations while successive governments seem unable to do anything to prevent it. Such sentiments are shared by a broad cross-section of society from politicians and intellectuals to farmers movements and environmental NGOs. However, condemnation of TRIPs is far from universal. Gupta notes that two influential farmers' organisations in India take quite opposite views towards TRIPS. The Karnataka Rajya Ryota Sangha (KRRS; Karnataka Farmers Association)

---

[34] As acknowledged in the CBD, at least that knowledge which is relevant to biodiversity and sustainable use of biological resources.

[35] According to Drahos: "[w]hile new forms of intellectual property in the form of protection for semiconductors or plant varieties have readily been minted for transnational industrial elites both nationally and internationally, the recognition of indigenous intellectual property forms has proceeded slowly or not at all. This selective approach to solving freeriding problems comes into sharp focus when one compares the evolution of protection for the semiconductor chip and protection of folklore. Prior to 1984 manufacturers of computer chips in the US had complained that existing intellectual property regimes often failed to protect their products. Their chips often failed to clear the patent hurdles of novelty and inventiveness . . . In 1984 the *Semiconductor Chip Protection Act* was passed . . . In contrast, the issue of protection for indigenous knowledge has largely remained just that, an issue". P. Drahos, "Indigenous Knowledge and the Duties of Intellectual Property Owners". (1997) 11 *Intellectual Property Journal*, 179.

is vehemently anti-TRIPS, whereas the Shetkari Sangathana (Farmers Union) is very much in favour.[36]

Recent Indian governments have been somewhat responsive to the concerns expressed by some of these movements and organisations. Internationally they have at times been quite outspoken in their criticisms of the global IPR regime, *inter alia* because it is considered to conflict in certain ways with the CBD. In 1997, the government submitted a paper to the World Trade Organisation's Committee on Trade and Environment which was critical of TRIPS on the grounds that the Agreement does not require patent applicants to declare and acquire the prior informed consent of the country of origin of the resource and/or traditional knowledge used in biotechnological inventions.

The Indian government has condemned the basmati rice patent and as we saw earlier it opposed the turmeric patent. Nevertheless, the government is frequently criticised for its failure to come up with appropriate national legislation or a comprehensive strategy to oppose the misappropriation of Indian resources and traditional knowledge. Many Indians appear to take the view that India did not benefit when biological resources were the common heritage of humankind and that for India to profit from its great biological wealth it must start by controlling the export of biological material. The present government seems to share this view and is developing appropriate biodiversity legislation. The most recent draft national biodiversity law would not only ban the export of genetic material without the prior informed consent of the government, but also requires that those intending to seek IPR protection over such material or related knowledge request prior authorisation to do so.[37]

5. Community Knowledge Documentation Projects

India is a culturally and biologically diverse country where traditional biodiversity-related knowledge can be divided into the classical systems that are documented in ancient texts, such as the Ayurveda, Unani and Siddha systems of medicine, and local folk knowledge which is not always documented. Traditional knowledge relating to plants is highly developed in India. For example, of the 25,000 plant species that exist in the Indian Subcontinent, as many as 7,000 are used

[36] According to KRRS leader, Dr Nanjundaswamy, "[w]e are going to launch a one-point programme — to drive out the multinationals. Our genetic resources are our national property" (*The Hindu*, March 4, 1993, p. 9 in Gupta). In contrast, Shetkari Sangathana leader, Sharad Joshi said "[w]hat's wrong with Dunkel? [the draft TRIPS Agreement] I prefer to pay royalty for good quality seeds than pick bad subsidised ones." One might add that neither of these leaders are themselves farmers. Nanjundaswamy was formerly a professor in Germany, while Joshi used to work for the United Nations in Switzerland (in Gupta *op. cit.*).

[37] A. Kothari, "India's Biodiversity Act: Finally, a Step in the Right Direction". Article submitted to listserv: BIO-IPR (December 1998).

medicinally.[38] Nevertheless, as in other countries, there is a tendency to undervalue traditional knowledge, especially that which belongs to the most marginalised communities. This section describes two programmes to deal with the situation by documenting traditional knowledge and ensuring that the communities and individuals responsible for generating such knowledge are the main beneficiaries in case of commercialisation.

5.1 People's Biodiversity Registers

The People's Biodiversity Registers Programme is sponsored by WWF India and co-ordinated with the Centre for Ecological Sciences of the Indian Institute of Science, and the Foundation for Revitalisation of Local Health Traditions (FRLHT), both in Bangalore. Among the main objectives of the People's Biodiversity Registers programme are:[39]

1. *To provide* a record of local knowledge for the use of present and future generations of village community people.
2. *To promote* the *revitalisation* of local knowledge by: (a) *recognising* the range of such knowledge; (b) *rewarding* outstanding knowledge, skills, techniques and conservation practices; (c) *validating* and *promoting* sound local knowledge and resource management traditions; and (d) *promoting* inter-community transfer of knowledge for capacity enhancement.
3. *To alert* conservationists about the need for action concerning threatened resources and the need for protection of local resource rights.
4. *To protect* local biodiversity and knowledge from misappropriation by companies such as through patenting of modified products, processes and biological resources.

More recently, even wider objectives have been attached to the programme: to improve environmental monitoring and management at the local level by building upon what local people already know. Accordingly, Prof. Madhav Gadgil of the Centre for Ecological Sciences considers that the PBRs should comprise information divided into ten modules as follows:[40]

1. *Identifying* different user groups in accordance with their use of local biological resources (the "Peoplescape")
2. *Mapping* the mosaic of ecological habitats of the study site (the Landscape)

[38] J. Lambert, J. Sristava, & N. Vietmeyer, *Medicinal Plants: Rescuing a Global Heritage*. World Bank Technical Paper No. 335 (World Bank, Washington DC, 1997) p.29.

[39] Foundation for Revitalisation of Local Health Traditions (FRLHT), *Beyond the Biodiversity Convention — Empowering the Ecosystem People* (FRLHT, Bangalore, 1995).

[40] M. Gadgil, "Conserving India's Biodiversity: Let People Speak", *Hindu Survey of the Environment — 1998.*

3. *Documenting* the ecological history of the study site
4. *Investigating* the extent and distribution of local collective and individual knowledge about different species of plants and animals and their uses (*i.e.* the knowledge base)
5. *Recording* the abundance, scarcity and distribution of living organisms
6. *Recording* patterns of economic (subsistence and commercial) utilisation of living resources
7. *Documenting* efforts to regulate uses of living resources or to conserve them, both by government agencies and local communities
8. *Recording* the development aspirations of local communities and how these relate to local biodiversity
9. *Documenting* divergences and agreements among the various local groups concerning management of natural resources
10. *Documenting* the emerging options for managing the natural resources of the study site, with particular focus on biodiversity conservation

The planners envisage a decentralised bottom-up system, recognising that people must have incentives to participate in the documentation of their knowledge. Promotion of traditional biodiversity-related knowledge primarily for the benefit of local communities is emphasised while regulation of access to information in the registers is considered a means to achieve this, rather than an end in itself. The long-term goal is a network of decentralised databases, all linked to "a [consolidated] national database which would give full credit to the origin of information at the level of an individual, a community or a village council".[41]

Documents are currently in preparation for villages throughout India. Each study involves a year-long process of talking to local individuals, groups of local people and public meetings. The documentation is carried out mostly with the collaboration of local educational institutions and voluntary organisations. The first People's Biodiversity Register (PBR) was completed and released in 1997.

Copies of each PBR will by held by *panchayats* (local elected councils) and educational institutions, and proposed district level institutions called "Biodiversity Cells" that will serve as repositories of computerised collections of the PBRs produced within the district.[42] However, it is not yet clear who will actually own the PBRs.

How will the system help to implement the CBD's provisions on traditional knowledge? Placing control of PBRs in the hands of local

---

[41] M. Gadgil, P.R. Seshagiri Rao, G. Utkarsh and P. Pramod, "New Meanings for Old Knowledge: The People's Biodiversity Registers Programme". Submitted as an invited paper to *Ecological Applications* (1999, in press).

[42] U. Ghate, *Village Biodiversity Registers: Promoting Sustainable Use and Equitable Sharing of Benefits in the Context of GATT, UPOV and CBD* (unpublished paper, 1997).

institutions has obvious advantages in terms of helping to preserve and maintain traditional knowledge, but it is recognised that effective incentive mechanisms are needed to encourage further development of existing knowledge. One idea is to grant *panchayats* the right to charge fees for access to PBRs. Another is to set up a national biodiversity fund, which among other things would provide financial support for *panchayats* and disburse special grants and awards to communities and individuals that make outstanding efforts to conserve biological resources and/or document knowledge.[43]

The proponents of this system argue that the existence of the PBR data banks will encourage mutually beneficial relationships between communities and corporations that will, subject to conditions set by local people, have access to a wealth of information on biodiversity. It is emphasised, though, that community claims over knowledge will not be at the expense of individuals. Individuals desirous to record claims to their own knowledge as a means either of protecting it or of exploiting it commercially can disclose only enough information to establish a claim without sufficient detail to make unauthorised use or commercial application possible. If communities or individuals decide to exchange biological material or knowledge with companies for financial or in kind benefits, the "biodiversity cells" can assist them in negotiating contractual arrangements. To help create a more level playing field in community-company negotiations, it is intended that they will also channel information on trade in biological resources, such as the volume of trade and prices of medicinal plants to local communities.[44]

Those involved in the programme do not take an anti-patent stand, but they argue that the success of the PBR system depends in part on changes to the patent system. They propose (as has Anil Gupta [below]) that patent applications based on use of genetic resources and/or traditional knowledge should include a statement as to the origin of genetic resources and proof that the prior informed consent of the holders of traditional knowledge was given.

5.2 SRISTI's Local Innovations Databases

The Society for Research and Initiatives for Sustainable Technologies and Institutions (SRISTI) of Ahmedabad, India, has for several years been developing databases of traditional knowledge and innovations in close collaboration with local community members. Anil Gupta, SRISTI's Director, emphasises the adaptive and creative nature of so-called "traditional" systems of knowledge and resource management, and rejects arguments that all traditional knowledge should be treated as communal property. He asserts that entitlements are not equal for all

[43] Gadgil 1998, *op. cit.*
[44] Gadgil *et al*, *op. cit.*

community members. This is because while some individuals within communities possess, conserve, generate and disseminate knowledge, and may deliberately engage in biodiversity-friendly practices, other community members (including some community leaders) may have no interest in innovation or conservation.

Gupta[45] advocates the establishment of a global registration system of local innovations along the lines of SRISTI's local innovations database. Such a system would enable individual and collective innovators to receive acknowledgment and financial rewards for commercial applications of their knowledge, innovations and practices, make it possible to build links between small investors, entrepreneurs and innovators for mutual financial benefits, and in some cases enable individuals or communities to seek IPR protection in such forms as inventors certificates and petty patents. Gupta also proposes that national patent offices should be able to access local innovation databases when carrying out prior art searches and examinations in order that patent applications which appropriate knowledge contained in these databases may be properly tested for novelty and inventive step.[46]

The ideal situation, he suggests, would be a global registration system that every national patent office could be able to access *and* universal acceptance that "prior art" should not discriminate against knowledge held in foreign countries.

6. Conclusions

It has been suggested in this article that documentation of traditional knowledge may in some cases be the only way to ensure that it does not disappear. However, protecting traditional knowledge cannot be achieved without also upholding the individual and collective human rights of traditional knowledge holders and their communities. Moreover, top-down documentation approaches should not be at the expense of initiatives that emphasise *in situ* conservation of knowledge. Documenting and storing traditional knowledge "on site" not only allows local people to control its use but also to refine it and develop it further to meet the challenges of a changing world. But whether such documentation is based upon a top-down or a bottom-up approach, serious consideration must be given to the question of who should own the databases and of how far access to them should be restricted. In neither of the above cases do these issues appear to have been

[45] Anil K. Gupta, "Technologies, Institutions and Incentives for Conservation of Biodiversity in Non-OECD Countries: Assessing Needs for Technical Co-operation". (presented at the OECD *Conference on Biodiversity Conservation Incentive Measures.* Cairns, March 1996); Anil K. Gupta, *Getting Creative Individuals and Communities their Due: Framework for Operationalising Articles 8(j) and Article 10(c).* (Submission to the Secretariat of the Convention on Biological Diversity, 1996).

[46] A. Gupta, (Anil) "Knowledge Network Among Grassroots Innovators: Emerging Applications of Information Technology", *Honey Bee* 9(3), (1998).

completely resolved one way or the other. With respect to the second issue, one can assert confidently that access restrictions lessen the possibility of information within them being misappropriated. On the other hand, keeping database information out of the public domain could in some situations make it harder to challenge misappropriation than if such knowledge were made publicly available. For example, a company might acquire knowledge about a medicinal plant from an indigenous group and then patent this knowledge. Depending on how "prior art" and "the public domain" are interpreted in the legal jurisdiction where the patent is held, challenging the patent could be less effective because the knowledge had only been recorded in a private database and not made available to the public through publication. It is essential that organisations co-ordinating traditional knowledge register initiatives explain to local communities the full implications of sharing their knowledge with all outsiders including themselves. Fortunately SRISTI, FRLHT and the Centre for Ecological Sciences do seem to do this.

It is very important also that respect, preservation and maintenance of traditional knowledge not be justified *solely* by its instrumental value. Traditional knowledge should not be respected, preserved and maintained merely *because* it is relevant to biodiversity conservation and sustainability; even less because some of it has industrial application. A great deal of traditional knowledge has no commercial potential whatsoever, but this does not make it any less worthy of respect or protection. The disappearance of traditional knowledge may be a tragedy for the world, but above all, it is a tragedy for those peoples and communities of the world that depend upon the integrity of their knowledge systems for their cultural and even physical survival.

6. Traditional knowledge systems and intellectual property rights "talking past each other": Current issues in New Zealand

Dr David V. Williams

With university qualifications in history, law and theology, he has taught law at Dar es Salaam (Tanzania) and Auckland (New Zealand). He is now an Independent Researcher engaged in legal history research. The primary focus of his work is research commissioned for hearings of the Waitangi Tribunal. This Tribunal is a permanent commission of inquiry which reports on claims against the Crown, both historic and contemporary, lodged by Maori, who are the indigenous population of Aotearoa/New Zealand. His most significant publication is *"Te Kooti tango whenua": The Native Land Court 1864–1909* (Huia Publishers, Wellington, 1999).

Traditional knowledge systems and intellectual property rights "talking past each other": Current issues in New Zealand

Introduction

The Treaty of Waitangi was a compact agreed to between the indigenous Maori tribes of New Zealand and the British Crown in 1840 at the outset of British colonial rule. Although often dismissed as a treaty of cession with no relevance to modern conditions, it contained a number of guarantees of Maori rights. These guarantees to respect the *tino rangatiratanga* or full authority of Maori over their lands and all treasured possessions were more notable for their breach than for their observance, particularly when the tide of incoming settlers in the late nineteenth century rendered Maori a marginalised minority within their own land. For many years the New Zealand courts held the Treaty to be a "simple nullity" or a "moral" obligation without legal significance unless incorporated into New Zealand law by legislation.[1]

The legal and political significance of the Treaty of Waitangi was greatly enhanced in 1975 when the Waitangi Tribunal was established by an Act of Parliament as a permanent commission of inquiry. It was empowered to make recommendations to the Government on claims by Maori relating to the practical application of the Treaty in the modern context. The Tribunal must determine whether laws and Crown policies were inconsistent with the principles of the Treaty. Since 1987 the Court of Appeal and the Waitangi Tribunal have evolved a considerable case law on the meaning and application of the "principles of the Treaty".[2]

Most of the 700 or so claims to the Tribunal by Maori have concerned colonial policy and practices in the past which devastated tribal control over land, forests, fisheries and other natural resources. The claim registered by the Tribunal as *Wai 262* is rather different. It is a multi-tribal claim which concerns a wide range of issues relating to *matauranga Maori* — that is, Maori knowledge systems and their protection of sacred wisdom. The claim's broad ambit has called into question the normal parameters of intellectual property law, has challenged the constitutional structures of law-making by Parliament

---

[1] *Wi Parata v. Bishop of Wellington* (1877) 3 N.Z.J.R.(N.S.) 72; *Te Heu Heu Tukino v. Aotea District Maori Land Board* [1941] N.Z.L.R. 590.

[2] A. Ward, *National Review, Volume II*, (Waitangi Tribunal, Wellington, 1997) "Appendix: The Principles of the Treaty of Waitangi".

without the consent of Maori and has questioned the automatic adoption in New Zealand of many international trade conventions based on neo-liberal globalisation principles.

Since 1997 a number of hearings have been held at tribal centres in different parts of the country to lay the claimants' grievances before the Tribunal. I had been commissioned by the claimants in 1996 to prepare a scoping paper identifying key issues raised by the claim. A substantial paper with accompanying document bank was lodged with the Tribunal. The paper which follows is based on my oral presentation to the Tribunal in September 1997 summarising that documentation.

The foundations of the *Wai 262* claim

The focus of my report to the Tribunal is a commentary on what evidence is available as to how Maori exercised and continue to exercise traditional authority and stewardship rights over the flora and fauna species mentioned in the claim. I commented on how oral testimony evidence might be confirmed by experts, and on how the past and present policies of the Crown appear to be inconsistent with Treaty of Waitangi obligations.

The starting point for the report is the first two paragraphs of the statement of claim. They assert that the Declaration of Independence (1835) and the Treaty of Waitangi (1840) affirmed the authority of Maori tribes as the absolute sovereign authority in Aotearoa (the name Maori usually use for New Zealand). The basic approach of the *Wai 262* claim prefers not to rely on the "principles of the Treaty" developed since 1987. Rather the claim is based upon the rights of Maori as *tangata whenua* — the indigenous people of these lands. Accordingly, the emphasis of the report is on evidence concerning the rights of indigenous peoples to self-determination and autonomous development. The rights claimed by indigenous peoples in relation to intellectual property issues have been set out in documents such as the "Mataatua Declaration on Cultural and Intellectual Property Rights" agreed to at Whakatane, New Zealand in 1993.[3]

My report challenges some of the usual assumptions adopted by the Crown — especially the automatic applicability of presumptions and doctrines derived from English law. A comparison is drawn with the orthodox legal view that Maori customary land was considered to be Crown land subject to native aboriginal title unless that title was lawfully extinguished by the Crown. This means that Maori were left with the burden of proving their title to land by providing evidence to various Crown agents including land purchase officers and the Native Land Courts.

[3] International Research Institute for Maori and Indigenous Education, *Cultural And Intellectual Property Rights, Volume Two* (Moko Productions/IRI, Auckland, 1997) pp. 5–6.

A similar analysis in respect of intellectual property notes the law's position that rights to intellectual property only accrue if Maori are able to demonstrate "human intervention" or "innovation" (value added) to create intellectual property in respect of traditional knowledge systems. Such assumptions are, it is argued, at odds with the full authority guaranteed by the Treaty. The "radical title" to all treasured possessions (including what is now understood as intellectual property) lies with the tribes. Thus the Crown should have the burden of proof to establish the rights it claims by demonstrating, if it can, that Maori traditional resource rights and knowledge systems have been subsumed by national law.

The Crown's reliance on current law may be compared with the now discredited imperial law view of territory that was considered *terra nullius*. If the Crown's assumption is that it has the monopoly right to legislate and Maori retain use rights to traditional resources only if they have established value added input, then its actions are liable to be impeached as breaches of the Treaty of Waitangi by the Tribunal hearing this claim.

The Crown has made similar assumptions in the realm of international trade agreements and other international law obligations. This is particularly important with recent obligations based on principles of globalisation and trade liberalisation relating to intellectual property law regimes. *Pro forma* consultation with some Maori at a few ad hoc meetings, or as minority members of advisory committees, has taken place *after* the executive branch of Government has already entered into binding international law obligations. The question for the Tribunal is whether this pattern of governmental conduct is consistent with the obligations of the Treaty of Waitangi.

The *Wai 262* claim therefore invites the Tribunal to advise the Crown on an appropriate mechanism to ensure constitutional priority for Maori knowledge systems, especially with respect to indigenous flora and fauna, stewardship of ecosystems, moveable cultural heritage objects and other treasures.

The report refers to a number of written accounts on the central importance for Maori of *whakapapa* — genealogy — and how that connects people to all the realms and manifestations of life forces. The traditional oral culture of Maori is replete with genealogical understandings of the holistic interconnectedness of humanity with ecosystems. There is a complete absence in Maori knowledge systems of anthropocentric claims to "full ownership" over flora and fauna, ecosystems or anything else.

The way questions are posed is all-important. How is it that the relationships of Maori with indigenous flora and fauna can be constrained by laws? What evidence can the Crown produce to show that intellectual property laws override Maori knowledge systems in a way that is consistent with the Treaty? What is the basis for the Crown's claims to "ownership" of traditional resources now vested in the

Department of Conservation, Crown Research Institutes, patent/copyright/trademark holders, museums and the like? Can the Crown explain why knowledge about medicinal plants used by Maori ought to be available to pharmaceutical companies without any regard to the prayers, protocols and traditional practices associated with gathering medicinal plants.

Can a Crown agency permit bio-prospecting or genetic modification of indigenous organisms and native species without regard to the Crown's duty of active protection for Maori relationships with all their treasured possessions?

"Talking past each other"

In the *Wai 262* inquiry there is a distinct danger of the participants "talking past each other", to use the memorable phrase highlighted by Dame Joan Metge in her analysis of cross-cultural communication.[4] These problems are compounded when the communications are from the language and thought processes of an indigenous people, but are conducted within a "Western" influenced culture and in the language of the colonisers. There are further difficulties when a word such as *kaitiakitanga* is inserted into the Resource Management Act 1991 and equated with "guardianship" and "the ethic of stewardship".[5]

Maori language concepts — such as *matauranga, kaitiakitanga, tino rangatiratanga* and *whakapapa* — will be frequently invoked during this inquiry in relation to flora and fauna species, natural phenomenon, ecosystems and cultural heritage objects. They cannot be readily translated, let alone assimilated into legal categories which purport to distinguish between real, personal and intellectual property rights; between ownership and possessory or use rights; between tangible and intangible items with economic exchange value.

The tension of cross-cultural communication is fully evident in the debate as to the complementarity or otherwise of traditional knowledge systems — *matauranga* — and "science". Definitions of *matauranga Maori* have been put forward as part of this debate. A Ministry of Research Science & Technology report considers that *matauranga Maori* "refers to that body of traditional knowledge which underpinned the traditional Maori society and provided the technological and philosophical skills of that community." It also points out diverging views on the suggestion that Western knowledge and developments are "science" whilst Maori knowledge and development is "either not science or is lore as opposed to law".[6]

---

[4] J. Metge & P. Kinloch, *Talking Past Each Other: Problems of Cross-Cultural Communication* (Victoria University Press, Wellington, 1984).

[5] M. Mutu, "The Use and Meaning of Maori Words Borrowed into English for Discussing Resource Management and Conservation in Aotearoa/New Zealand", Conservation Board Chairpersons' Conference, February 10, 1994.

[6] Ministry of Research, Science and Technology, *The Interface Between Matauranga Maori and Mainstream Science* (Wellington, 1995).

It is not helpful, in my opinion, to engage in debate about the "science" label. I prefer the approach of Professor M.H. Durie[7]:

(i) *Matauranga Maori* belongs to iwi [tribes] and should remain under Maori control;
(ii) there are signs that the Crown's policies for science, research and technology could lead to the assimilation of *matauranga Maori* to mainstream knowledge systems;
(iii) *Matauranga Maori* is different to science and should not be confused with it;
(iv) Maori participation in science and technology should be encouraged but is not a goal which is directly linked to *matauranga Maori*;
(v) whilst the Government bears some responsibility for the protection of *matauranga Maori* and should make funding available for its transmission and development, we should not confuse that issue with Maori participation in science.

What is important, therefore, in the hearing of the *Wai 262* claim is that indigenous knowledge is entitled to respect and validation in its own right rather than by reference to the paradigms of Western science.[8]

Traditional Ecological Knowledge and Ethnobotany

There is an international context for understanding the nature of claims by indigenous peoples to the protection of their traditional ecological knowledge. The Wai 262 claim is not an isolated phenomenon. Indigenous peoples throughout the world are networking to preserve their cultural traditions and way of life from the ever-threatening impact of modernisation and development. Greater awareness of these issues was brought to international attention at the "Earth Summit" in Brazil in 1992.[9]

The United Nations Research Institute for Social Development has produced important discussion papers. They examine the general characteristics of indigenous peoples' sustainable resource management practices, review the challenges faced by indigenous peoples in maintaining the viability and sustainability of their traditional forms of production. Most importantly, in the context of this claim, there is discussion of recent experience with returning control of natural

[7] M.H. Durie, "Matauranga Maori, Iwi and the Crown: A Discussion Paper" (James Henare Research Centre, University of Auckland, September 26, 1996).
[8] M. Peters, *Post-Modern Science in Aotearoa? Conservation, Cosmology and Critique*, (Auckland Research Unit for Maori Education, University of Auckland, 1993); M. Roberts, "Teaching Indigenous Knowledge and Western Science" (Centre for Pacific Studies, University of Auckland, 1996).
[9] D.A. Posey, "International Agreements and Intellectual Property Right Protection for Indigenous Peoples" (Institute for Cultural and Social Anthropology, Oxford, 1994).

resources to indigenous peoples and the extent to which this has contributed to sound resource use and conservation.[10]

One consequence of the burgeoning interest in the issues raised by indigenous people has been the development of a field of academic study generally known as "traditional ecological knowledge". Dr M. Roberts suggests that the term is not entirely apt but it has become accepted. A paper she co-authored with several leading Maori activist women brings out the importance of Maori cosmology and highlights the fundamental importance of genealogy and the personification of natural phenomena in the belief systems of Maori.[11]

Then there is the field of study known as "ethnobotany". This is the study of the interactions beween people and plants — how people, especially indigenous people, use and relate to plants.[12] In February 1988 there was an "International Workshop on Ethnobotany" held in Christchurch, New Zealand. Two of the *Wai 262* claimants — Saana Murray and Dell Wihongi — played significant roles in that conference. It was then that they became aware of the work of Dr D. Yen in sustaining stocks of ancient tubers for kumara (sweet potato). Once held by the Department of Scientific and Industrial Research, they had been declared surplus to the Department's research and would have been lost forever except that Dr Yen transported them to Japan. Kumara were a crop of the utmost importance in the traditional life of Maori. The Department had not consulted any Maori about their decision to dispose of the tubers. Del Wihongi's evidence to the Waitangi Tribunal spoke of her eventually successful efforts to ensure the return of those kumara tubers to the "National Ethnobotanical Garden" she runs (known as "Te Wao Nui a Tane").

Traditional ecological knowledge and ethnobotany are emerging fields of inquiry. They have the capacity to play an increasingly important role in the steps some international organisations and national governments are tentatively initiating in order to limit the massive loss of biological diversity which has resulted from industrialisation and colonisation, particularly in the last two centuries. Both scientific developments and governmental policy will be critical to conserving the planetary environment by maintaining biological diversity. Traditional ecological knowledge may provide important information in the search for urgently required solutions. This will only be possible if indigenous peoples are properly empowered to continue to

[10] M. Colchester, *Salvaging Nature: Indigenous People Protected Areas and Biodiversity Convention* (United Nations Research Institute for Social Development, Discussion Paper No 55, 1994); M.P. Pimbert & J.N. Pretty, *Parks, People and Professionals: Putting Participation into Protected Area Management* (United Nations Research Institute for Social Development, Discussion Paper No 57, 1995).

[11] M. Roberts, W. Norman, N. Minhinnick, D. Wihongi & C. Kirkwood, "Kaitiakitanga: Maori Perspectives on Conservation" (University of Auckland).

[12] M.J. Parsons, "Ethnobotany — A Maori Perspective" in *People, Plants and Conservation: Botanic Gardens into the 21st Century: Conference Proceedings* (Royal New Zealand Institute of Horticulture, Wellington, 1992).

fulfil their customary role as guardians of some of the planet's most fragile ecosystems.

International Law and Domestic Responses

Since 1984 successive New Zealand governments have been at the leading edge of the international trend towards policies of market liberalism and globalisation in international trade. They have enthusiastically endorsed the establishment of the World Trade Organisation (WTO). The GATT agreement on Trade Related Aspects of Intellectual Property Rights (GATT: TRIPS) was rapidly implemented into nine new Acts of Parliament as a result of the GATT (Uruguay Round) Bill 1994. In none of those Acts is there an explicit safeguarding of Treaty of Waitangi rights. This was a matter of deliberate omission, as a result of a close vote in the House of Representatives during the second reading of the Bill.

Later, in the Hazardous Substances and the Organisms Act 1996, section 8 requires that those exercising powers and functions under the Act to "take into account the principles of the Treaty of Waitangi (Te Tiriti o Waitangi)". Until the commencement of the *Wai 262* hearings, however, there had been no significant scrutiny of Treaty of Waitangi implications for trade and intellectual property law reforms

There are diverse and contradictory developments occurring in the drafting of international treaties and conventions. On the one hand there are developments towards a globalised economy and free trade market liberalism. Then there are conventions seeking to maintain biological diversity. At the same time, and not necessarily in congruence with these trends, are the international law developments towards identifying and enhancing the rights of indigenous peoples. The WTO Committee on Trade and Environment has recognised this tension in a report to the WTO Ministerial Conference held in Singapore in November 1996. The report touched upon the status of traditional and indigenous knowledge and asked whether or not the TRIPs agreement should accord recognition to traditional interests and rights holders.[13]

The only significant consultation between Crown and Maori on trade related intellectual property right issues has been initiated by the Ministry of Commerce. The Ministry's paper identified two key questions:

> Can the Plant Varieties Rights (PVR) Act be used to prevent Maori from using native plants in traditional ways?
> Can the Patents Act be used to prevent Maori from using native plants in traditional ways?

---

[13] Information and Media Division of WTO, "Report of the WTO Committee on Trade and Environment", Press/TE014, November 18, 1996.

The answers provided by the Ministry of Commerce to these questions were "No".[14]

In my view neither of these "key questions" nor their answers address the fundamental questions arising in the *Wai 262* claim and in the Mataatua Declaration. I would also question the answers and the accompanying assurances that were given by the Ministry. The WTO has already foreshadowed that it may place member governments under an obligation to ensure unrestricted and unpaid access to plant genetic resources and the free movement of plant genetic resources. It is apparent that scientists in developed countries are determined to expand the coverage of patent law in a manner which detrimentally affects developing countries and indigenous populations. For example, the Indian Government has had to file a case against an United states patent granted in 1995 in favour of two scientists to use a powder extracted from turmeric which has been commonly used in India for healing wounds for many centuries.[15]

A quite different approach to international law developments, which validates and seeks to promote self-determination of indigenous peoples, is to be found in the works of Dr D.A. Posey.[16] By great good fortune he was in Aotearoa/New Zealand attending the 6th International Congress of Ethnobiology in November 1998 and he was called as an expert witness to give evidence for the *Wai 262* hearings. In his writings Dr Posey argues that it is preferable for indigenous peoples to develop their own systems for protecting the bundle of rights he labels as "traditional resource rights", rather than relying solely upon laws of intellectual property which are purely economic in nature. Support for recognition of traditional resource rights may be found in numerous international conventions and agreements which are already legally binding upon states, including New Zealand. In addition, many non-binding international agreements (or "soft laws" as Dr Posey calls them) are fully consistent with domestic jurisprudence concerning the Treaty of Waitangi.

The importance of non-binding international law ought not to be minimised. Dr Posey's approach seems to be consistent with views on "aboriginal autonomy" recently expressed by the Waitangi Tribunal, with specific reference being made to the International Decade of Indigenous Peoples and the Draft Declaration on the Rights of Indigenous Peoples.[17] Moreover, international law does not assume that

[14] Ministry of Commerce, *Intellectual Property Law Reform Bill: Maori Consultation Paper* (Wellington, 1994).

[15] A. Agarwhal & S. Narain, "Pirates in the garden of India", *New Scientist*, October 26, 1996.

[16] D.A. Posey & G. Dutfield, *Beyond Intellectual Property: Toward Traditional Resource Rights for Indigenous Peoples and Local Communities* (International Development Research Centre, Ottawa, 1996); D.A. Posey & G. Dutfield, *Traditional Resource Rights: International Instruments for Protection and Compensation for Indigenous Peoples and Local Communities* (IUCN The World Conservation Union, Cambridge, 1996).

[17] Waitangi Tribunal, *The Taranaki Report: Kaupapa Tuatahi* (G. P. Publications, Wellington, 1996) pp.19–20.

nation states will adhere only to the minimum standards of binding international laws. Much international diplomatic effort is expended in producing non-binding agreements which are intended to be hortatory — that is, states are encouraged and exhorted to move towards the loftier requirements of those agreements rather than abide by the lowest common denominator of prior state practice. In particular, if the Brazil Earth Summit is to have meaning for indigenous peoples and for their future generations, then the Convention on Biological Diversity to which New Zealand is a party needs urgent implementation. The guarantees in the Treaty of Waitangi provide excellent domestic law reasons for the Government to be urged to meet fully the aspirations of indigenous peoples set out in non-binding international law. The Tribunal's consideration of the *Wai 262* claim should be welcomed as an opportunity for a thorough going reassessment of national legislation and constitutional arrangements affecting indigenous peoples rights to self-determination over their traditional resources rights.

Crown policies

Crown policy from the outset of colonial rule in 1840 promoted emigration from Britain and the settlement of large numbers of people — the vast majority of whom were European — in New Zealand. Imperial government instructions to New Zealand governors contained extensive comment on the imperative nature of settling the "waste lands" of the colony. With the advent of government controlled by settler politicians in the 1850s the pace of immigration increased dramatically and the impact upon Maori became brutally evident during the war period from 1860 to 1872. The New Zealand Settlements Act 1863 provided for the outright confiscation of substantial areas desired for settlers. In addition there were numerous Acts explicitly devoted to the promotion of wholesale settlement throughout the country along lines dictated by the Government. Perhaps the most important of these was the Immigration and Public Works Act 1870.

A feature of Crown settlement policy for many years was that new settlers were required to remove all indigenous forest cover from their blocks in a very short period of time, with penalties imposed on those who were tardy in clear felling. Indeed as late as 1963 to 1982, the Land Amendment Act 1963 established a Marginal Loans Boards which bought and promoted development of marginal land for onward disposal to holders of otherwise uneconomic areas of farmland.

The impact of a mere century and half of settlement upon the indigenous flora and fauna has been so dramatic that towns, cities and farmlands now cover most of the territory of the country. Fragments of indigenous ecosystems are now to be found almost exclusively in the Crown's conservation estate almost all of which comprises mountainous high country or outlying islands. G Park has written a book which graphically describes the pitiful lack of indigenous forest or swamp lowlands remaining after the ruthless implementation of settlement policies.[18]

For many years, with only one or two exceptions to the rule, the Department of Scientific and Industrial Research (and successor institutes) have been primarily concerned with research and development into non-indigenous species of flora and fauna.

In addition to settlers and their exotic grasses, hedges, trees, crops and other plants that were encouraged to be introduced, the Crown also had a policy to encourage the importation of foreign animals and fish for commercial production, game hunting and other recreational purposes. Acclimatisation Societies were strongly encouraged which played a significant role in the repeated introductions into New Zealand habitats of non-indigenous fish, birds and animals designed for sport and recreation. The importing of huge numbers of exotic species, and the devastation of indigenous swamps and forests in favour of agricultural developments, inevitably meant that native bird and fish populations that once existed in abundance were rendered extinct or faced extinction as a consequence of Crown promoted settlement policies.

Furthermore, as time went by, legislation began to impose more and more restrictions upon Maori exercising traditional resource rights to customary harvests. This regime began in the Wild Birds Protection Act 1864 with a partial prohibition on hunting indigenous wild duck, paradise duck or pigeon. Increasing numbers of species were incorporated into the Animal Protection Acts' provisions (including at one time the opossum — perhaps the worst introduced pest in the country). The current law, Wild Life Act 1953, includes absolute prohibitions on taking virtually all native birds.

A similar pattern may be observed in Crown policies relating to indigenous forests. The New Zealand State Forests Act 1855 commenced with an important preamble which emphasised the importance of preservation of forest growth "in elevated situations". The converse was that lowland areas should be entirely deforested and that was the policy that was articulated by the Royal Commission of Forestry (1913). The Commission insisted there should be:[19]

> . . . a general principle that no forest land which is suitable for farm lands, except it is required by scenic or climatic reserve, should be permitted to remain under forest if it can be occupied and resided upon.

The Government quickly adopted this policy and arranged to eliminate native forests growing in lowland swampy ecosystems. It also

[18] G. Park, *Nga Uruora: The Groves of Life* (Victoria University Press, Wellington, 1995).

[19] *Report of the Royal Commission on Forestry* (Appendices to the Journals of the House of Representatives, 1913) C–12, p. xxiv.

proceeded to acquire large tracts of the dwindling areas of Maori land, often compulsorily, if they remained under forest because this was seen to be an unproductive land-use.

The Royal Commission on Forestry did recognise the merits of absolutely protected reserves for the survival of some indigenous flora and fauna. This approach, described as "Yellowstone model", was named after the first national park created in United states about 1872. It involved the forced removal of indigenous people in order to develop wilderness preserves. The adverse consequences of this model have been highlighted in modern publications by the World Wild Life Fund for Nature and the Sierra Club.[20]

Some totalitarian examples of the creation of special reserves for conservation purposes are highlighted by the *Wai 262* Statement of Claim. Takapourewa (Stephens Island) and Hauturu (Little Barrier Island) are islands which were compulsorily acquired in the 1890s. Any Maori remaining on the islands were then forcibly evicted from their ancestral home.

With regard to protected conservation areas on the mainland, the origins of the Crown's policy lay in a desire to protect "scenery". The policy began in the early 1900s and was a belated effort to save a few scraps of scenery from the ongoing "progress" of further settlement. One result was that as a large proportion of the remnants land covered by indigenous flora were Maori owned, it was Maori who were called on yet again to sacrifice their own interests for that of the national good. The provisions of the Scenery Preservation Acts were strengthened so that Maori land could be compulsory acquired under the Public Works Act for scenery purposes. It mattered not that the land included Maori sacred sites. Maori leaders were not silent bystanders. For example, Heke, the MP for Northern Maori in 1903, argued for the protection of native forests in Northland but objected strenuously to the compulsory acquisition of Maori land under the Public Works Act.[21] Whilst there are supposed to remain certain rights for former Maori owners of such land under the Reserves and Domains Act 1953, including rights to take or kill birds and other hunting rights, the rights are meaningless as all native birds are absolutely protected under other legislation.

A recent governmental initiative that has provoked heated debate is the New Zealand Conservation Authority's 1994 discussion paper on "Maori Customary Use of Native Birds, Plants and Other Traditional Materials". The assertions of the *Wai 262* claim find many echoes in the notes taken by Conservation Authority staff of statements made at many meetings around the country in 1994 and 1995. The majority of non-Maori responses were stridently critical of proposals to permit

---

[20] E. Kemf (ed.), *Indigenous Peoples and Protected Areas: The Law of Mother Earth* (Earthscan, London, 1993 foreword by Sir Edmund Hillary).

[21] Park, *op. cit.*, pp. 142–146; Heke, *N. Z. Parliamentary Debates*, vol. 126, 1903, pp. 710–711.

cultural harvests of some species in limited circumstances. Debate focussed on "icon species" such as native wood pigeons and albatross. Most Maori supported traditional customary use of native plants, animals and materials such as bone and feathers.

Concluding comments

In my view it is important that the Waitangi Tribunal should carefully seek from those who have learned Maori wisdom in the old ways some indication of traditional rights and responsibilities of guardianship. It is also important for the Tribunal to gather evidence of appropriate developments in Maori understandings since the beginning of colonial rule. Although some ethnographers have shown much interest in recording traditional usages and knowledge of the "old-time Maori", much less interest is shown in how Maori tribes have adapted and responded to the use of modern technologies. There are a number of occasions upon which the Waitangi Tribunal has discussed "new technologies and the right to development" implicit in Treaty arrangements between the Crown and Maori.[22]

Counsel for the *Wai 262* claimants may well wish to argue for the right of development in respect of the numerous aspects of the claim, not least the use of whatever modern technology management practices can be relied upon to ensure sustainable ecosystems for indigenous flora and fauna. However, the Human Genome Diversity Project is one development that is quite contrary to the tenor of the *Wai 262* claim. On the contrary, outrage at the aims, purposes and methods of that project was expressed by the Mataatua Declaration 1993 dealt explicitly with this issue. A Maori perspective sternly critical of the project is to be found in an article by Aroha Mead and Nin Tomas.[23] Similar issues arise in relation to a 1996 Ministry of Environment document raising issues concerning genetically modified organisms. Clearly the right to development needs further elaboration and while Maori ought not to be restricted to 1840 technology and information in exercising Treaty rights, neither should it be assumed by the Crown that Maori should to agree to every new proposal for bio-prospecting involving indigenous flora and fauna.

The *Wai 262* claim seeks the assistance of the Tribunal in moving debate away from a nihilistic and unproductive assigning of blame for historic events as between Maori and non-Maori settlers. The focus should be on the best ways and means that the remaining indigenous flora and fauna can now be conserved and on appropriate mechanisms for acknowledging the importance of Maori knowledge systems and

---

[22] Waitangi Tribunal, *Muriwhenua Fisheries Report* (Brookers, Wellington, 1988) pp. 234-235, citing the Canadian case: *Simon v. The Queen* (1985) 24 D.L.R. (4th) 390, 402 [See also *Ngai Tahu Sea Fisheries Report 1992* and *Te Arawa Geothermal Resources Report 1993*].

[23] A. Te P. Mead & N. Tomas, "The Convention on Biological Diversity: Are Human Genes Biological Resources?", *N. Z. Environmental Law Reporter*, July 1995, pp. 127–132.

traditional resource rights. At the end of the day, the *Wai 262* claim brings into focus the fact that Maori people, their sacred knowledge and indigenous flora and fauna have but one home on this increasingly fragile planet. That home is this country of Aotearoa/New Zealand. If all that is distinctive and important and only found in Aotearoa is to survive and maybe to flourish again, then it must happen here. For Maori as the indigenous people there is and can be only one land which sustains them. The Waitangi Tribunal has the opportunity to refocus the attention of the Crown and members of the wider public upon these facts as intellectual property law reforms are considered. Without such a salutary reminder, it is probable that the government will continue to give undue attention to the globalisation of universalised norms which promote rapid advances in the new frontier of bio-technological scientific development rather than actively protecting the rights of indigenous peoples to self determination.

7. Intellectual Property Aspects of Biological Resources—The Malaysian Perspective

Dr Ida Madieha Azmi

Assistant Professor, Kulliyyah Of Laws, International Islamic University. She obtained her doctorate in Law at QMW College, University of London and has written in the areas of the history of intellectual property, the prehistory of IP and IP under Islamic law. Dr Azmi has also written extensively on Malaysian IP law.

Intellectual Property Aspects of Biological Resources — the Malaysian Perspective

1. Genetic Resources and The Traditional Exploitation of Forest Produce

Malaysia is one of the principal habitats of the world's biologically diverse species of plants and animals. Statistics have shown that the countries rich in genetic resources are mainly in the Third World: there are 12 megadiversity countries which include Malaysia (and among others Brazil, China, Mexico, Australia, Indonesia, Peru, Ecuador, India, Zaire, Madagascar and Colombia). These countries collectively house 60 to 70 per cent of the world's plants and animals.[1] The recent debates on the desirability of conserving biodiversity in view of the potential economic benefits in preserving the natural heritage for future research on and development in biotechnology has spurred more interest in the manner in which we traditionally exploit natural resources.

Traditionally, the main source of income from forestry has been timber. In 1993, timber products constituted a 27.6 per cent share of the overall primary commodities in Malaysia.[2] Despite the effort to shift to indigenous manufacturing activities, timber is still an important source of Malaysia's GNP. This can be seen from the Sixth Malaysian Plan (1991-95).[3] During the Fifth Economic Plan the annual felling rate of logs increased by 5.8 per cent to 41 million cubic metres in 1990. Out of the total production, Sabah and Sarawak contributed 73.2 per cent, with Sarawak accounting for 50 per cent or 20.5 million cubic metres. The importance of timber and timber products is also evident from the recent 1997/98 reports. During the first seven months of 1997, total export earnings of saw logs increased by 6.3 per cent to RM 1,310.4 million,[4] underpinned by a 10.5 per cent increase in export unit value to RM 352.4 per cubic metre.

Because of the economic significance of timber products for Malaysia, the regeneration process has been assumed to ensure the continued supply of timber and timber products. Under the Sixth Malaysian Plan, reforestation is administered under a scheme known as the Compensatory Forest Plantation Project. In seven states in Peninsular Malaysia, 35,200 hectares of degraded forests have been replanted with fast-

[1] See the report in the *New Straits Times,* November 5, 1995.
[2] See Economic Report 1993/94, Ministry of Finance, Malaysia.
[3] Sixth Malaysia Plan, 1991–1995, National Printing Department, Kuala Lumpur.
[4] Economic Report 1997/98, Ministry of Finance, Malaysia, p. 128.

growing timber species such as *Gmelina arborea, Acacia mangium* and *Paraserianthes falcataria.*

The patenting of biotechnological products has paved the way for the commercial exploitation of natural resources of a considerable magnitude and hence, the demand for natural biological resources. This, in turns, calls for a renewed evaluation of forestry and conservation. The expansion of property rights into genetic resources, unfortunately, has created other problems. The most important of all is the relationship between intellectual property rights and ownership of genetic resources. Intellectual property rights do not afford recognition to the provider of the biological resources (*i.e.* the country of origin of genetic resources). At the same time, in the framework of intellectual property rights, the role of the indigenous people in the preservation of knowledge pertaining to natural resources is not considered. These associated implications of propertisation of genetic resources were instrumental to the reinvigoration of the debate between the North and the South.

This chapter attempts to appraise the present controversy on biological diversity in Malaysia and addresses the inadequacy of the law, in particular intellectual property laws, in dealing with matter. While this review is not intended to provide a definitive analysis, it will offer worthwhile insights into the prospects for biodiversity in Malaysia and the implication of the propertisation of genetic resources.

The present debate on the need to conserve biological diversity has to a certain extent been sparked by the discovery of two potent substances in the deep forest of Sarawak for the cure of AIDS and the extent of screening activities carried on by foreign multinational companies in the Malaysian rain forests.

2. Appropriation of genetic resources in Malaysia

In the deep forests of Sarawak, as a result of a routine scientific expedition funded by the United States National Cancer Institute, scientists have stumbled upon two potent substances known as *Calanolide A* and *Castatolide. Calanolide A* is extracted from the Bintangor tree, a tree that is common in Sarawak. Both the substances have been successfully laboratory-tested in connection with AIDS and, as reported in the Far Eastern Economic Review,[5] the substance "acts on a key enzyme that affects the AIDS virus' ability to replicate". With such findings, it is highly possible that the substance may produce drugs, which are less costly and less toxic than *AZT*, the AIDS treatment produced by an American drug firm Burroughs Wellcome. The National Research Institute has successfully applied for a patent for *Calonide A* in the United states.

[5] "Nature's Laboratory, Sarawak Tree Yields Potential Aids Treatment", *Far Eastern Economic Review* , March 24, 1994.

Costatolide, which is the sap of another species of wild tree known as *Calophuyllum Teysmanii Innophylloide*, has been identified as suitable for commercial exploitation. This substance produces more yields per raw material and is easier to extract. Reports highlighted that it will take some time for the substance to be the generating income because the substance need further test and refinement.

More and more screening activities are to be undertaken in Malaysia. They are mostly performed by foreign scientists with the collaboration of local scientists. In one development area,[6] 26 local and seven foreign scientists are involved in 33 research projects on identifying wild species in 290,000 hectare of the Belum forest in Hulu Perak. Positive discoveries have been made of wild species that have pharmaceutical potential. Among them are wild fruit trees, species of palm, fungi, trees, shrubs, ornamental plants and a spectrum of flora and fauna. Other discoveries include new species of beetles and moths. In another development undertaking, the local Forest Research Institute of Malaysia (FRIM) had signed a joint venture with a Danish pharmaceutical company to engage in research on local biological diversity. Because Malaysia does not have the requisite capacity either to identify or screen the genetic diversity in our tropical forest, a substantial portion of the wild species have yet to be identified.

It is clear that with the recent breakthrough in biotechnology, the future potentials of these resources for humankind are limitless. Unfortunately, we have not been able to see how this surge in interest and the hunt in biological resources will economically benefit Malaysia. This is conceded by the leader of the Belum expedition himself, Dr Yap Son Kheong. He lamented that if Malaysia has "high technology, the local pharmaceutical industry will benefit from the expedition". Additionally, Malaysia does not possess the necessary financial resources to acquire the requisite technology and to conduct training in expertise to expedite screening.[7] Most expeditions in Malaysia are funded by foreign bodies. In the case of the Sarawak expedition, the fund came from the National Research Institute; a U.S based research institute. As for the expedition in Belum forest, in Perak, the bulk of the expenditure came from the German government which has contributed DM50,000 (about RM$80,000) for the cost of equipment, staff salaries and also camp maintenance.

The development in biotechnology has challenged the traditional concept of development. In Malaysia, rapid growth of development has led to the massive clearing of forests and lands. This practice has often been justified as the price for material growth. However, it should be conceded that genetic resources could be a potential economic source. A reversal of attitude is necessary from one championing

[6] See the report in the *New Straits Times*, April 8, 1995.

[7] This is one of the problems identified as the obstacles to the full documentation of biological diversity in Malaysia. See Dr M. Manokaran's comment in *The Star* November 10, 1996.

pure material development to one focussing on sustainable development. The cause of the change can be attributed to the evolution of a new thinking, *i.e.* the "new ecological paradigm".

3. Conservation and the "new ecological paradigm"

The concept of the "new ecological paradigm" requires the elevation of biodiversity preservation above other considerations in managing natural resources.[8] This paradigm calls for the reordering of traditional priorities by exercising real prudence and restraint before land is developed or resources harvested. On top of that, it advocates the establishment of an extensive system of ecological reserves — one that is large enough to protect the different types of ecological systems in order to buffer species populations against human encroachment.[9]

The priority of biodiversity preservation is important, as it has been identified that the main source of current day problems is the consumption ethic. This philosophy has long dominated natural resource development policy and gives primacy to economic and other utilitarian considerations.

Another main concern relates to the present method in conserving animal and plant species. Currently, animals and plants are not subject to conservation except those species, which are considered as facing the threat of extinction. In Malaysia, regarding wild life, for example, only those considered to be the endangered species are protected under the Wild Life Act 1972 (Act 70).[10] Clearly, these laws extend limited legal protection to biological resources. They do not establish substantive standards for protecting species against habitat alteration or population loss.

To overcome the backdrop of traditional conservation policy, Keiter has suggested the elevation of biodiversity conservation to a position of primacy within public land and resource law. This calls for the preservation of biodiversity for no other reason than the intrinsic value of biodiversity itself. Steps can be taken to enhance biodiversity levels on multiple-use public lands. The reform options include the creation of buffer zones, the revision of the prevailing standards, and the adoption of ecosystem management policies.

The new ecological paradigm is a powerful tool, if adopted, in preserving biological diversity. However, it must be conceded that this line of thinking may be too advanced for developing countries. Their primary concern is to develop their countries, which may, in the course

[8] Robert B. Keiter, Conservation Biology and the Law: Assessing the Challenges Ahead (1994) 69 *Kent Law Review* 911. See also, William M. Flevares, Ecosystems, Economics, and Ethics: Protecting Biological Diversity at Home and Abroad [1992] 65 *Southern California Law Review* 2039.

[9] See Keiter, *ibid.*

[10] This is clear from the definition under the Wild Life Act 1972 whereby "protected wild animal" or "protected wild bird" means a wild animal or wild bird described in Sched. 2 and Sched. 5 or Sched. 4.

of action, result in the destruction of natural habitats. This practical difficulty is further compounded with the fact that the present intellectual property regime does not provide enough incentive to the owners of biological diversity.

4. Intellectual property and bio-piracy

The South alleges that the patenting of biotechnology has resulted in the plundering of biological resources or the appropriation of biological resources without proper compensation given to them.[11] Added to this, most new plants are being obtained with the assistance of traditional knowledge about the medicinal value of biological resources.

The contribution of traditional knowledge to biotechnology and the pharmaceutical industry cannot be denied. According to one source, out of the 121 pure chemical drugs currently in use worldwide, 45 are derived from 39 plant species originating in and around the tropical rainforest.[12] Many of the drugs derived from the rainforest are very important drugs, which still defy production by synthesis. Examples are:

- antimalarial quinine, antiar rhythmic quinidine from *Cinchino ledgeriana;*
- antigalucoma pilocarpine from *Pilocarpus jaborandi;*
- tropical anaesthetic cocaine from *Erythoxylum coca;*
- anticancer vincristine and vinblastine from *Catharantus roseus;* and
- tranquilliser rescinnamine and reserpine from *Rauvolfia serpentia.*[13]

Statistics have shown that of the 120 active compounds isolated from plants and widely used in modern medicine, 75 per cent show a

[11] There is an interesting argument as to who steals from whom and the extent of the North-South conflicts. In this regard, Shiva argues that the wealth of Europe in the colonial era was to a large extent based on the transfer of biological resources from the colonies to the centres of imperial power, and the displacement of local biodiversity in the colonies by monoculture of raw material for European industry. This is done on the basis that biological materials are common heritage of humanity, which should therefore be available to all without restriction. See Shiva, *Biodiversity, A Third World Perspective* (Third World Network, Malaysia) p. 14. This position is radically furthered by the International Undertaking in Plant Genetic Resources which was passed in 1983 and adopted by many countries under the auspices of the United Nation's Food and Agriculture Organisation (FAO). The undertaking asserts that: "Plant genetic resources are a heritage of mankind and consequently should be available without restriction". It also went on to specify that this included "elite and breeding lines (for example, genetically altered biological materials) to be within the rubric of common heritage." See Food and Agriculture Organisation of the United Nations, Plant Genetic Resources Report of the Director General, FAO, C83/25, 1983, Rome, p.6. See also A. Gillespie, Common Property, Private Property and Equity: Clash of Values and the Quest to Preserve Biodiversity [1995] *Environmental and Planning Law Journal* 388.

[12] See "Medicinal Products from the Tropical Rainforests of the East" (a chapter from Salleh Mohd. Nor *et al* Prospects in Biodiversity Prospecting), referred to in Carolyn Hong, "Ensuring Biodiversity Benefits Host Countries", *New Straits Times,* November 5, 1995, p.12.

[13] C. Hong, *op. cit.*

correlation between modern and traditional use of the plant. In addition to this, the leads from indigenous people given to the world market for medicinal plants has resulted in an estimated profit of US$43 billion (RM109.7 billion); and the value of crop varieties improved by traditional farmers is estimated to be $15 billion (RM38.3 billion).[14]

The crucial point is that despite the relevancy of traditional sources and the role of indigenous people for the pharmaceutical industry and biotechnology, no proper protection exists in intellectual property law for them.[15] Nor are they given any incentive or recompense for their effort. Furthermore, legally, these knowledge, as they are often undocumented and passed orally from one generation to another, is not considered as "prior art" for the purpose of patenting. Because there is legal uncertainty with the criteria for "state of the art", the indigenous people's knowledge and usage of a medicinal art would not bar the eventual patentability of inventions using their information.[16] Hence, paradoxically, the knowledge of the traditional medicine is not at par with modern cognition.[17] Historically, the knowledge possessed by indigenous people of a plant's exact value and use has existed from centuries of shared knowledge, although it may be described it in folklore rather than scientific jargon.[18]

Malaysia is rich with traditional pharmaceutical resources. The extent of use of these materials for traditional medicine is yet to be documented in detail. Because of the extensive use of local plants for pharmaceutical use, there is a potential problem associated with the patenting of genetic materials particularly when a substance is locally

---

[14] C. Hong, *op. cit.*

[15] Gurdial Singh, a well known activist for third world countries commented that while the product itself is found in nature, the knowledge is surely not "found in nature" as such, as the people had to know the correct species, part to be used, its preparation and so on. Gurdial said there must be a rights regime recognising the local community to be the owners of the knowledge. Any commercial use of the knowledge must be paid for, he said, suggesting that the Government or an NGO (non-governmental organisation) act on their behalf. For this he proposes two Acts to achieve these purposes — a Community Intellectual Rights Act, and Collectors of Biological and Plant Genetic Resources (Control and Licensing) Act. See C. Hong, *op. cit.*

[16] Legally, an invention is patentable in Malaysia if it satisfies three requirements as laid down in s.11 of the Patents Act 1983. The section reads: "An invention is patentable if it is new, involves an inventive step and is industrially applicable." while section 14 explains the meaning of novelty in these terms:

"An invention is new if it is not anticipated by prior art.

(2) Prior art shall consist of —

(a) everything disclosed to the public, anywhere in the world, by written publication, by oral disclosure, by use or in any other way, prior to the priority date of the patent application claiming the invention;

(b) The contents of a domestic patent application having an earlier date than the patent application referred to in paragraph (a) to the extent that such contents are included in the patent granted on the basis of the said domestic patent application."

[17] See Shiva's view on this. She maintains that there is a need to recognise the farmers' and tribal contributions to the evolution and protection of biodiversity — by treating their knowledge systems as futuristic, not as primitive. See Biodiversity: A Third World Perspective, *op. cit.* at p. 25.

[18] C. Hong, *op. cit.*

known to have medicinal properties and has been used in traditional medicines. Added to that, most of the traditional medicines are not patented or even registered. Below is an illustration of the types of plantations, which have been, known traditionally to have medicinal properties.

Table 1. Plants known to have medicinal value and have been used in traditional medicine in Malaysia.

Species	**Local Name**	**Medicinal**	**Properties**
Ananas comosus	pineapple	*bromelain*	proteolysis agent
Areca catechu	*pinang*	*aerokaline*	*anthelmintics*
Carica papaya	papaya	*kimopapain*	proteolysis agent
Centella Asiatica	*pegaga*	*asiatikosid*	*vulneraria*
Cantharus roseus	*kemunting*	*vinblastine*	anti-cancer
		vincristine	anti-cancer
Curcuma longa	*kunyit*	*kurkumin*	*koleretik*
Datura metel	*kecubung*	*skopololamin*	sedative
Dioscorea triphylla	*gedung*	*diosgenin*	contraceptive
Ricinus communis	*jarak*	*jarak oil*	laxative

Source A. Latif (1992)[19]

The issue of bio-piracy or the plundering for profit of the biological inheritance of indigenous peoples was raised at the second meeting of the World Biodiversity in Jakarta from November 13 to 15, 1992.[20]

Perceptions of inequality of access to the genetic resources of the South has led to the call for the control of the appropriation of genetic resources. The then Deputy Prime Minister at the First Meeting of the Inter-Governmental Working Group on the Global Forest, Datuk Seri Anwar Ibrahim, announced the need to formulate strategies jointly to control access to the developing countries' genetic resources by countries with advanced technology.[21] He maintained that there could no longer be unconditional and unlimited free access to these resources. The Deputy Prime Minister further criticised the attitude of the developed countries by saying that "these advanced countries are vocal on biodiversity but are highly protective of access to biotechnology".[22]

The above analysis demonstrates that the expansion of property rights over genetic resources has resulted in a backlash from the donors of genetic resources, as under the present regime pecuniary benefits do not flow to them. Compelling arguments can be drawn from the above

[19] Extracted from Zakri A. Hamid, Kepelbagaian Biologi Biakbaka Tumbuhan dan Bioteknologi: Implikasi Kepada Dunia Selatan (Universiti Kebangsaan Malaysia, 1993) p. 54.
[20] David Robie, "Row Over Bio-Prospecting in the Pacific, NST, November 3, 1995.
[21] The objective of the meeting is to facilitate dialogues and consolidate approaches to the management, conservation and sustainable development of the world's forests.
[22] See *New Straits Times,* April 20, 1994.

discussion and from the experience of other countries to augment our proposition that the law in Malaysia with regard to appropriation of genetic resources needs a major overhaul.

The Legal Regulation of Biological Conservation in Malaysia

In Malaysia, certain species are gazetted as endangered animals under the Wild Life Act 1972 (Act 70).[23] Conservation of animals and wild life habitat is ensured through the creation of wild life natural parks and sanctuaries. Entrance to these wild life reserves is restricted to those who possess the licence to enter. Such licence can be granted by the Director/Deputy Director/Assistant Deputy Director for Wild Life and National Parks.[24] This licence will either be conditional or non-conditional as the Minister is free to set some conditions attached to the licence as underlined in section 31 of the same Act.[25] Licence is needed for all kinds of activities. A written permission from the Director for Wild Life and National Parks is necessary to enter into a wild life reserve[26] even for purposes of research and study.[27] Failure to do that will result in the commission of an offence with possible liability for a fine.[28] Section 49 of the same Act further prohibits the commission of actions, which amounts to the disturbance of natural harmony of wild life.[29]

Another relevant statute is the Forestry Act. The Act clearly states that all forest produce from a permanent reserved forest or state land is the property of the state Authority.[30] Certain use permits need to be obtained while certain activities are not allowed[31] under section 32.

---

[23] See Sched. Two, Four and Five of the Wild Life Act 1972 for a list of protected animals.

[24] s.30 provides the procedure in granting licences by the Director or Deputy Director/Assistant Director of the Wild Life and National Parks.

[25] s.31 provides the instances whereby the Minister may prescribe conditions, in particular with regard to the shooting, breeding or keeping and killing of wild animals.

[26] s.48(1) provides that no person shall enter a wild life reserve or a wild life sanctuary unless he first obtains a written permit from the Director for Wild Life and National Parks.

[27] s.51(A) stipulates that written permission from the Director General of the Wild Life and National Parks is necessary to do research or study in a wild life park.

[28] s.81 provides that the entrance into a wild life sanctuary without a permit is an offence, punishable to a fine not exceeding three thousand ringgit or to a term of imprisonment not exceeding two years or to both.

[29] s.49 prohibits the commission of certain acts in a wild life sanctuary which includes:
(a) to shoot, kill or take any animal or bird (wild or otherwise);
(b) to take, disturb, damage or destroy the nest or egg of any animal or bird (wild or otherwise);
(c) to disturb or remove any timber or vegetation,
in a wild life sanctuary.
See also s.31(5) of the Protection of Wild Life Act 1972, which prohibits the disturbance, or removal of any timber or vegetation in a wild life sanctuary.

[30] s.14 provides that all forest produce situated, lying, growing or having its origin within a permanent reserved forest or State land shall be the property of the State authority.

[31] s.32 prohibits the carrying out of certain of occupations and activities in permanent reserved forest, unless the person is the holder of a use permit.

Such use permits can be granted for the purposes of research, recreation and education and training.[32] These use permits do not extend to the appropriation of forest produce.[33] It would seem that though micro-organisms are not expressly provided for in the present legal framework,[34] any type of collection of samples may not be taken under the National Forestry Act 1984 (Act 313).[35]

The Native Plants Protection Act 1934 regulates the conservation of native plants. Although it was expressly provided under section 4 of the Act that it is an offence to remove protected native plants from any place, section 6 of the Act provides the Minister with discretion to authorise the taking of any protected native plants.

Another relevant statute is the Fisheries Act 1985. (Act 317). This Act provides for the establishment of marine parks or reserves.[36] Under this Act, the removal of any aquatic animal or plant[37] or part thereof whether dead or alive is not allowed without the permission of the Director General of the marine park.[38]

---

[32] s.34 regulates the issuance of use permits by the Director for the purposes of undertaking research; education or training; recreation and the use of water resources except for the construction or operation of hydroelectric dams.

[33] s.35 clearly specifies that the use permits are not to be issued for the purpose of taking forest produce unless:
- (a) the taking of such forest produce is incidental to or necessary for the purpose for which the use permit is issued; or
- (b) such forest produce is, under the use permit, allowed to be grown by the holder thereof.

[34] See the definition of "forest produce" under the National Forestry Act, 1984 (Act 313).
"Forest produce" includes—
- (a) the following when found in or brought from a permanent reserved forest: guano, peat, rock, sea-sand, river-sand, sea-shells, shell-sand and surface soil;
- (b) the following when found in or brought from a permanent reserved forest or State land:
  - (i) trees and all parts or produce not herein mentioned of trees;
  - (ii) plants including climbers, creepers and grasses, and all parts or produce of such plants;
  - (iii) silk, cocoons, honey, wax and edible bird's nest;
- (c) the following when found in or brought from a permanent reserved forest, state land, mining land, reserved land or alienated land: timber, fuel wood, charcoal, getah, getah taban leaves, wood oil, bark, extracts of bark, damar and attap.

[35] To "take" in relation to forest produce includes every activity involved in:
- (a) the harvesting, collecting, tapping, mining, quarrying or removing, of any forest produce;
- (b) the injuring or damaging of forest produce; or
- (c) the grazing of cattle upon the forest produce.

[36] See s.41 of the Act.

[37] Although the term "plant" is not defined under the Fisheries Act 1985, reference can be made to the Plant Quarantine Act 1976 (Act 167) where "plants" have been defined to mean "any species of plant or any part thereof whether living or dead and includes the stem, branch, tuber, bulb, corn, stock, budwood, cutting, layer, slip, sucker, root, leaf, flower, fruit, seed or any other part of product whatsoever of a plant whether severed or attached but does not include any plant product that has undergone a process of heat and drying treatment".

[38] s.43 provides for certain offences under the Act which includes:
- (a) fishing or attempts to fish;
- (b) taking, removing or being in possession of any aquatic animal or aquatic plant or part thereof, whether dead or alive;
- (c) collecting or being in possession of any coral, dredges or extracts any sand or gravel, discharging or depositing any pollutant, altering or destroying the natural breeding grounds or habitat of aquatic life, or destroying any aquatic life; and;
- (f) Destroying, defacing or removing any object, whether animate or inanimate, in a marine park or marine reserve.

From the above analysis, it is clear that there is a need to improve the present legislations on conservation. At the moment what are protected are those specific species under the Act, which are regarded as precious and in the danger of extinction. With regard to natural forest resources, our laws are confined to products, which are situated in permanent reserved forest or state land; they do not cover private lands.

Recently, the National Biodiversity was released by the Ministry of Science, Technology and the Environment. The policy outlines 15 strategies to improve scientific, knowledge base, enhance utilisation of the components of biodiversity and develop a centre of excellence in industrial research. The policy has identified areas where new legislation or major enhancements to existing legislation are needed for which includes intellectual property and other ownership rights. Despite the poignant points, which the Policy has addressed, no suggestion was mooted therein as to the mechanism of protection.[39] With regard to the regulation concerning prospecting of genetic resources, there are bits and pieces in the existing National Forestry Act, Fisheries Act and Wildlife protection Act, which are adaptable to regulate removal of genetic materials. But these Acts, drafted years ago, do not provide for the new elements of prior informed consent and sharing of benefits.

The main disadvantage with licensing is that parties' obligations are drawn on a contractual basis, which in turn depends on consensual agreement. With unequal bargaining power, contracts are not the most optimum form of ensuring biological conservation. However, in any attempt to create regulations on genetic resources, guidance would have to be sought from the provisions of the Rio Biodiversity Convention.

Conclusion

The importance of biotechnology cannot be denied. In Malaysia, research involving biotechnological engineering has been successfully concluded involving rubber and palm oil, two of Malaysia's main agricultural commodities.[40] In particular, with regard to rubber, a lot has been done to improve rubber yields through biotechnology, since the introduction of rubber from Brazil and West Africa more than 100 years ago.

Research has also been undertaken by MARDI to improve the current variety of local fruits. Most of the research on local fruits is still at their infancy. The emphasis of this research is to produce superior varieties of local fruits such as *durian*, *rambutan*, mango and star fruit.

[39] This policy was drawn up by a task force headed by Universiti Kebangsaan Malaysia's Deputy Vice Chancellor for Academic Affairs Datuk Professor Dr Zakri Abdul Hamid and Dr N. Manokaran from National Technical Committee on Biodiversity of the Forest Research Institute, Malaysia.

[40] See Zakri A. Hamid, *op. cit.*

On top of that MARDI has also been successful in creating a new variety of rice which is resistant to disease such as *penyakit merah (tungro)* and also *penyakit karah (Pyricularia oryzae)*.

Due to the importance of biotechnology, the need to preserve our biological diversity becomes more crucial. However, the more daunting task would be to regulate the appropriation of our biological resources, in view of the fact that these resources are yet to be identified fully in Malaysia. As a first step, there is a need to buffer the present laws on conservation. Access to biological resources may no longer be free and non-conditional. One of the requirements, which can be imposed, relates to the exchange of information or the transfer of technology. Secondly, the authorities may also emphasise participation in research, which is consistent with Article 19 of the Rio Biodiversity Convention. Thirdly, on the line of the "use tax", a royalty can also be imposed on the donee on the sales of all products derived from genetic material discovered in any developing country. Legislation is the best mode in determining the equitable appropriation of biological resources. In this way, no problem is foreseeable with ensuring compliance from a dissatisfied donor.

Co-ordination in the management of biological diversity is equally important. The present mechanism whereby different bodies manage different conservation areas and are responsible for issuing licences for activities to be carried out should be changed. In its place there should be a central body in charge of the administration of the various conservation areas, the monitoring of the issuance of licences and the appropriation of biological resources. Currently, the Director of the Wild Life and National Parks issues licences for entrance in forests while, licences pertaining to activities in the sea is issued by the Director General of the Fisheries Department.

There is more to be done in the area of biological prospecting. A nexus between the licence to take and to use genetic resources/ biological materials should be established in place of the present mechanism whereby "licence" is needed for the appropriation of genetic resources but not the exploitation of these resources by way of intellectual property. Licence to screen and appropriate biological materials should be mandatory regardless of whether it is carried out in restricted areas or private lands. Hence, all forms of appropriation of all types of species, fauna, flora and plant available in nature within Malaysian land should be monitored.

As far as contractual agreements on bioprospecting is concerned, a lot can be learned from the Merck in bio-agreement. In all instances, the application to screen local flora and fauna would have to depend on many factors such as the availability of assistance in screening, the transfer of technology either in relation to the conservation or the exploitation of genetic resources in the form of intellectual property rights, the exchange of information and in certain cases joint development of technology especially it has been developed to commercial product. In sum, the prospect of gaining access to biological diversity in Malaysia depends on whether the whole arrangement is a smart partnership which serves and benefits both parties, financially and technologically.

From the global perspective, the preservation of biological diversity in Malaysia should not be seen as a moral duty, which would have to be upheld by the Malaysian government and Malaysians alone. In fact, the conservation of biological resources is a long-term investment for the good of humankind as a whole. Viewed this way, this duty would have to be shared with other nations, in particular, in terms of financial resources and technical assistance.

More fundamentally, the problems arising from the extension of intellectual property rights into the domain of biological diversity demands a fresh outlook of how we view these rights and the basis for protecting them. The focus of intellectual property rights should not be to recoup investment and to maximise profits solely. There should be a more balanced and fair approach, which accommodates both the rights of the intellectual property owners, on the one hand, and the legitimate expectation of the donors of biological resources, on the other. The main obstacle would be the lack of international consensus on how this can be done. It is unfortunate that all the main regime of international framework of intellectual property rights does not take any stand on this issue. The Rio Biodiversity Convention has advanced an interesting outlook of how this can be done. However, in the absence of any backing from the intellectual property regime, the measures suggested by the convention will only remain as a mere conjecture.

8. Intellectual Property Protection of Traditional Medicine and Treatments in Malaysia

Ong Chui Koon

B.Sc.(Honours)(Biochemistry), University of Malaya, Kuala Lumpur, M.Sc.(Managing Intellectual Property), QMW, London. Currently, working towards a Ph.D. in Intellectual Property at QMW, London. Mr Ong started his career as a Research Officer at the Standards and Industrial Research Institute of Malaysia (SIRIM). Prior to embarking on his doctoral research, he was Head, Patent Information Unit, SIRIM. In Malaysia, he has served, amongst other things, as a Patent Consultant to the Malaysian Patent Office in training the Patent Examiners, in the Committee on TRIPS and Committee on Patents (Amendment) Law. He was an Executive Committee Member, Malaysian Invention and Design Society (MINDS) from 1994–1996.

Intellectual Property Protection of Traditional Medicine and Treatments in Malaysia*

1. Introduction

Throughout history, traditional medicines[1] have long contributed to the health of people around the world and mankind as a whole.[2] In Malaysia, traditional medicine is extensively used both by the urban and rural population. It has been practised by the various ethnic groups[3] long before the introduction of modern medicine into the country and is an integral part of Malaysian culture. In particular, the use of medicinal plants or herbs[4] as condiments is a common household practice and have been used empirically from one generation to another throughout the country.[5] Traditional medicine has played an important role in the study and development of new

---

* The author would like to thank Dr Noel Byrne, Dr Peter Drahos, Dr Spyros Maniatis, Dr Yun Joo Lee and Miss Caroline Wilson for their helpful discussions and suggestions and Dr Uma Suthersanen for her encouragement.

[1] Examples of some of the world's major traditional system of healthcare are Ayurveda (Science of Life), traditional Chinese medicine (including Chinese herbal medicine and acupuncture), Homeopathy, Unani, Oriental medicine (Korean traditional medicine), Kempo (Japanese medicine), Siddha, European folklore medicine, Amchi (Tibetan medicine) and Dzangkho (Bhutanese medicine). Katiyar, C.K., "Traditional Knowledge Basic Notions and Current Issues", WIPO Asian Regional Seminar On Intellectual Property Issues in the Field of Traditional Medicines, New Delhi, October 7–9, 1998.

[2] The World Health Organisation estimates that 80% of the people in developing countries still rely on traditional medicine for their primary health care needs. Norman R. Farnsworth, "Screening Plants for New Medicines", In Biodiversity 83 at 91. E.O. Wilson (ed.), (National Academy Press, Washington DC, 1988).

[3] Malaysia is a multinational and multi-cultural country. Its main ethnic communities include the Malays, Chinese and Indians.

[4] Malaysia, being a tropical country, is richly endowed with natural resources among which are more than 15,000 species of higher plants containing diverse types of chemical compounds. Azizol Abdul Kadir and Ng Lean Teik, "Research and Economic Potential of Biodiversity in Malaysia", FRIM Report, Forest Research Institute Malaysia (FRIM).

[5] Herbs have long been used in Malaysia as medicine for treating and preventing disease. They are also commonly consumed as condiments. For example, the Malaysian herb plant known as Pegaga *(Cantella asiatica)* is commonly consumed as a vegetable among the Malays, as a cooling drink by the Chinese and as a tonic for the brain by the Indians. Symptoms of dizziness one sometimes experiences when fresh leaves of Pegaga are chewed alone is due to the high concentration of neurotransmitter precursors of catecholamines, tyrosine and phenylalanine. These amino acids may also influence the mechanisms which regulate the brain function, thus explaining why the herb is used as tonic for the brain and also recommended for treating hystero-epilepsy. The usefulness of this herb throughout history is indicated by the fact that laboratory analysis has found that nearly all those natural ingredients utilised by local communities do in fact register some sort of biological effect. Ng Lean Teik, "Towards Developing a New Medicinal Plants Industry", FRIM Report, Forest Research Institute Malaysia (FRIM).

drugs[6] and has been a pointer towards many of the drugs that we use today.[7] Given the economic and social significance of traditional medicine, it is desirable that these values be recognised and protected. This is even more so in the light of recent developments where public traditional knowledge is being converted into private property[8] and traditional wisdom pirated without sharing out the benefits.[9]

This article looks at the intellectual property[10] that is available for the protection of traditional medicine and treatments in Malaysia. In particular, it examines the availability of patent protection to the end-products of traditional medicine and treatments. Further, it discusses briefly the origin, practice, characteristics, status and end-products of traditional medicine and treatments, and analyses and assesses the application of patent law to each of the end-products of traditional

[6] The application of traditional medical knowledge has been the source of development of a number of useful drugs derived from plants recently. The rosy periwinkle (*Catharanthus roseus*) was the source for vincristine and vinblastine which are drugs used against childhood leukaemia. The rosy periwinkle was used in folk medicine as treatment for diabetes. Reid, Laird, Meyer, Gamez, Sittenfeld, Janzen, Gollin and Juma, *Biodiversity Prospecting,* (World Resources Institute, USA, 1993).

[7] Good examples of important drugs are well documented in the annals of science — the common aspirin (used as analgesic), quinine (antimalarial), reserpine (antihypertensive), digitalis drugs (cardiac glycosides) and morphine (narcotic analgesic).

[8] U.S. Patent No. 5401504 granted on March 28, 1995 to Suman K. Das and Harihar P. Cohly on the use of turmeric in wound healing. The inventors are Indian-born faculty members at the University of Mississippi's medical center in Jackson. After moving to the United States and becoming chief of plastic surgery with a lab at the medical center, Das decided "to check out the old mother's tale" that turmeric could heal scrapes and wounds. In 1991, he and Cohly began experiments on rats and found that there was definitely an enhancement of healing with turmeric. *In vitro* studies with human endothelial cells also showed a growth-enhancing effect. They then moved to clinical trials in patients and the results indicated that using turmeric was better than no therapy in "healing some ulcers which had been written off" as untreatable. Their patent lists the university as owner and itemises six claims, based on the primary claim to "a method of promoting healing of a wound in a patient, which consists essentially of administering . . . an effective amount of turmeric powder". This patent has now been revoked by the United States Patent and Trademark Office following protest by the Indian Government. *SCIENCE,* vol. 277, September 5, 1997, p. 1429.

[9] U.S. Patent No. 5047242 (the Neem patent) granted to W.R.Grace. Grace claimed that sales of Neem product accounted for only a "fraction" of its total sales of US$5.1 billion. Outside estimates has placed the revenues from Neemix, the agricultural product, at around US$60 million annually from sales within the U.S. The product is sold mainly in the U.S. and the Middle East, and Grace has reserved patents in other key markets. Cited by Shayana Kadidal in "Subject-matter imperialism? Biodiversity, Foreign Prior Art and the Neem Patent Controversy", *IDEA,* Vol. 37, No. 2 (1997), 371 at 377, n.32. In the opinion of Anil K. Gupta, the patentees should at least share a part of their profits with the local Indian communities. After all, they did not stumble upon neem tree based knowledge randomly. The contribution of the local communities had made the innovation possible. Anil K. Gupta, "Rewarding Creativity for Conserving Diversity in Third World: Can IPR Regime Serve the Needs of Contemporary and Traditional Knowledge Experts and Communities in Third World? July, 1997, Indian Institute of Management, Ahmedabad.

[10] Intellectual property in Malaysia covers copyright, trademarks, patents and registered designs. Confidential Information, know-how and technology transfer are also included under it. There is currently no protection for plant varieties. The Agreement on Trade Related Aspects of Intellectual Property Rights, Including Trade in Counterfeit Goods of which Malaysia is signatory, requires that an effective *sui generis* system for the protection of plant varieties be developed. For this purpose, the Government of Malaysia has formulated a "Protection for Plant Varieties Bill". The "Protection for Plant Varieties Bill" has been passed by the Parliament but has not yet come into force.

medicine and treatments. An issue which this article addresses is whether Malaysian patent law offers adequate protection to the end-products of traditional medicine and treatments; and it concludes that existing patent law does not protect adequately the end-products of traditional medicine and treatments. This prompts the author to suggest relevant amendments to the Patents Act. Finally, there is a review of current international efforts and initiatives; and a *sui generis* system to protect traditional medicine and treatments is examined.

2. Definition

Traditional medicine may be defined as the sum total of all the knowledge and practices, whether explicable or not, used in the diagnosis, prevention and elimination of physical, mental or social imbalance and relying exclusively on practical experience and observation handed down from generation to generation, whether verbally or in writing.[11] It is a solid amalgamation of dynamic medical know-how and ancestral experience[12] and comprises those practices based on beliefs which have been in existence, often for hundreds of years, before the development and spread of modern scientific medicine, and which are still in use today. Its acceptance by a population is largely conditioned by cultural factors and much of traditional medicine is therefore not easily transferable from one culture[13] to another. According to the observation of the World Health Organisation (WHO), the essential differences among the various systems of traditional medicine arise not from the difference in the goals or effects, but rather from the cultures of the peoples who practise the different systems.[14]

Traditional medicine is not static. Cultural change and development take place with the acquisition of new knowledge or with a change in the surroundings of the people, who need to adapt in order to survive or to achieve a new equilibrium. Thus, traditional methods of treatment are usually specific to a particular country or to a particular community in that country,[15] although some of them, such as acupuncture, are used worldwide.

---

[11] World Health Organisation, "WHO Meeting on the Promotion and Development of Traditional Medicine", Geneva, November 28 to December 2, 1977, Technical Report Series 622, 1978, p. 8.

[12] *ibid.* at 8.

[13] Culture was defined generally as the sum total of the life-style, society patterns, beliefs, attitudes and the commonly accepted organised ways in which a community attempted to solve its life problems. *ibid* p. 9.

[14] *ibid.* p. 9.

[15] This is particularly true for Malaysia where there are various ethnic groups. In Malaysia, traditional Malay medicine has to be modified to meet the needs of the Chinese and the Indians where certain methods of treatment are a taboo to them. Radin Supathan, N., "Treatment of Drug Addiction by Malay Traditional Medicine", Proceedings: Malaysian Traditional Medicine, Kuala Lumpur, 1988, pp. 49–53.

3.0 Traditional Medicine and Treatments in Malaysia

3.1 Origin, Practice, Characteristics and Status

Local Malaysian traditional medicine has four sources, namely Chinese medicine (introduced from China), Indian medicine (introduced from India), Malay village medicine (including Orang Asli[16] medicine) and miscellaneous (including those introduced by Javanese, Sumatrans, Arabs, Persians and Europeans).[17] Chinese traditional practitioners comprise the *sinsehs* (Chinese physicians) and herbalists. The Indian practitioners are made up of Ayurvedic, Siddha and Unani as well as Yoga and spiritual therapists. The Malay traditional practitioners comprise the bomoh (Malay medicine man), *tukang urut* (masseurs), *mudin* (circumcision specialist) and *bidan* (midwives).[18]

Chinese and Indian traditional medicines have a rich cultural heritage recorded in precise documentation, with systematic records of nearly 2000 plants and detailed information on the uses of medicinal plants, such as dosages, modes of preparations and collection methods.[19] On the other hand, Malay village medicine and Orang Asli medicinal knowledge is passed on from generation to generation by word of mouth.[20] In specialised areas, for example bone-setters, midwives or traditional birth attendants and herbalists, knowledge of different plants and healing techniques are restricted to certain classes of persons, and the healing properties of particular plants is often kept secret. Practitioners acquire their knowledge through oral tradition and apprenticeship.[21] According to a study conducted by Haliza, most if not all the practice of traditional medicine had been associated with the family practice, *i.e.* practitioners or healers came from families some of whose members had practised traditional medicine. Among the Malay practitioners, most had either one of their grandparents involved in the practice; and the same is true for Chinese and Indian practitioners.

---

16 The Orang Asli are the aborigines of Peninsular Malaysia. The Orang Asli comprise the Semai, the Negrito and the Melayu Asli or Proto Malays. Carey, I, *The Orang Asli: the Aboriginal Tribes of Peninsular Malaysia* (Oxford University Press, Kuala Lumpur, 1976).

17 A. Latiff, "Some Noteworthy Botanical Aspects of Malaysian Traditional Medicine", Proceedings: Malaysian Traditional Medicine, Kuala Lumpur, 1988, p. 2.

18 Haliza Mohd Riji, "A Study on Practitioners and Users of Traditional Medicine in the Federal Territory and Selangor", Proceedings Malaysian Traditional Medicine, Kuala Lumpur, 1988, pp. 235–244.

19 Goh, S.H., "Chemical and Pharmacological Constituents in Traditional Medicine", Proceedings: Malaysian Traditional Medicine, Kuala Lumpur, 1988, p. 9.

20 It is only recently, with the view of developing a Malaysian herbal industry, that the Forest Research Institute Malaysia (FRIM), the Malaysian Agricultural Research and Development Institute (MARDI) and the Institute for Medical Research (IMR) have initiated several programmes to document the medicinal plants and to provide the necessary scientific data with respect to efficacy, safety and toxicity. Abdul Razak Mohd Ali, Azizol Abdul Kadir and Ng Lean Teik, "Commercial Production of Selected Herbs", National Conference on Agroindustry: Investment Opportunities and Towards Country Self-Sufficiency, November 3–4, 1998, Kuala Lumpur, Malaysia.

21 n.18, at 237.

Although no data is available to show that practitioners run family undertakings, it seems clear the profession is very much influenced and trained informally by family members with knowledge in the field.[22]

The concept of illness and disease in traditional medicine is very different. In traditional medicine, there is the spiritual side of the medicine and this is indigenous to a particular race or community.[23] Haliza noted in her study that the kinds of illnesses usually referred to Malay traditional practitioners were those believed to be caused by spirits. The next common were illnesses related to reproductive organ, pregnancy and those concerned with the urinary and alimentary systems. Patients of Chinese traditional medicine included both chronic as well as "mild" illnesses such as cough and cold. Most commonly treated by sinsehs were those associated with the central nervous system, respiratory system, methods of achieving pregnancies, sprains, fracture, rheumatism, and discomfort of general nature or of unknown cause. Among Indian traditional practitioners, the illnesses commonly referred to are disorder of the respiratory, digestive and musculo-skeletal system.[24]

The study undertaken by Haliza showed that traditional practitioners did not use sophisticated instruments to diagnose an ailment or disease. Rather their methods are based on observation, physical examination and a study of the history of the ailment or disease. Diagnosis is simple deductive process. The Malay practitioners diagnosed an illness by analysing the history of the patient's illness taken directly from the patient or from the family members. In situation where the illness is said to be spiritually caused, use of spiritual means is adopted in order to get a clearer diagnosis. Most formally trained Chinese sinsehs use stethoscope, sphygmomanometer and thermometer, and other specific instruments for diagnosing an illness. Informally trained Chinese sinsehs, who eschew medical instrumentation, tend to specialise in sprains, bone-setting and rheumatic disease. The Indian practitioners begin diagnosis by taking note of the history of the illness. In addition, physical examination is done. The use of instruments is not commonly practised.[25]

The traditional methods of treatments used by the Malay, Chinese and Indian traditional practitioners vary and are based on social, cultural and religious background as well as on the knowledge, attitudes and beliefs that are prevalent in the community.[26] Both

[22] n.18, at 237.

[23] For example, according to the Chinese, hypertension is caused by the imbalance of the so called "Ying and Yang" of the body. Chinese medicine divides hypertension into three types (a) hyperactivity of the Liver-Yang, (b) hyperactivity of Yang due to deficiency of Yin, and (c) deficiency in both Yin and Yang. Ngeow Sze Chan, "Treatment of Hypertension by Chinese Medicine", Proceedings: Malaysian Traditional Medicine, Kuala Lumpur, 1988, pp. 37–48.

[24] n.18, at 238.

[25] *ibid.*

[26] *ibid.*

medicinal and non-medicinal therapies are used in the treatment of a disease or an ailment. Medicinal therapy is normally used for non-spiritually caused illness whereas non-medicinal therapy is used to treat illness which is spiritually caused or of unknown cause.[27]

In medicinal therapy, the traditional practitioner issued a prescription to the patient. The prescribed medicine may consist of various parts of plants, with or without animal parts or mineral materials. The plants and/or animal parts and mineral materials are brewed in a pot to produce an extract. Depending on the prescription, the patient is advised to use a certain number of bowls of water to brew the mixture for between one hour to several hours. When brewing is completed, the patient then drinks the extract either hot or cold in single or multiple dosage, as directed by the traditional practitioner.[28] The extract consisting of a mixture of dilute active substances is used to treat one or more diseases.[29] The various ingredients for medicinal therapy are usually obtained locally although some are imported and can be purchased from medical halls.

For external injuries or for the treatment of musculo-skeletal ailment (fracture, sprains and rheumatism), herbal preparations are used in traditional Chinese medicine. Herbal preparations take a long time to brew, normally more than six months and are usually prepared by the practitioners themselves. Most herbal preparations used alcohol instead of water as solvent for brewing. The art of preparing a quality herbal preparation is often a guarded secret, and a long brew allows the preparation to "mature". For treating musculo-skeletal ailment, the herbal preparation is used in the form of a poultice.[30]

Non-medicinal therapy utilises various techniques such as acupuncture, chiropractic, osteopathy and other physical, mental, spiritual and mind-body control,[31] and it is not uncommon for patients to follow a strict diet and to be required to stay indoors for a certain period of time.[32] The "do's" and "don'ts" for non-medicinal therapy vary among the Malays, Chinese and Indians although there are some overlaps.[33] For illnesses which are spiritually caused, holy water and prayers are used simultaneously in the treatment. In addition, the patient's body is

[27] Personal communication and interview with Sinseh.
[28] *ibid.*
[29] This is due to the fact that various metabolites can be extracted from different plant parts such as the roots, leaves and shoots separately. It is estimated that about 85% of traditional medicine involves the use of plant extracts. Norman R. Farnsworth, "Screening Plants for New Medicines", in Biodiversity 83, at 91 (E.O. Wilson (ed.), National Academy Press, Washington DC, 1988).
[30] Flingoh Oh, C.H., "Herbal Medicinal Preparations for External Injuries and Rheumatic Pains", Proceedings: Malaysian Traditional Medicine, Kuala Lumpur, 1988, pp. 264–266.
[31] Zhang, Xiaorui, "Significance of Traditional Medicine in Human Health Care", WIPO Asian Regional Seminar On Intellectual Property Issues in the Field of Traditional Medicines, New Delhi, India, October 7–9, 1998. (Document No. WIPO/IP/MED/DEL/98/3).
[32] Radin Supathan, N., "Treatment of Drug Addiction by Malay Traditional Medicine", Proceedings: Malaysian Traditional Medicine, Kuala Lumpur, 1988, pp. 49–53.
[33] *ibid.*

inscriped with holy verses so as to prevent the spirit from coming back.[34]

Although modern medicine is now available in Malaysia, traditional medicine has maintained its popularity because of its historical and cultural impact. Even today in modern Malaysia, traditional medicine is still being practised either as an alternative or supplement to modern medicine. People believe in it, and it is still effective against many common diseases. Urban dwellers seek not only treatment at the modern health establishments but they also go to traditional practitioners residing in the towns as well as in the rural areas.[35]

3.2 End-Products

Based on the general characteristics described above, it is possible to group the end-products of traditional medicine and treatments as follows:

(a) Traditional knowledge

This includes traditional practices, beliefs, experiences and observations which have been handed down from generation to generation, knowledge on the identity and medicinal properties of plants;

(b) Methods of treatments

This includes diagnosis, medicinal and non-medicinal therapies, bonesetting, healing techniques, circumcision, methods of achieving pregnancies and midwives; and

(c) Products and processes

This includes plants, animals, mineral materials, plant and animal extracts, plant and animal products, condiments, herbal preparations, collection and preparation methods.

---

[34] Kamarulzaman Yahya, "Perubatan Tradisi di Kalangan Masyarakat Orang Asli", Proceedings: Malaysian Traditional Medicine, Kuala Lumpur, 1988, pp. 226–228.

[35] The reasons are, first, traditional systems of treatment are more culturally acceptable, and are able to meet the psychological needs in a way modern medicine does not. Secondly, many people do not have the economic capacity to be treated for long periods with synthetic drugs because of their expense. Traditional medicine and treatments not only provide basic health care which is not only effective, but affordable, especially to the poorer people. Traditional practitioners in Malaysia normally do not charge a consultation fee but a donation or contribution of between 10 to 30 ringgit seems to be the common range. Thirdly, patients resort to traditional medicine because of failure from modern therapy. This is evidenced by the withdrawal of several synthetically produced drugs such as thalidomide, terfenadine, mexaform and ketorolac from the market. Fourthly, it is sometimes claimed that traditional remedies have less serious adverse effects than modern medicine, such as in chemotherapy. The practitioners of traditional medicine, in particular herbal medicine, believe that their processing of herbal plants based on their traditional methods may modify the adverse effects of the active principles or that the various constituents present may interact with each other resulting in the moderation of the adverse effects of the individual constituent. Fifthly, plants can be obtained from diverse geographical habitats and are therefore easily accessible to the local people.

Each of the possible end products may form a suitable subject-matter for patent protection. In the next part of this article, an assessment on the availability of patent protection for each of the end-products will be considered in turn.

4. Patent Protection

In order to assess properly the protection afforded, it is necessary to examine each element of patent law as it is applied to each of the end products.

4.1 Protectable Subject-Matter

Not every subject-matter is patentable — only that which constitutes an "invention" may be the subject of a patent. The Patents Act provides that an "invention"[36] means "an idea of an inventor which permits in practice the solution to a specific problem in the field of technology and may either relate to a product or a process".[37] Not every invention is patentable. Among the things which are excluded from patent protection include discoveries, plant varieties and methods for the treatment of the human body by surgery or therapy and diagnostic methods practised on the human body.[38]

(a) Traditional knowledge

Patent law will not permit the patenting of knowledge *per se*. Knowledge *per se* such as traditional practices, experiences, observations, beliefs,

---

[36] This definition follows exactly the definition in s.112(1) of the WIPO Model Law for Developing Countries on Inventions, Volume 1 — Patents. In the United Kingdom Patents Act 1977, there is no definition of "invention" as such, although a list is provided in s.1(2) of things which are not considered inventions. For the purposes of the 1977 Act, s.125(1) defines an invention as "that specified in a claim of the specification of the application or patent, . . . as interpreted by the description and any drawings contained in that specification, and the extent of the protection conferred by a patent or application for a patent . . .". In the European Patent Convention, there is also no definition of "invention". Art. 52(1), EPC provides that "European patents shall be granted for any inventions which are susceptible of industrial application, which are new and which involve an inventive step. Art. 52(2), EPC provides a list of things which shall not be regarded as inventions within the meaning of Art. 52(1). Art. 52(4) EPC specifically provides that "methods for the treatment of the human or animal body by surgery or therapy and diagnostic methods practised on the human or animal body shall not be regarded as inventions . . .".

[37] Patents Act 1983, s.12.

[38] Patents Act 1983, s.13(1).

Notwithstanding the fact that they may be inventions within the meaning of section 12, the following shall not be patentable:

(a) discoveries, scientific theories and mathematical methods;

(b) plant or animal varieties or essentially biological processes for the production of plants or animals, other than man-made living micro-organisms, micro-biological processes and the products of such micro-organism processes;

(c) schemes, rules or methods for doing business, performing purely mental acts or playing games;

(d) methods for the treatment of the human or animal body by surgery or therapy, and the diagnostic methods practised on the human or animal body..

knowledge on the identity and medicinal properties of plants are not inventions within the definition of patent law.[39]

The need for an invention was discussed by the Court of Appeal in *Genentech v. Wellcome*[40] and in *Biogen v. Medeva*[41] relating to genetically engineered products. In both these cases, the courts had raised the question that claims relating to genetically engineered products generally did not amount to an "invention" within the confines of the 1977 United Kingdom Patents Act. Lord Justice Mustill in *Genentech v. Wellcome* had argued that in the light of section 1(1), which essentially duplicates Article 52(1) of the European Patent Convention, that the "fundamental requirement" of invention must be fulfilled.[42] He opined that the question whether the claim discloses anything which can be described as an invention must be answered in the affirmative before compliance with the other four conditions set out in section 1(1) becomes relevant.[43]

It is submitted that it is unlikely that patenting a plant solely on the basis of the knowledge that the plant has medicinal properties will be permitted under existing law.

(b) Methods of Treatments

A method for the treatment of the human body by surgery or therapy, and a diagnostic method practised on the human body is a non-patentable invention.[44] The term surgery is held to mean the field of medicine involving the healing of diseases or accident injuries, or remedies against physical defects by means of a surgical intervention performed on a live body. Consequently, not only operations performed on the human body by means of a scalpel are excluded, but also those using other medical instruments.[45] Treatment by therapy implies the curing of a disease or malfunction of the body through prophylactic methods.[46] The term "treatment by therapy" also include treatment of health disorders (pain, physical complaints or diminishing abilities) and reactions to environmental conditions.[47] The term "diagnostic" is to be understood in the medical sense as recognition, differentiation and localisation of pathological conditions.[48]

---

[39] Patents Act 1983, s.12.
[40] (1989) R.P.C. 147.
[41] (1995) R.P.C. 25; (1995) F.S.R. 4.
[42] (1989) R.P.C. 147, 262. See also Lord Justice Purchas, at 226–229. For a comment, see Sherman, (1990) 21 I.I.C. 76, 82.
[43] [1989] R.P.C. 147, 262–263.
[44] Patents Act 1983, s.13(1)(d).
[45] For a detailed analysis on the exclusion of surgical methods, see Rainer Moufang, "Methods of Medical Treatment Under Patent Law", (1993) 24 I.I.C. 18 at 37.
[46] Malaysian Patent Examination Manual 1996, s.2.8, Chapter IV.
[47] Case T81/84 — Dysmenorrhea/Rorer, [1988] O.J. E.P.O. 207, (1988) 19 I.I.C. 803. Here the Technical Board of Appeal held that a method of alleviating menstrual symptoms was unpatentable. See also discussion by Lancon, "Patentability in the Field of Therapy and Diagnosis", (1991) 22 I.I.C. 893 and Panchen, "Patentability in the Field of Therapy and Diagnosis", (1991) 22 I.I.C. 879.
[48] Rainer Moufang, "Methods of Medical Treatment Under Patent Law", (1993) 24 I.I.C. 18 at 45.

It is submitted that any invention relating to the traditional way of diagnosing an illness, the various techniques such as acupuncture, chiropractic and osteopathy used in non-medicinal therapy, bonesetting techniques for fractures, healing techniques for wounds, circumcision, methods of achieving pregnancies and midwifery will fall under this exclusion list and are not protectable subject-matter.[49] This provision however does not apply to products used in any such methods.[50] This means that a medicament consisting of a poultice for use in treating sprains or rheumatism may be patented, subject to meeting the patentability criteria.

(c) Products and Processes

Products of nature do not fall within the ambit of patentable subject-matter.[51] It follows that plants and animals which are found either in the wild or domesticated and mineral materials are not protectable subject-matter. In order to be patentable, there must be a man-made invention, not a creation of nature.[52] Likewise, finding a new medicinal plant in the wild is mere discovery[53] and is a non-patentable invention.[54] In order to be patentable, discoveries must be embodied in some practical, technical or industrial application.[55] One cannot patent a new medicinal plant just by being the first to catalogue it.[56]

Similarly, a plant variety discovered in a population produced by crossing two medicinal plants is also a non-patentable invention. The Act specifically exclude plant varieties from patent protection.[57]

---

[49] However, skilful formulation of claims can overcome obstacles raised by s.13(1)(d). See for example, Case T290/86 — ICI/Cleaning Plaque (1992) O.J. E.P.O. 414; (1992) 23 I.I.C. 815.

[50] s.2.8, Chapter IV, Malaysian Patent Examination Manual, 1996.

[51] *Funk Brothers Seed Co. v. Kalo Inoculant Co.* (1948) 76 U.S.P.Q. 280; (1948) 333 U.S. 127; *General Electric Co. v. De Forest Radio Co.,* (1929) 278 U.S. 656.

[52] *Diamond v. Chakrabarty,* (1980) 206 U.S.P.Q. 193; 447 U.S. 303.

[53] N.J. Byrne, "Mere Discoveries Are Not Patentable", in *The Scope of Intellectual Property Protection for Plants and Other Life Forms — Part 1* (Intellectual Property Publishing Limited, 1989), p. 16.

[54] Patents Act 1983, s.13(1)(a); s.2.4, Chapter IV, Malaysian Manual of Patent Examination, 1996.

[55] In the Patent Court, Whitford J. in his judgment said: "It is trite law that you cannot patent a discovery, but if on the basis of that discovery you can tell people how it can be usefully employed, then a patentable invention may result. This in my view would be the case, even though once you have made the discovery, the way in which it can be usefully employed is obvious enough". *Genentech Inc.'s Patent* (1987) R.P.C. 553 at 566, subsequently approved by Purchas and Dillion L.JJ. in *Genentech v. Wellcome,* (1989) R.P.C. 613 CA at 208 and 240.

[56] *Genentech Inc.'s Patent,* (1989) R.P.C. 147, CA. *Genentech* concerned a patent for human tissue plasminogen activator (t-PA). Natural t-PA exist in small amounts in human tissue where it helps activate an enzyme which is capable of dissolving fibrin in blood clots. *Genentech* was the first company to devise a practical process for the production of sufficient quality and quantity of t-PA as a therapeutically acceptable product on a commercial scale. Its claims were for t-PA and any process by which t-PA could be produced by rDNA technology. The United Kingdom Court of Appeal held that the isolation of gene sequences constituted a mere discovery, and thus was not itself patentable. The Court held that although the amino acid sequence of t-PA had not previously been determined, one cannot patent a known substance just by being the first to determine its structure. (In this paper, rDNA means recombinant DNA as distinct from ribosomal DNA which is also abbreviated as rDNA. DNA is the short term for Deoxyribonucleic acid.).

[57] Patents Act 1983, s.13(1)(b).

A typical traditional remedy in the form of an extract or condiment and consisting of active substances in the form of a dilute, not a pure form of the substances, and which is obtained through the brewing of parts of various plants is not an invention. Patent law only allow the patenting of a single pure active substance isolated from natural sources.[58]

However, plant and animal products, herbal preparations for use in poultice and collection and preparation methods may be protectable subject-matter, subject to meeting the patentability criteria.

4.2 Patentability Criteria

Not every invention is patentable. To be patentable, an invention must be new, involve an inventive step and be industrially applicable.[59] This part assesses the application of each of the patentability criteria to the following end-products, namely plant and animal products, herbal preparations, collection and preparation methods.

4.2.1 New

An invention shall be taken to be new if it is not anticipated by prior art.[60] The newness of an invention is assessed in comparison to the prior art[61] at the time of the application. The assessment of newness also require an investigation as to whether an invention has already been made publicly available.[62]

(i) Plant and Animal Products and Herbal Preparations

Various plant and animal products and herbal preparations have been used by users of traditional medicine for a very long time in Malaysia. These plant and animal products and herbal preparations which are already available to the public will clearly lack newness.[63]

---

[58] *Merck v. Chase* (1967) 155 U.S.P.Q. 139 — Vitamin K; *Bergstrom and Sjovall* (1970) 166 U.S.P.Q. 256 (CCPA 1970) — Prostaglandins.

[59] Patents Act 1983, s.11.

[60] Patents Act 1983, s.14(1).

[61] Prior art consists of everything disclosed to the public anywhere in the world, by written publication, by oral disclosure, by use, or in any other way prior to the priority date of the patent application claiming the invention, and including the contents of any pending patent applications having an earlier filing date or priority date. Patents Act 1983, s.14(2)(a), (b). The priority date is defined in s.27A of the Patents Act 1983. Malaysia acceded the Paris Convention for the Protection of Industrial Property and became a member of WIPO on January 1, 1989. The width of this definition should be noted. There are no restrictions whatever as to the language in which the relevant information is made available to the public nor any age limit is stipulated for the documents or other sources of the information. This means that a document even if published in an obscure publication and which is not generally read by the public will be publicly available and will be taken into consideration for novelty assessment. T.A.Blanco White, "Patents for Inventions", (5th Ed., 1983, Stevens & Sons, London), p. 72.

[62] *Formento v. Mentmore* (1956) R.P.C. 87, CA.

[63] *ibid.* Making pens embodying the invention available to the public before the priority date of the patent means "publication through use".

This is true even if the active substances present in the plant and animal products and herbal preparations are not yet identified. According to Lord Hoffmann when deciding the *Merrell Dow*[64] case, it was not necessary for a active substance to be identifiable or reproducible for it to have made available to the public. He gave the example of the Amazonian Indians who had known for centuries that cinchona bark can be used to treat malarial and other fevers, but only in 1820 was quinine isolated from the bark. The Amazonian Indians, who believed that the effect of cinchona was due to "the spirit of the bark" could, said Lord Hoffmann, be said to "know" about quinine even though he did not know its name or its chemical structure.[65] Taking the cue from the decision in the *Merrell Dow* case, it is submitted that the plant and animal products and herbal preparations are all lacking in novelty even if there are no public knowledge of the presence of active substances.

(ii) Collection and Preparation Methods[66]

The collection and preparation methods have been used both by the users of traditional medicine and the traditional practitioners themselves for generations. These methods are available to the public and clearly lack novelty.

4.2.2 *Inventive Step and Industrial Application*

Because the end products are either not protectable subject-matter or lacking in newness, it is submitted that the criteria of inventive step and industrial application therefore cannot be met.

5. Limitations of Patent Law

Based on the analysis in the part of this article immediately preceding, it is submitted that there are difficulties in applying patent law to protect the end-products of traditional medicine and treatments. This section discusses the problems and the lack of special provisions in patent law to protect the end-products.

---

[64] *Merrell Dow Pharmaceuticals v. Norton & Co.* (1996) R.P.C. 76.

[65] In contrast, in the *Mobil* case, the EPO Enlarged Board of Appeal decided that the word "available" carries with it the idea that, for lack of novelty to be found, all the technical features of the claimed invention in combination must have been communicated to the public, or laid open for inspection. Under the European Patent Convention, a hidden or secret use, because it has not been made available to the public, is not a ground for objection to validity of a European patent. *Mobil/Friction-Reducing Additive* (1990) O.J. E.P.O. 93; (1991) 22 I.I.C. 85.

[66] In this article, collection methods refer to the procedure used in collecting the plants or plant products either by the traditional practitioners or by the users of traditional medicine. The procedure used for collecting plants or plant products include certain time of the day, during dry or wet season, plants growing on the hill-slope or in the valley, age of the plants and drying techniques. Preparation methods refer to the procedure of brewing or boiling the plants or plant products, amount of water to use, duration of brewing/boiling and addition of any other ingredients, for example animal parts and mineral materials.

5.1 Problems

(a) Traditional Knowledge

In traditional medicine, what constitutes an "invention" is the knowledge. "Invention" in traditional medicine is different from "technical invention" as defined in patent law.[67] In traditional medicine, the "identity" of a medicinal plant and the "knowledge as to which part of the plant" is suitable for use as an ingredient in the preparation of a medicament for the treatment of an ailment or disease are the "inventions". It is this information that is required protection.

(b) Methods of Treatment

One of the differences between methods of treatment in traditional medicine and modern medicine is the use of physical, mental and spiritual therapies in the treatment of an illness. These methods of treatment are influenced by the culture and beliefs which are prevalent in a particular community. Physical methods of treatment involve muscle manipulation and massage. Mental methods of treatment involve self discipline. This could be in the form of a strict diet, staying in-doors for a certain period of time (especially for new mothers) and following the many "do's" and "don'ts". Spiritual methods of treatment involve prayers and use of holy water. The subject-matters that require protection are the physical, mental and spiritual therapies that are used in traditional treatments.

(c) Products and Processes

In traditional medicine, the plants, animal parts and mineral materials are consumed or used as a multi-component system in the form of an extract or as a herbal preparation. Different types of plant or animal extracts are used for the treatment of different ailment or disease. A plant extract which is obtained through brewing the roots of a particular medicinal plant is different from a plant extract which is obtained through brewing the leaves of the same plant. Each plant or animal extract is a different "invention" in traditional medicine.

Likewise, the practitioners of traditional medicine believe that the processing of herbal plants based on their traditional methods may modify the adverse effects of the active principle, thus making the traditional remedy having lesser adverse effects than modern medicine, such as in chemotherapy. Each traditional method of processing herbal plants therefore constitutes an "invention".

5.2 Lack of Special Provisions

The current Patents Act does not have any special provisions for the protection of end-products of traditional medicine and treatments. The

[67] Patents Act 1983, s.12.

closest section of the Act that might be of some help is subsection 13(2). This subsection provides that:

> "Where the Registrar[68] is uncertain as to the patentability of any items specified in section 13(1), he may refer the matter to the examiner[69] for an opinion and shall thereafter decide whether to include or exclude such item as being patentable or otherwise".

This provision however is untested. There is as yet at this point in time any patent application for traditional medicine and treatments being filed at the Malaysian Patent Office. Furthermore, there is no Patent Examiner who is trained to evaluate and examine such an application. At best, any application for the protection of traditional medicine and treatments will be examined in accordance with the procedures set out in the Patent Examination Manual. A decision to reject the application as non-compliance under sections 13(1) and 14(1) of the Patents Act is therefore anticipated.[70]

6. Summary of Findings

In the previous parts of this article, the effectiveness of patent protection for the end products of traditional medicine and treatments was assessed. It was found that the end-products could not meet the requirements of patent law and hence patent protection could not be afforded. Furthermore, it was found that there were problems in fitting the end-products within the confines of patent law. There is therefore a gap in providing effective protection for traditional medicine and treatments.

It is submitted that since there are no special provisions in the patent law to cover and protect traditional medicne and treatments, it is desirable to amend the existing patent law or to develop an appropriate protection scheme to fill this gap.

7. Towards Protecting Traditional Medicine and Treatments

The final part of this article discusses, first, the amendments to the Patents Act, 1983 and second, the possibility of introducing other protection schemes, such as for example a *sui generis* system for the protection of traditional medicine and treatments. The proposal to amend the Patents Act by including a special provision specifically for

[68] The Registrar of Patents includes any Deputy Registrar of Patents or Assistant Registrar of Patents.
[69] "Examiner" means any person, government department, unit, organisation or any foreign or international patent office or organisation appointed by the Patents Board.
[70] Personal communication with Patent Examiner, Patent Office, Intellectual Property Division, Ministry of Domestic Trade and Consumers Affairs, Malaysia.

the protection of the end-products of traditional medicine and treatments is to be considered as an interim measure. The reasons are first, to quickly provide a form of protection for traditional practitioners who have developed new plant and animal extracts or find a new use of a known extract, and secondly, the development of a *sui generis* system takes a long time.

7.1 Amendments to the Patents Act

Although the Patents Act provides for the protection of a new use of a known compound,[71] this provision however is not suitable for the protection of plant or animal extracts. The reason is patent law only allows the patenting of single pure active substance, not a complex mixture.[72]

In order to overcome this obstacle, it is proposed that a special provision be provided specifically for the protection of plant and animal extracts. Towards this end, it is proposed that two new subsections be introduced into the existing Act, namely:

(a) a new subsection 12(3) to include plant and animal extracts within the definition of invention; and
(b) a new subsection 14(2)(c) to address the issue of prior art.

Under this special provision, in order to be patentable, the new extract or a new use of a known extract shall not have been made available to the public and shall not be part of the prior art. The assessment of newness for a newly developed extract or a new use of a known extract is conducted by comparing the "new extract" or the "new use of a known extract" with any recorded prescriptions available or published in Malaysia.[73]

The examination of a patent application claiming an invention in the field of plant or animal extract can be carried out under the International Patent Classification (IPC)[74] group A61K dealing with

---

[71] Patents Act 1983, s.14(4).

[72] See *Merck v. Chase* and *Re Bergstrom and Sjovall*, above.

[73] Towards this end, the Forest Research Institute Malaysia in collaboration with the Institute for Medical Research are currently doing a systematic documentation of all medicinal plants used in traditional medicine. Included in the documentation are scientific evidence on claims made in traditional medicine with respect to efficacy, toxicity and safety, prescriptions currently used in traditional medicine and methods of preparations. Personal communication with Dr Azizol Abdul Kadir, Director, Medicinal Plants Division, Forest Research Institute Malaysia.

[74] The International Patent Classification, abbreviated as IPC is based on an international multi-lateral treaty administered by WIPO. This Classification subdivides technology into 8 sections, 20 subsections, 118 classes, 624 subclasses and over 67,000 groups. Each of the sections, classes, subclasses, groups and subgroups has a title and a symbol, and each of the subsections has a title. The symbol or symbols of at least the subclass or subclasses to which the technical invention described in any patent document belongs are indicated generally on the patent document by the industrial property office of the country where the application is filed. Thus, the document is retrievable according to its subject matter, with the help of the IPC. World Intellectual Property Organisation, *Intellectual Property Reading Material* (2nd Ed., WIPO, Geneva, 1998) p. 293.

pharmaceutical inventions. In view of the perculiar characteristics of traditional medicine, the Malaysian Patent Examination Manual[75] should accordingly be reviewed and revised so as to reflect the special examination procedures for plant and animal extract inventions.

7.2 Traditional Medicine and Treatments As Intellectual Property Rights of the Indigenes

Outside the traditional international intellectual property conventions[76] there are a number of international instruments which have incidentally addressed the issue on the protection of traditional medicine and treatments.

For example, Article 29 of the Draft Declaration on the Rights of Indigenous Peoples recognised the right of indigenous peoples to:

> . . . special measures to control, develop and protect their sciences, technologies and cultural manifestations, including human and other genetic resources, seeds, medicines, knowledge of properties of fauna and flora, oral traditions, literatures, designs and visual and performing arts".[77]

In this Draft Declaration, the issue of "medicines, knowledge of properties of fauna and flora, oral traditions" was clearly spelt out.

Apart from the United Nations, various international groups have also recognised the need for the protection of traditional medical knowledge of the indigenous people. For example, in 1988 the International Society for Ethnobiology (ISE) issued "The Declaration of Belem" calling for worldwide attention to protect the intellectual property rights of the indigenous peoples.[78] One of the points highlighted in the Declaration of Belem is that

> all medical programs include the recognition of and respect for traditional healers and the incorporation of traditional health practices that enhance the health status of these populations.

Likewise at the Fourth World Conference on Women held at Beijing in 1995, it was agreed that the intellectual property rights of indigenous woman be "protected, respected and maintained". The language covers "knowledge, innovation and practices . . . including practices

[75] Last reviewed in 1996.

[76] Namely the Berne Convention for the Protection of Literary and Artistic Work and the Paris Convention for the Protection of Industrial Property.

[77] The final version of the Draft Declaration on the Rights for Indigenous Peoples which was agreed upon by members of the United Nations Working Groups on Indigenous Populations at its 11th session in 1993.

[78] The Declaration of Belem, Adopted at the First International Congress of Ethnobiology in Belem, Brazil in 1988.

relating to traditional medicines, biodiversity and indigenous technologies".

These Declarations are all about the need to recognise and to protect traditional medicine and treatments and underscore the importance of traditional medicine and treatments as a source of knowledge and for providing primary health care.

The significance of these international instruments has been recognised in Malaysia. At a recent seminar entitled "Environmental Economics and Transforming Technologies of Indigenes in Malaysia", the issue of intellectual property protection and intellectual property rights of the indigenes was discussed.[79] It is submitted that putting traditional Malay village medicine and Orang Asli medicine under intellectual property rights of the indigenes is one alternative method of protection.

7.3 A *Sui Generis* System

At the international level, the limitations of patent law to provide adequate protection for traditional medicine and treatments has been recognised by the World Intellectual Property Organisation, WIPO. Recognising the need to address this issue, WIPO in collaboration with the Government of India had on October 7 to 9, 1998 organised a regional seminar at New Delhi to discuss intellectual property issues in the field of traditional medicine.[80] Among the ideas put forward at this seminar was to form a task force at international level to discuss the mechanisms and the possibility of a *sui generis* system[81] for the protection of traditional medicine and treatments.

On the development of a *sui generis* system, WIPO can help to formulate an international treaty and to develop a model law. Currently, at international level, such a treaty is yet to be formulated. As to the WIPO Model Law, it can be drafted along the lines of the WIPO/UNESCO Model Provisions for National Laws on *Sui Generis* Protection of Expressions of Folklore Against Illicit Exploitation and Other Prejudicial Actions.[82]

[79] Expert Group Workshop and Meeting on "Environmental Economics and Transforming Technologies of the Indigenes in Malaysia", August 8–9, 1997, Penang, under the sponsorship of National Council for Scientific Research and Development, Ministry of Science, Technology and the Environment, Malaysia, in collaboration with School of Social Sciences and School of Distance Education Studies and The Orang Asli Department, Ministry of National Unity and Social Development, Malaysia.

[80] Two officials, one from the Malaysian Patent Office and one from the Forest Research Institute Malaysia participated in this seminar.

[81] This idea was mooted because of development of *sui generis* solutions providing for the protection of intellectual property rights in plants varieties, integrated circuits and databases. The availability of *sui generis* solutions means that the categories of intellectual property rights are not closed. Michael Blakeney, "Communal Intellectual Property Rights of Indigenous Peoples in Cultural Expressions". 1 J.W.I.P. 6, 985 at 986.

[82] See document UNESCO-WIPO/Folk/PKT/97/19 dated March 21, 1997.

In view of the social significance of traditional medicine in providing primary health care to people living in developing countries, a *sui generis* system should take into account the fact that the larger public interests must have precedence over commercial interests. This is to ensure that traditional medicine and treatments will and still be available to the society as it has been available to everyone for generations. At present the biotechnology industry is free to utilise the traditional medical knowledge and gaining monopoly rights over the identified active substances of plants which have been selected for screening based on such knowledge.[83] A *sui generis* system for the protection of traditional medicine and treatments can help level the playing field.

8. Conclusion

A special provision in the patent law along the lines outlined above is an immediate solution for the protection of traditional medicine and treatments. In the absence of a national legislation, protection of traditional medicine and treatments as intellectual property rights of the indigenes is another viable alternative. A *sui generis* system appears to be the most appropriate scheme for the protection of traditional medicine and treatments. A *sui generis* system will be able to accomodate the perculiar characteristics of traditional medicine and treatments and to ensure that public traditional knowledge will not become private property. It will also prevent the surreptitious use of traditional medical knowledge by bioprospectors and ensure the sustainable use of traditional medicine and treatments for many generations to come.

---

83 See U.S. Patent No. 5047242, above.

9. Indigenous Peoples and The Protection of Genetic Resources in Brazil

Maria Thereza Mendonça Wolff

Industrial Chemist and Chemical Engineer of the Federal University of Rio de Janeiro, Brazil, she began her professional career as a Chemist-Analyst in the Institute of Chemical Agriculture of Rio de Janeiro (Embrapa). She has graduated in Experimental Physics in the Unversity of Aachen (Germany) in the area of Radioisotopes; in Brazil she was successively a researcher in Radioisotopes at the CNPQ, Chemist-technologist in INT (National Institute of Technology) working with sugars and alcohol and for 20 years has been a partner of Dannemann, Siemsen, Bigler & Ipanema Moreira (Rio de Janeiro). She is the Co-ordinator of Biotechnology in the Brazilian Association of Intellectual Property (ABPI) and a member of the Brazilian Society of Microbiology and a member of the Brazilian Society of Genetic Engineers.

Indigenous Peoples and the Protection of Genetic Resources in Brazil

Biodiversity in Brazil

Brazil exhibits from 55 to 60 thousand different species. This is equivalent to 22 per cent of the near 250 thousand species existing on earth, of which more than 7 per cent exist only in Brazil. Brazil has 55 species of primates (24 per cent of the total in the world), 3000 species of fresh water fish (three times as high as the number existing in any other country), 3000 species of terrestrial vertebrates (of which 310 species are currently at risk of extinction), 468 species of reptiles (fourth in the world), 1622 species of birds (of which 191 species are currently at risk of extinction) and 10 to 15 million different insects. The different terrestrial and marine microorganisms are innumerable.

The tables below indicate the development of pharmaceutical and other products from Brazilian resources and the Brazilian derivation of products in respect of which foreign patents have been sought.

Known medicaments based on Brazilian genetic resources

Name	**Plant or genetic resources**	**Indications**
Pilocarpina	Jaborandi *(Pilocarpus jaborandi)*	treatment of glaucoma and alopecia
Capoten or Captopril	Veneno de Jararaca *(Bothrosps Jararaca)*	treatment of arterial pressure
Quelicin or Anectine or Sucostrin or Tubocurarina	Curare *(Chondodendron tomentosum)*	muscle relaxant
Oncovin or Velban	Boa-Noite *(Catharantus rosens)*	treatment of leukemia and/or tumours

Source of research: Brazilian Journal: "O Estado de São Paulo" of November 5, 1998

Pharmaceuticals based on Brazilian plants, patented in foreign countries

Name	Country	Indications
Quebra-Pedra *(Phyllanthus corcovadensis)*	USA	against hepatitis b and for the removal of kidney stones
Guaraná *(Paullinia Cupania)*	USA	anti-thrombolytic
Espinheira Santa *(Maytenus ilicifolia)*	Japan	anti-inflammatory and anti-histaminic
Sangue-de-Drago *(Croton urucrana)*	USA	anti-viral and anti-diarrheic in HIV cases
Marapuama *(Hirtella sp)*	Japan	aphrodisiac
Pfaffia	Japan	anti-tumoral
Rupununine *(Octoteadodioli)*	England	contraceptive and anti-tumoral
Cumaniol *(Clibalium sylvestre)*	England	neuromuscular active agent and reversible heart blocking agent

Source of research: Brazilian Journal: "O Estado de São Paulo" of November 5, 1998

The Convention on Biological Diversity

The Convention on Biological Diversity (CBD) imposes a variety of requirements on contracting parties which deal with access to genetic resources and the remuneration of source countries and communies. These include Article 15, which provides that in order to share in a fair and equitable way the results of research and development and the benefits arising from the commercial and other utilisation of genetic resources, each contracting party shall take legislative, administrative or policy measures.

Article 16, paragraph 2 also provides that access to and transfer of technology to developing countries shall be provided and/or facilitated under fair and most favorable terms and that in the case of technology subject to patents and other intellectual property rights, such access and transfer shall be provided on terms which recognise and are consistent with the adequate and effective protection of intellectual property rights. Article 16, paragraph 5, provides that the contracting parties, recognising that patents and other intellectual property rights may have an influence on the implementation of this Convention, shall co-operate in this regard subject to national legislation and international law in order to ensure that such rights are supportive of and do not run counter to its objectives.

Article 18, paragraph 4, provides that the contracting parties shall, in accordance with national legislation and policies, encourage and develop methods of co-operation for the development and use of technologies, including indigenous and traditional technologies, in pursuance of the objectives of this Convention. For this purpose, the contracting parties shall also promote co-operation in the training of personnel and exchange of experts.

Article 19, paragraph 2 provides that each contracting party shall take all practicable measures to promote and advance priority access on a fair and equitable basis by contracting parties, especially developing countries, to the results and benefits arising from biotechnologies based upon genetic resources provided by those contracting parties. Such access shall be on mutually agreed terms.

As can be seen from the above Articles, the terms of the Convention are wide enough to leave each member-country the delimitation of its jurisdictional scope.

The Biodiversity Convention in Brazil

Brazil signed the Biodiversity Convention on June 5, 1992 and ratified it on February 2, 1994. The Convention came into force on May 29, 1994, the date of publication of its ratification. This chapter surveys the Brazilian perspective concerning the rights of patentees and the distribution of benefits to the country and to indigenous and local communities for pharmaceutical products obtained or derived from Brazilian plants. Prior to the Convention, coming into force, federal Decree no. 98,839 of January 1990 provided for the collection of scientific data and materials by foreigners, and applied to all field activities performed by all foreign individuals or legal entities having as an objective the collection of data, materials, biological specimens and minerals and pieces integrating the native and popular culture, which are intended for study or research. This decree was not revoked after ratification of the Biodiversity Convention and remained in force.

This decree established that activities will only be authorised if there is co-participation and co-responsibility of a Brazilian institution with related competence. The decree states the requirements for collection procedures and where information about the origins of the resources and the authorisation to disclose scientific work shall appear, thereby regulating, *inter alia*, the possibility of shipment abroad.

State Bioprospecting Legislation

There were two state laws in force in Brazil, prior to the Biodiversity Convention, which were relevant to bioprospecting. These were the law no. 1235 of July 9, 1997 of the state of Acre and the law no. 0388/97 of the state of Amapa.

The Law of the state of Acre contained the following definitions, which are relevant to the consideration of biodiversity conservation and bioprospecting:

> "Ex situ Conditions: conditions where the biological diversity components are conserved outside their natural habitats.
>
> In situ Conditions: conditions where the biological resources exist within ecosystems and natural habitats and, in case of domesticated or cultivated species, the surroundings where they have developed their distinctive properties.
>
> Domesticated or Cultivated Species: species within which the evolutionary process has been influenced by human activity.
>
> Synthesised Product: substance obtained by a synthetic process from genetic information or other biological molecules. It includes the semi-processed extracts and substances obtained through transformation of a product derived by a synthetic process (hemi-synthesis)".

Such definitions encompass, compounds obtained from genetic resources such as, for example, medicinal active substances found in plants, microorganisms, genes, cultivars, *inter alia,* under which protection by intellectual property is subject to authorised access.

The decree requires bioprospecting to be subject to an Agreement of Access in which the parties are:

a) the state;
b) the applicant for access; and
c) the furnisher of traditional knowledge or the domesticated agricultural crop.

The state is represented by the Department of Environment of the state of Acre. This Department will sign Agreements of Access with third parties for genetic resources that are deposited at centers of *ex situ* conservation established within the state territory. The Law provides that no individual rights of intellectual property registered inside or outside the state which use universal knowledge held by local communities or which have been acquired without a certificate of access and the state exit license will be recognised.

Foreign biotechnologies will be used provided that they adhere to the law and biosafety rules and the candidate company undertakes full liability for any damages they may cause to health, environment or local crops, presently, or in the future.

The state Law of state of Amapa establishes a similar bioprospecting regime. Authorised individuals or legal entities with access to Brazilian genetic resources are obliged to communicate to the competent authorities any information concerning the transportation of collected specimens, not involving the authorisation of access to its shipment abroad. The utilisation of genetic resources for research, conservation or commercial or industrial applications that does not have the access certificate is forbidden.

Post-CBD National Legislation

Bill no. 306/95 concerned with the recognition of the rights of indigenous persons to intellectual property rights arising from bioprospecting activities was introduced by Senator Marina Silva. This was approved by the Senate on November 4, 1998 and is currently under evaluation by the National Congress The Bill creates a Commission for Genetic Resources which to authorise access to Brazilian genetic resources. This Commission comprises representatives from the Federal Government, state Governments, scientific community, local communities and indigenous groups, access agencies, non-governmental organisations and private companies. Under the Bill parties to access agreements are:

(a) the state,
(b) the applicant for access,
(c) the access agency, and
(d) the furnisher of traditional knowledge and domesticated agricultural crop.

The Bill introduces definitions for terms such as "Derived product" which is an isolated natural product of biological origin, or onto which it is structurally based, or yet which has otherwise been created from the use of a traditional knowledge associated thereto. From this definition, there will be included among derived products, any products based on a natural product, thus including active substances and genes.

With regard to compensation, Article 35 provides for fair compensation among applicant, access agency, furnishers of traditional knowledge and other parties to access contracts. Article 36 provides that compensation shall include a contribution to a special fund for conservation, research and inventory of genetic richness.

Article 41 provides that rights over genetic resources and derived products obtained in breach of this law will not be recognised. Applicants for intellectual property rights over biotechnological inventions or cultivars based on any genetic resources or traditional knowledge, as well as those, based on cultural or artistic traditions of local communities or indigenous groups, are required to certify approval by said communities and groups, obtained prior to the application for legal protection of the invention and in accordance with the laws of the country of origin of the genetic resources.

The rights of the local and indigenous communities to collectively profit from their traditional knowledge and be compensated by the conservation of the genetic resources is recognised in Article 44. Article 45 provides that "local and indigenous communities hold the full rights over their traditional knowledge and the assignment of those rights shall be by them and by according to prescribed forms of contract". Article 46 assures to the local and indigenous communities the right to benefits arising out of the access to genetic resources from their region. Access will be denied where the local and indigenous communities consider such activities threaten the integrity of their natural or cultural richness.

Article 47 provides that rights to intellectual property on products or processes related to traditional knowledge associated to genetic resources or derived products the access to which is not done in accordance with the law shall not be recognised.

The Federal Government, responding to Senator Marina Silva's Bill, created an Interministry Group of Access to Genetic Resources. The Interministry Group of Access to Genetic Resources is under the co-ordination of the Ministry of Environment and is comprised of several related Ministries, such as Justice, Navy, Health, Agriculture, Industry and Commerce and further entities directly interested in this matter. This Interministry Group was established in order to evaluate and propose improvements on the Bill first submitted by the Senator. Finally in August 1998 it offered a substitute Bill which will be submitted for vote. The substitute provides less stringent regulation so as to allow an exchange of information. It acknowledges the right of the traditional knowledge holder in deciding upon access of third parties to the information regarding such knowledge, and assures the local and indigenous communities' right of participation in the distribution of benefits arising out of the use of such knowledge.

The substitute Bill contains no definition of the term "derived product". Article 11 of the Bill requires that "the benefits arising out of the economic exploitation of product or process developed from a specimen of a component of the Genetic Richness, obtained by a national institution or one established abroad, shall be shared in a fair and equitable way with the Union."

This is amplified by Article 12, which defines that this sharing shall be by way of:

I. partition of profits and royalties arising out of the economic exploitation of processes and products developed from a specimen of components of the Genetic Richness;
II. transfer of technologies;
III. licensing, free from encumbrances, of products and processes; and
IV. qualification of human resources.

Article 16 requires that an Agreement on Utilisation of Genetic Richness and Distribution of Benefits shall clearly indicate the contracting parties, namely:

I. on one side:
   (a) the Union;
   (b) the region's owner or Indigenous Community Representative or Local Indigenous Community Representative;
II. on the other side:
   (c) the national institution authorised to carry out the access; and
   (d) the addressee institution.

Conclusion

Brazil is playing an active role in the discussions concerning the revision of the biotechnology patent provisions of the WTO Agreement on Trade Related Intellectual Property Rights (TRIPs) and also in the harmonisation of the CBD with TRIPs. Its legislative initiatives in the recognition of the rights of indigenous peoples and local communities in bioprospecting provides a useful perspective and experience in this debate.

Index

(All references are to page numbers)